Menachem Michelson
Right-Hand Man

Right-Hand Man

The Biography of Yehiel Kadishai
Chief of Staff and Confidant of Menachem Begin

Menachem Michelson

Translated by: Jessica Setbon

gefen גפן
publishing house בית הרצאה לאור
JERUSALEM ● NEW YORK Est. 1981

Originally published in Hebrew as *Yad Yemino*
Gefen Publishing House, Ltd., 2013

All photographs were received from the personal collection of Yehiel Kadishai,
and every effort was made to locate their lawful owners. The photographs appearing
without mention of source are from the private collection of Yehiel
and Bambi Kadishai.
The cover photo and photo of Kadishai on the back cover were taken by
David Rubinger, with the generous permission of *Yedioth Aharonoth*.

Cover Design and Typesetting: Irit Nachum

ISBN: 978-965-229-736-5

1 3 5 7 9 8 6 4 2

Gefen Books, Ltd.
11 Edison Place
Springfield, NJ 07081
516-593-1234

Gefen Publishing Ltd.
6 Rehov Ha-Zvi
Jerusalem 94386, Israel
++972-2-538-0247

www.gefenpublishing.com

Printed in Jerusalem

Library of Congress Cataloging-in-Publication Data

Mikhalson, Menahem, author.
[Yad yemino. English]
Right hand man : the biography of Yehiel Kadishai, chief of staff and confidant of
Menachem Begin / Menachem Michelson ; translated by Jessica Setbon.
    pages cm
ISBN 978-965-229-736-5
1. Kadishai, Yechiel, 1923- 2. Begin, Menachem, 1913-1992. 3. Jews–Israel–
Biography. 4. Politicians–Israel–Biography. 5. Israel. Misrad rosh ha-memshalah. I.
Title.
DS126.6.K16M5413 2015
956.9405'4092–dc23
[B]
                                    2015020944

Our God wants it, and the Messiah is here, too.

There's a plow for the homeland, and ten thousand youths for the army.

There's the gold, and there's the goldsmith waiting

To strike the coin: For the freedom of Israel

But who doesn't want it? – Evil Fate,

Dragging us forever through fire and blood:

From the teeth of Christianity to the teeth of Islam.

Uri Zvi Greenberg

From "Ezor Magen u-Ne'um Ben ha-Dam" [A Shield of Defense and the Word of the Son of Blood] (Jerusalem: Sadan, 1930)

CONTENTS

INTRODUCTION

I first met Yehiel Kadishai in May 1981, on the eve of elections for the Tenth Knesset, in which the Likud won forty-eight mandates and Menachem Begin began his second term as prime minister. I had gone to the Prime Minister's Bureau in Jerusalem as a journalist for *Yedioth Aharonoth* to join a trip to an election convention in Ashkelon, at which Begin was to be the sole speaker.

The office was something else. I was bowled over by the unbuttoned atmosphere. There was much coming and going of ministers and senior officers, along with guests from abroad who had come to express the support of the Jewish community of Miami or Glasgow, and for the photo opportunity with Begin, to be published in the *Miami Jewish Review* or the Scottish *Jewish Echo*.

Amid them all was Yehiel Kadishai, Begin's chief of staff, clapping the shoulder of one, exchanging half a word with another, joking with the secretaries, extolling the scent of the aftershave of a senior Treasury official who was waiting for Begin, asking a foreign guest about a mutual acquaintance from their days in the Jewish Brigade. He would pop in and out of Begin's room, disappearing for a few minutes at a time, then returning in high spirits.

I then met with Begin and traveled on with him to Ashkelon – but that's not the story. The story is that the figure of Yehiel Kadishai remained with me for many years afterward, even when Begin became a memory and Yehiel retired. Over the years, I came across scholarly research with harsh criticism of the management of the Begin office as "unprofessional," when in fact it had been managed smoothly and reached far beyond the achievements of other Israeli PMOs.

Begin's perfectionism and Kadishai's Jewish-style informality combined to create a unique historical phenomenon – more than an Israeli office, Begin's was a Jewish office, run by a real *mensch*. So when I was approached by Herzl Makov, director of the Menachem Begin Heritage Center in Jerusalem, and Hart Hasten of Indianapolis to write Yehiel's biography, I was delighted – not only because I was curious about Yehiel, but because of the challenge of writing his story and trying to pinpoint the secret of the man who was party to the secrets of Menachem Begin.

I hope I've been successful.

Now, a disclosure: this book could not have been published without the assistance of my good friend, the journalist and writer Shlomo Nakdimon, from whose work I drew; Amira Stern, director of the Jabotinsky Institute Archives, who assisted me greatly with advice as well as knowledge; Rami Shtivi of the Begin Heritage Center Archives, who was always at the right place at the right time; the many individuals I interviewed, who joined in the effort by diving into the past, and who came back up to the surface with many treasures; and of course, it would not have been possible without Yehiel and his wife Esther (Bambi), whom I inconvenienced many times, even at unconventional hours.

Above all, I wish to thank my wife, Nechama, for her insightful and valuable editing and comments.

Menachem Michelson

CHAPTER 1

LOW TIDE, HIGH TIDE

It was Sunday night, June 21, 1948, one week after the holiday of Shavuot. On the beach at Kfar Vitkin (today Beit Yannai Beach) lay a pile of equipment that had been unloaded with great effort from the *Altalena*, a boat used by the Irgun (Irgun Zva'i Leumi, the National Military Organization, an underground resistance group also known by its acronym, Etzel) to smuggle immigrants and weapons into Palestine. Medical equipment, army uniforms, and about 250 rifles were heaped in a pile on the sand. The 930 immigrants who had reached Palestine aboard the *Altalena* had debarked earlier and had then been quickly dispersed to immigrant housing in Hadera, Netanya, and Ra'anana, so now only a hundred or so Irgun members remained on the beach. Most were locals who had come to assist in unloading the weapons, along with a few of the newly arrived immigrants. Menachem Begin, the Irgun commander, was also there along with other Irgun leaders.

A storm of controversy raged around the *Altalena*. The Irgun and its rival Haganah paramilitary group had entered into a somewhat uneasy truce, to the point that the Irgun had contributed battalions to the Haganah-led Israel Defense Forces. But the fledgling Jewish government, under the leadership of David Ben-Gurion, feared that the Irgun battalions were about to rebel, reinforced with the new arms shipment. The air in the newly formed country was filled with the terrible scent of civil war. Unknown to the group on the beach, they had already been surrounded by soldiers of the Alexandroni Brigade, whose commander, Dan Even, had received orders directly from Yigael Yadin, head of the Operations Branch of the General Staff, to close in on them and confiscate the weapons.

About an hour and a half after midnight, Begin received a typewritten note at the Kfar Vitkin beach. The note contained an ultimatum from the brigade commander: surrender within ten minutes and relinquish the weapons, as well as the boat and its arms, into the possession of the Israel Defense Forces.

The Irgun leaders were shocked by the terse demand. They had never before been given only ten minutes to comply with an ultimatum. Not one of the Irgun members considered submitting to it under any circumstances. The next afternoon at 5 p.m., after consultation with other Irgun leaders also present, Begin decided to hold a roll call. He would personally explain the development of the negotiations to the Irgun members who had helped unload the boat, then sail to Tel Aviv to accelerate the remainder of the unloading.

The atmosphere during the roll call was tense. The Irgun members arranged themselves into a U formation on the beach, with Begin standing opposite. Several senior Irgun commanders stood beside him.

One of those standing anxiously at attention next to the small pier, his back to the sea, was a slim Irgun member named Yehiel Kadishai. He had just returned from Europe on the *Altalena* after completing his mission at the DP camps there. This was the second time he had ever seen Menachem Begin. Of course, at that moment he had no inkling that his future would be linked to that of Begin, the national leader and eventual prime minister. Nor did he have time to ponder this. His thoughts were wandering to his parents' home in Tel Aviv, which he hadn't seen in many long months, and where he planned to go as soon as roll call ended.

Begin began to speak: "'The Stand' [Hama'amad, another name for the Irgun] was right again—" He hadn't even finished his sentence when suddenly, with no advance warning, the concealed Alexandroni Brigade began to fire at the Irgun members as they stood at attention, listening to their commander. Perhaps the Alexandroni Brigade commander had interpreted the Irgun's delay as a refusal to comply.

The men immediately dropped to the ground, seeking refuge behind any rise, burying their faces deep in the sand, praying that they would not be hit, that the ground would swallow them up until danger passed. Their natural instinct was to return fire, but they were unarmed and could not reach the large weapons cache that was close at hand.

Yehiel lay behind a dune some twenty yards from the pier, alongside which was a pile of grease-covered English SMLE 4 rifles. He looked yearningly at the rifles, then began to crawl toward them. Inch by inch he approached the cache, pulled out a rifle from under the blanket covering the pile, and crawled back to his dune. He was well acquainted with this rifle from the days of his service in the British military. All the while, bullets from the direction of Kfar Vitkin continued to whistle overhead, spraying stone shards and dust. Aside from the fear of being wounded, Yehiel was filled with frustration – he now had a weapon, but no bullets.

During the chaos of the attack, Menachem Begin was rushed out of the fray to the docked *Altalena*. He ordered the captain to sail out of shooting range. The boat turned its prow westward, and then changed direction and headed south.

In the meantime, darkness had fallen, lit only by the flash of bullets that flared like memorial candles. Suddenly Yehiel heard a whisper at his side. He turned his head. It was his friend, Aharon "Aharonchik" (Dov) Heichman, who was crawling among the people on the ground, handing out torn undershirts to wipe the layers of grease off the weapons. No less importantly, he was also carrying a basket full of bullets. Yehiel filled his fist with bullets and stuffed more into his pockets. Then he quickly wiped off the grease, loaded the rifle, and began to return fire at his attackers.

He was no stranger to firing a weapon. But up until then, he had only shot during training sessions at firing ranges. This time, not only was he shooting at real live attackers and aiming to kill, he was forced to shoot back at his brothers, his fellow Jews. He was trapped in a terrible reality of brother attacking brother, brother bearing arms against brother. The thought flashed through his mind: when Jews shoot at Jews, is it the end of the dream of founding a Jewish state?

Another man took refuge next to Yehiel – this was Shlomo "Shloimele" Kontovsky, twenty years old, born in Warsaw, and one of Yehiel's trainees in the DP camp in Italy. He had survived the trials and tribulations of the concentration camps. In the refugee camps of Austria and Italy, he renewed his connections with Betar, which he had joined when he was only ten years old. He later joined the Irgun. Suddenly, Yehiel heard Shloimele groan. Yehiel twisted his head toward him, and saw the young man contorting in pain. He later found out that Shloimele had been hit by a bullet in the calf. Shots continued to fly over their heads, preventing them from coming to the aid of the wounded man. His blood ran like water. They had no tourniquet with which to try to save him, and even if they had, they could not get to him. He lost too much blood, fell unconscious, and toward morning, he died.

The cruel drama ended around 10 a.m. A cease-fire was declared on the public address system. Yehiel looked to his right and left and saw people standing up out of the sand. Here and there, single shots were fired. He knew that these were the most dangerous bullets. He noticed a figure rising up, heard a shot, and saw the figure collapse on the ground, lifeless. This was Avraham Oded, twenty years old, who had moved with his comrades to Zichron Ya'akov after the Irgun came out from the underground, then joined the Israel Defense Forces as part of the Irgun battalions. He was one of those who had rushed to Kfar Vitkin to assist in unloading the immigrants and weapons from the *Altalena*. He was one of those who paid for the operation with their lives.

On that bitter morning, six Irgun members (including Oded) and two IDF soldiers were killed, even before the tragedy that was to unfold on the Tel Aviv beach late that night. After the declaration of the cease-fire, military jeeps raced to the area, removed the dead, and rushed the wounded to hospitals.

After the conflict on Kfar Vitkin beach, Yehiel was overcome with exhaustion and he fell into a deep, dreamless sleep. He was awakened by the powerful rays of the afternoon sun beating down on his head. He got up, looking left and right, incredulous that after the noise and confusion of the previous night, quiet had returned. Only the breaking of the waves could be heard. He brushed the sand from his clothes, straightened them, and washed his face with water from a container he found on the beach. Then he went out to the road and hitchhiked to Netanya, to the Irgun headquarters. He felt he was returning to normal life.

The next day, he went on to Tel Aviv, where he met with his parents, who had no idea what had happened to him in Kfar Vitkin. Yehiel had heard the radio reports of what had happened to the *Altalena* on the Tel Aviv beach. The IDF had fired on her, killing ten more Irgun members (as well as another IDF soldier) and destroying the boat and her valuable military cargo. By the time Yehiel reached the beach, he saw only the burned-out shell of the boat, which stood in the shallow waters long afterward as a memorial of the catastrophe.

When he came home, he and his parents commemorated his twenty-fifth birthday, which had taken place nine days earlier. With a little less luck, it could also have been his memorial day.

At the time, Yehiel had no idea that thirty long years later, the leader who for many years had been wanted by the British, who had been admired by the fighters of the Irgun underground but hated by most of the organized Yishuv, the Jewish community in the nascent State of Israel, would earn the Nobel Peace Prize, the world's most prestigious award, as prime minister of Israel. Yehiel also could not know that he would accompany Begin on this path, serving for decades as Begin's personal aide, his right-hand man. Indeed, the prime minister and his assistant were spoken of in the same breath, as they were as close as brothers.

The Nobel Prize was granted to Begin as the leader who achieved the unimaginable: the first peace agreement between Israel and a bitter enemy state – Egypt, the largest and strongest of the Arab nations.

Hundreds of millions of viewers around the world watched with eyes glued to their screens as 250 guests in elegant dress entered the glittering Christian IV hall in the breathtakingly beautiful Akershus Castle, which was built in 1301 and stood atop a windswept hill overlooking the icy water of the fjord of Oslo, the capital of Norway. They saw the castle ushers in dark evening dress, wearing white bow ties, and listened to the chamber orchestra as it played works by Grieg and Sibelius. They observed King Olav V and Crown Prince Harald and his wife Sonja, and followed the excited expressions on the faces of the various prizewinners.

Begin and his wife Aliza (Ala to all who knew her) had arrived in a helicopter, which landed in the courtyard of the castle. Sayed Marei, who represented Egyptian president Anwar Sadat, arrived by car. (Sadat shared the prize with Begin, but was absent from the ceremony.) As the individual who knew Begin better than anyone else, except, of course, for his wife, Yehiel's heart beat at the same rate as that of his leader and friend.

After Begin received the Nobel Prize certificate and gold medal, he made a speech that included a poem in praise of peace.

Peace is the beauty of life. It is sunshine. It is the smile of a
child, the love of a mother, the joy of a father, the togetherness
of a family. It is the advancement of man, the victory of a just
cause, the triumph of truth.

There on the roof of the world, Yehiel could not help but recall that terrible
day when he lay on the sand, returning fire to his fellow Jews, a step away
from death, while his admired but controversial leader sailed the *Altalena*
weapons boat on to another harsh Jewish conflict that ended with dead
and injured and an open wound that never healed. There in distant Oslo,
Yehiel had no choice but to recall Shloimele, who had survived the Nazi
concentration camps only to be struck down by a bullet in the national
homeland, and Avraham, the Irgun fighter from Zichron Ya'akov, who
was felled by the weapons of brothers, but not by friendly fire.

Chapter 2

Sanctity and Sand

Yehiel was almost a sabra. When his parents made aliyah, he was a baby of just three months. He was born in Warsaw, Poland, on the eve of the holiday of Shavuot, 5 Sivan 5683 (May 20, 1923), twenty-five years before his life hung by a thread on the Kfar Vitkin beach.

Yehiel was the fifth child of Ze'ev Velvel Kadishson and Zipporah Feige (née Beckerman). His oldest sibling was Yitzchak, born in 1912; then came Leah (later Segal) in 1915, Shoshanna (Shelkovitz) in 1918, and Hava (Sheige) in 1921. Yehiel himself was born in 1923, and the last was Shmuel, the only true sabra in the family, born in Israel in 1926. The boys all kept the last name Kadishson, except for Yehiel. His teacher at Tachkemoni School in Tel Aviv, Mordechai Raziel, considered it a Diaspora name, inappropriate for life in Israel, and renamed him Kadishai. (This teacher was the father of David Raziel, the first Irgun commander, who was killed in Iraq in May 1941.)

Years later, when Yehiel was sixteen, he went to the office of the regional governor, the British Ministry of the Interior on Ha-Sharon Street in Tel Aviv, to get his identity card. He was quite pleased that he did not have to pay the British the twenty-five *grush* to have his name changed, as he presented himself using the name Kadishai.

His father's brother, Yisrael Yosef, who made aliyah in 1938, also changed his name from Kadishson, but preferred to call himself Ben Kayam. This new name came from a popular saying that when a male child was born, he ought to be named "Ha-Kaddish" (the Kaddish, the prayer recited for the dead), as this was the child who would recite Kaddish for his father after the father lived a long life of 120 years. Yehiel's uncle chose to transmute this to Ben Kayam, "the son who exists," meaning, the son who will recite Kaddish now exists. Yehiel's father's sister, Tova, during whose birth their mother died, made aliyah in 1933. Two of her granddaughters were songwriter Nurit Hirsch (the daughter of Tova's daughter Leah and Viennese opera singer Otto Hirsch) and actress Orly Zilberschatz. The muses of the arts played an important role in the family; in addition to these two relatives, Yehiel's nephew, son of his brother Yitzchak, is the musician Rafi Kadishson.

Further back, Yehiel's paternal grandparents were Yitzchak David and Sheindel Gittel. The oldest of Yehiel's brothers, Yitzchak, was named after this grandfather, and Yehiel's sister Shoshanna was originally called Sheindel after this grandmother. However, when the family moved to Israel, Sheindel Gittel was sent to kindergarten in Tel Aviv. When the teacher asked her name, the girl whispered softly, "Sheindel Gittel." On hearing this name from the Diaspora, the teacher burst out laughing. She then put on a serious face and said, "Here in Israel we don't use those names anymore." She thought for a moment, then decided, "From now on, your name is Shoshanna." Why Shoshanna, since the name Sheindel Gittel means "beautiful" and "good," and translates easily into the Hebrew names "Yaffa Tova"? Perhaps because *shin* is the first letter of both Sheindel and Shoshanna. Yehiel was named after the Admor and founder of the Alexander Chassidic sect, Rabbi Yehiel Danziger (1828–94).

Yehiel's maternal grandfather was Shmuel Chaim Beckerman, a *shochet* and *bodek* (ritual slaughterer and inspector) in Plonsk, birthplace of David Ben Gurion. His maternal grandmother was named Charke.

The Kadishson family had earned a reputation in Russia and Poland for the high-quality ink they manufactured. Two and three generations before Yehiel was born, members of the family worked in ink manufacturing. They also produced yellow adhesive made from gum arabic (acacia gum), a natural gum made of hardened sap from the acacia tree, which grows in Africa. The sap is used for many purposes, such as adhesive to bind paint pigments, shoe polish, and cosmetics, as well as adhesive on the back of stamps. As for the ink – fast forward to one Shabbat in 1978, when Yehiel went to services at a synagogue in New York City. On his right sat Elie Wiesel, while two seats down to his left sat a nonagenarian Jew. At one point in the service, the elderly man noticed Yehiel. He leaned toward him and said, "You're not Kadishai – you're Kadishson. I remember it as if it was this morning – the giant signs hanging above Warsaw, many years before the First World War, that said: 'Buy Kadishson's Ink.'" These signs, so he related, that advertised Kadishson Tint (ink), were written in Cyrillic letters, as Poland was then part of czarist Russia, and the ink was sold throughout the czar's empire.

One of the stories told about Yehiel's grandfather Yitzchak David was that one day he created a new color mixture that was revolutionary in the field. He took a risk on this mixture and invested a fortune in it, but there was a hitch in production and all the color came out black. Yitzchak David went to the Rebbe of Radzymin for advice.

"Rebbe, *gevald* (help)!" moaned Yitzchak.

"What happened?" asked the Rebbe.

"What will become of me?" said Yitzchak, wringing his hands. "I'm about to lose everything I have!"

The Rebbe answered, "Everything will be all right."

The grandfather asked, "What will be all right? How will it be all right?"

"Have you come to argue with me or to receive my blessing?" the Rebbe rebuked him.

Yitzchak fell silent and returned home. Two days later, Czar Nicholas died and the decree was made: every house in the empire must raise a black flag, and woe to the inhabitants of any home that did not have a black flag waving over it! But who had black dye in enormous quantities? Kadishson. He flooded the empire with black flags, earning back his initial investment with interest. But Yehiel called this a very nice story that was only a legend.

The Kadishson family, which had roots in Poland going back several generations, was also known for owning printing presses. One of these, a press that belonged to Yehiel's grandfather's brother, Menashe Kadishson, was located on 5 Ganesha Street, and in 1890 he printed a well-known compendium of Torah readings, known as *Hok le-Yisrael*.

Yehiel's parents' home was religious in the Chassidic style. His father and mother lived the life of the Chassidic community and religious Judaism, and were strictly observant in their home. They kept Shabbat and the holidays, with matzah at Passover, a sukkah and the four species at Sukkot, and at Shavuot, dairy foods as well as the all-night study session and morning services at the break of dawn. On Hanukkah, candles flickered inside the house, but not on the window toward the street, so as not to rouse the antisemitic bears from hibernation. They celebrated Purim according to tradition. On Tisha B'Av, they mourned for the destruction of the First and Second Temples with true emotion, not out of mere habit.

The family was stable financially, even well off. Aside from the family ink business, Yehiel's parents also had a fabric store they had received from their parents after they were married, to give them a stable base with which to start off. But his father did not think, like most of the family, that Poland was a place meant for the Jewish people, nor did he think it was a godly place at all.

Thus it was natural that his father would turn towards the Land of Israel not only in the Shemoneh Esreh prayer, but in his day-to-day life. He knew that his stay in the Diaspora was only temporary. He was not a Pole who happened to be Jewish. He was a Jew who was living temporarily in Poland, because historical circumstances had led him there. He lived with Jews, studied with Jews, and did business with Jews. Yiddish was his *mamme loshon*. He later told Yehiel with some pleasure that Yehiel himself (who had lived in Poland only for the first three months of his life) had never spoken with a non-Jewish Pole. "What have I got to do with them?" his father asked rhetorically.

The Chassidic way of life that characterized the household was not monolithic, but had its own uniqueness: his father was a Gerer Chassid, but he was also very close to the Alexander Chassidic sect. These two sects were the most well known within Polish Jewry. The winds of political Zionism that were blowing through Europe at that time did not reach Yehiel's father. He aspired to return to Zion without being a formal Zionist. "You don't have to be a Zionist to live in Eretz Israel," he once responded to someone who asked him if he was a Zionist. "Every Jew should live in Eretz Israel; there is no room for Jews in the Diaspora."

Thus, when he made the decision to make aliyah to Eretz Israel, he did what every Chassid did in such a situation – he went to his Rebbe to get his blessing.

To his surprise, the first Rebbe he approached refused – Yehiel's father did not tell his family which one this was, although it is not difficult to guess. The Rebbe fixed him with a penetrating gaze and said, "You aren't going to Eretz Israel, because I'm not giving you my blessing."

Velvel Kadishson was astonished, but he did not give up. He went to the second Rebbe, who granted his blessing. Velvel did not wait long before making aliyah with a large sum of money he planned to invest in business, five hundred British pounds, a sizable fortune. He lived in Eretz Israel for some time, inquiring into businesses in which he might invest the sum. He sent his wife glowing letters "from our homeland, which is built with the help of God, may His Name be blessed, and lacks nothing, where oranges in the winter and grapes in the summer are sold practically for free." When he had finished the preparations, Velvel sent a letter to his wife, Faygele, to come join him.

The well-known Yiddish American writer Dr. Hillel Zeidman, who published mainly in New York's Yiddish newspaper *Der Morgen Zhurnal*, once wrote a poetic article about Yehiel after he became Begin's right-hand man, in which he described the family's aliyah:

> In 1923, a Jewish woman from Warsaw makes aliyah with her five children to the shores of little Tel Aviv, where her husband, who arrived earlier, awaits her. In one hand she holds their youngest child, three months old, and in the other she holds a Torah scroll. The name of the child is Yehiel Kadishson. I look at the picture and my vision clouds. Through my tears, I don't see just any ordinary new immigrants. I see a Jewish mother, the quintessential Jewish mother, who saves two Torah scrolls from the threat of the conflagration a quarter century later: One is a Torah scroll of parchment; the other a Jewish child, who is also compared to a Torah scroll.

This description is emotional and literary, and touching, but ignores the small problem of how the mother with five children had reached the shore. Mother and children had begun their journey by train from Warsaw to Constanta, Romania, where they boarded a boat that sailed to Jaffa. They had no baggage, except for some canned goods and crackers that Faygele took with her, for God only knew what *treyf* food they would be given, if they were given anything at all. They were not worried about the journey, since they had the Rebbe's blessing.

The youngest, Yehiel, was but three months old, and Faygele carried him in her arms. The other four, a boy and three girls, were tied with ropes to a belt wound around her apron so that they wouldn't get separated from her along the way, and also so that they would not slip on board the boat. In reality, the Torah scroll was carried not in her other hand but in the arms of Moshe Zachsenhaus of Warsaw. He was an acquaintance who had sailed on the same boat and made aliyah with them, and later became a cart driver in Tel Aviv. Velvel Kadishson had given Moshe the responsibility of bringing over the Torah scroll that had been handed down in his family.

When the boat reached Jaffa port, there was no jetty or platform for disembarking passengers. How were they supposed to reach the shore? In small boats and barges. But how would they reach the boats and barges, as their ship had no stairs? The answer was simple – on the shoulders of the Arab porters.

Yehiel related: "Mother saw how the men were carrying the women on their shoulders, and she announced, 'There's no way I'm going down to shore like that.' So what will you do, she was asked. Her reply was clear and simple: 'I'm going back to Warsaw.' In the meantime, my father stood across from her on the jetty. He saw and perhaps also heard about Mother's plans, that she would do anything to avoid a man carrying her on his shoulders, and he shouted to her as she stood on deck: 'Come down, Faygele, come down, it's okay!' Finally, Mother and her children were tossed up in the air. They landed on the porters' shoulders and were carried to shore."

There in Jaffa port, the family was reunited. Yehiel's father, who had waited for them at the port in anticipation, lovingly welcomed his wife and children, whom he had not seen for a long time, as well as the Torah scroll. He took them to a hotel that he had rented and would eventually buy. On that day, the once homemaker became hotel manager and cook. Faygele went into the kitchen, and only left it after a difficult decade, when Velvel eventually sold the hotel.

While the rest of his family had been getting organized to make aliyah and then making the journey, Velvel Kadishson did not waste his time. He scoured the streets of little Tel Aviv searching for a good business, preferably a bargain. He found one. In 1923, he rented a two-story building in the newly constructed Rosenfeld quarter on the seashore. The building had a dozen rooms, six on the first floor and six on the second. Velvel purchased beds and closets, and transformed the building into a hotel facing the ocean. This was Tel Aviv's first hotel on the beach.

The Rosenfeld quarter, or "Rosenfeld Homes," was constructed that same year by an American immigrant named Shimon Rosenfeld. He purchased the land from the Hachsharat Ha-Yishuv company, which in turn had obtained it from an Arab family in Jaffa who did not consider it worth keeping. The neighborhood occupied an area that eventually became Herbert Samuel Promenade along the seashore, from the corner of the future Trumpeldor Street in the north down to the future Yarden Street in the south. The Kadishsons' hotel was the southernmost building. The trademark of the long two-story buildings was their rounded tin roofs, which were shaped like barrels turned on their sides.

Before the hotel was constructed, the *Daily Mail* newspaper wrote, "This hotel, with a large flag flying over it, is strange to the site. Even the camels carrying sand and merchandise along the seashore on their way from the fields of Sheikh Munis and Sumeil to Jaffa Port look askance at the strange building that is to become a hotel. We all know that this is how our country will be built, as well as our hotels. We love you, our new pioneer who joins your older brother, the Rosenfeld quarter."

Velvel set aside a few of the first-floor rooms for his own family's living quarters and a dining room and kitchen. He named it the Vershevsky Hotel, after his hometown of Warsaw, as an auspicious sign for a prosperous business. The second-floor rooms were designated for guests. Sometimes, when the hotel was full, guests stayed in the first-floor rooms that belonged to the family. The building had a broad roof, and some of the first-floor rooms had steps leading down to the beach. The hotel catered to Jewish tourists from Europe, attracting many observant Jews, rabbis, and Chassidic leaders, with whom Velvel enjoyed discussing Torah, earning the hotel on the shores of Tel Aviv a reputation among European Jewry.

"Father was strictly observant, and he was a scholar of Talmud," Yehiel related. "He used to tell me, 'Read everything that's printed, but stay away from the Zohar and Kabbalah.'"

The hotel was somewhat of a success, depending on the time of year. It turned a profit mainly in the summer season, when Jews from overseas came to visit Eretz Israel, including eminent Chassidic Rebbes. In the winter, when the tide rose and seawater penetrated the building, revenue was at low tide. "Seawater often leaked into the hotel in the winter," Yehiel recounted. "The water didn't damage the heavy iron beds, but other furniture was made of wood, and each winter a few items were swept out to sea with the tide." In the summer, when the tides were at the low point, profits reached their height.

Many guests filled the hotel, and sometimes it was fully booked. Velvel, the owner and manager, adopted worldly customs, purchasing a suit of sky-blue and white that gave him the look of a refined businessman. To complete the picture, he even bought a Rolls Royce motorcar from British military surplus, and used it to transport tourists from Jaffa port to the hotel, or into town, as everything was nearby.

Velvel was a seasoned hotelier. One of the stories that was passed down in the family told of a pampered Jew from Europe who wanted a room near the sea. Velvel took him to the balcony of the largest room, which was also the most expensive, stood behind him, and announced in his best tour guide voice, "Here, this is your room – and here, right here, is the sea."

The tourist gazed out at the white tops, looked back into the room, scratched his forehead and finally exclaimed, "No, no! This is no good."

"Why?" asked Velvel. "What's wrong?"

"Because I can't sleep with the noise from the waves," declared the tourist.

"What do you mean?" Velvel replied, unfazed. "Look at that distance – the room is right here, and the sea is way over there…"

Years later, seasoned journalist Gabriel Tsifroni wrote in *Maariv* newspaper (under the pseudonym Y. Getz): "Word reached Jerusalem of the kosher hotel on the shores of Tel Aviv, and praise of the delicacies of Zipporah Feige's kitchen tempted the wise among the well-off ultra-Orthodox vacationers. In the summer months, they usually went to swim

at Jaffa beach and stayed in the Neve Shalom and Neve Tzedek hotels."
A few months after the family arrived, the great wave of the Fourth
Aliyah began, breathing new life into Eretz Israel in general and Tel Aviv
in particular. The Vershevsky Hotel was among the beneficiaries of this
inundation.

The secularist glitter that sparkled from the nearby cafes did nothing
to harm the decorous ambience that the Jerusalem notables desired on
their holidays. The family atmosphere of the Vershevsky Hotel won them
over. Guests from abroad were plentiful in those days of glory. The hotel
reached the pinnacle of fame in the ultra-Orthodox world when the Rebbe
of Amshinov, who came to Eretz Israel to visit his followers, stayed there
with his entourage.

Jews from Poland who were visiting Eretz Israel also came to the hotel.
Yet they were eager to return to the land they really loved, Poland, which
would soon repay their love with lethal hatred. They found a million
reasons why life in Eretz Israel was unlivable. Once, when Yehiel was
eight, he overheard one of these tourists as the guest sat in the salon – it
was not yet called a lobby – and sipped a glass of tea. The guest said to
Velvel, "I don't understand how you can live in this country! The sugar
here is so bitter!"

Velvel, trying desperately not to burst out laughing, replied, "Yes, it's
really quite strange. We brought that sugar over straight from Poland, in
sealed wooden boxes…"

Velvel made great efforts to convince his relatives to make aliyah,
running between the various government offices to try to obtain
"certificates" for them. Most did not come, as they could not foresee the
terror that awaited them around the corner, but finally, his efforts bore
fruit: his sister, Tova, and her husband, Yehudah Zilberschatz, made
aliyah in 1933.

Other relatives, who visited Eretz Israel and stayed in the hotel, getting
soaked by the rains in winter and drowning in the humidity of summer,
sighed heavily, "How can you live here? For six months the rain falls on
you, and the other six months the rain falls off you…"

But the boy Yehiel feared neither rain nor humidity.

Yehiel's childhood was filled with the view of the sea, the murmur of the waves, the salty taste of the water, and the soft sand that swallowed his footprints. Yehiel was a child of the sea, like Elik, the main character of the book *Bemo Yadav: Pirkei Elik* (With His Own Hands) written by Elik's brother, the well-known author Moshe Shamir, who lived next door to the hotel.

"The sea is where we were constantly – in it, or next to it," Yehiel related. "We mostly waded in the shallows, but we also went in after we learned to swim, by ourselves. We collected shells, we built beautiful, richly imaginative sand castles. Once, when I was little, I almost drowned. I went into the water and suddenly I felt like something was pulling me in. I tried to fight the stubborn wave, but it was bigger than me. Suddenly one of the swimmers saw me, stretched out his hand and grabbed me, and that's what saved me. When I returned home, I didn't even tell my mother, because what was there to tell? Nothing happened to me. I did not tell her about other, worse incidents, so why should I tell her about this? My brother Yitzchak, who was a good swimmer, was once caught up in a whirlpool, and escaped by a miracle. There were always dangerous currents in the ocean."

Sometimes the beach was profitable, not just for business owners, but for children as well. In the 1920s, Tel Aviv residents began developing the beach area as a site for leisure and tourism. This was during the Fourth Aliyah, when the bourgeois who made aliyah were permitted by the British Mandate to bring money into Palestine. The social worldview of these new immigrants was individualistic and inspired them to take advantage of the potential of the seashore for monetary profit. Some areas of the Tel Aviv seashore were not fit for swimming, and rocks along the beach had to be removed. The Tel Aviv municipality rented an additional area from the Mandate, at the end of Allenby Street, where they erected three swimming stations. These were buildings on the seashore with staircases on the second floor from which one could descend directly into the water. These swimming stations were privately owned, and their owners removed the rocks from the water. One of these buildings was declared the "Hot Seawater Bathhouse" by a big sign displayed on the large wooden structure, which was constructed on pillars next to the waterline. The initiative of a Tel Aviv resident named Sordotovitch, this building was divided into small booths, each one with a bathtub for sitting in, which stood on metal legs, and a heater for the water inside the tub. In order to enter and enjoy a *mehaye* in the baths, customers had to pay half a *grush*. (A *grush* was equal to 1/100 of a British pound.) The boys on the beach, Yehiel among them, used to crawl under the building and use an improvised net to collect coins that fell from the pockets of the bathers at the Hot Seawater Bathhouse. They used the coins to buy an assortment of candies they didn't have at home.

"Once I broke my leg, and I didn't tell my mother about it," Yehiel said. "It happened on Allenby Street on the corner of Mea Shearim Street, today Ha-Kovshim Street. On the corner of the street there was a small house, six feet (2 m) lower than the street. This was the home of painter Zionka [Siona] Tagger, the mother of Avraham Katz-Oz, a former Knesset member. We kids easily climbed onto the roof of the house by grabbing onto boards and other projections. We jumped off the roof into piles of sand – the height was reasonable, and it was great fun.

"I wanted to do something unusual, because it wasn't anything special to jump onto a pile of sand, so I jumped onto a concrete platform – and broke my ankle. The pain was sharp. I limped on one leg all the way down Allenby Street to our home. I considered what I should do so that my parents wouldn't find out what had happened – I didn't yet know that it was a break. I concluded that the situation demanded an act of daring.

"In those days, people left the doors to their homes open, as they had no reason to fear thieves. When I got home, I knocked on the unlocked door. My sister Shoshanna opened the door wide, and I fell on the floor and acted as if I had just hurt myself. I groaned heavily. My mother, sisters, and brothers ran over to me, lifted me off the floor, and carried me to the kitchen table. They sent for a long-bearded Yemenite who was known for his supreme powers of healing. He asked us for a small bowl, filled it with olive oil, and gave me a massage, which was not worth beans. The next morning my brother Yitzchak took me on his bicycle to orthopedist Dr. Ya'akov Weinshall. His clinic was on the first floor of a building next to the Great Synagogue. He looked at my foot, touched it here and there, and I jumped to the ceiling in pain. He identified the problem at once, but did not give me any preparations, just wrapped my foot in a cast. Two weeks later, he removed the cast and continued treatments with a blue lamp. Soon after I was healed, I rode at high speed on a scooter down Geula Street toward the beach, hit something and was thrown into the air. I landed hard, and the result was a broken arm – and another cast."

As befitting for the precious child of an Orthodox family, at age three and a half Yehiel was sent to learn his letters at the *cheder* near Kerem Ha-Teimanim. The *cheder* was next to Ezrat Achim Synagogue, no more than a large tin hut. Beside it was a small building in which the teacher labored to teach the boys to read and write. Yehiel sat on the bench together with ten other young boys and learned his letters. Later he attended the Sefat Emet *cheder*, which was run by the Ger Chassidic movement. On his head he wore a beret, and he always wore short pants, even in winter.

He attended the *cheder* until he was six. Then he went to the Histadrut Ha-Haredim school in Simchat Beit Ha-Sho'eva Lane, on Allenby Street in Tel Aviv, which was a private boys' school with an aristocratic name. The curriculum was mostly Torah studies, with some English and math. The institution was established by Yosef Fetter, a Belgian millionaire and founder of the Belgium-Eretz Israel Bank and a substantial agricultural estate in Gedera. Yehiel continued at that school until the end of sixth grade, when he switched to Tachkemoni School, run by the Mizrachi movement

Two brothers from the Chelchinsky family, who were in Yehiel's class, came from Ir Shalom, a neighborhood in the area of today's Ramat Ha-Sharon. We can learn something of the atmosphere of the times from the fact that the brothers came every day to school riding together on the back of a hefty brown donkey, which they tied to a post with a rope. They left it with a bag full of hay and a bucket of water, and it waited for them with donkey-like patience until the end of their studies around 3 p.m., when they rode it back home.

Yehiel's Bible teacher was Dr. Dov Plato, who wrote a commentary to the book of Jeremiah together with writer Ephraim Zoref. It goes without saying that Dr. Plato required his students to purchase his book.

"The price he asked for the book was very high," Yehiel related. "It cost eighteen *grush*. To get some idea of what this was worth, in my father's hotel this was almost equal to the price of five meals of five full courses each. Each meal cost four *grush*. Most of us – myself and my good friend for many years Nachum Slonim, who sat next to me at the same desk in class – did not have enough money to buy Plato's book. Most of the boys in the class were from poor families. Plato used to walk among the rows and peek at our books to see which ones we were using. Once, when he saw that we didn't have his book, he shouted at us, 'Where's the book?!' Nachum replied, speaking for myself as well, 'My father said, What's wrong, Rashi's not good enough anymore?'"

Later, Nachum Slonim confided to his father, "Dr. Plato is treating me unfairly because I didn't buy his book." Slonim's father replied, "Nonsense. Be a good student, and you'll get good grades." Two weeks later, they had a test in class. Nachum didn't know the material as well as Yehiel, so while Nachum scribbled something on paper as if he were writing, Yehiel wrote the answers for both of them using carbon paper. The copies were identical, except that Yehiel Kadishai's name appeared at the bottom of the original, while Nachum Slonim signed his name at the bottom of the copy. When they received their graded tests back, Yehiel had received an A minus, while Slonim received an F.

Like anyone else, Dr. Plato was trying to improve his financial situation, so every Shabbat at 11 a.m. he gave a lecture at the local community center. The hall was large, but the number of listeners was meager – a small handful of Jews who were not in a hurry to go home after synagogue. They were occasionally joined by a few pupils from the school who were less interested in Plato's lecture than in implementing the plot they had hatched. Once every few weeks, no sooner had Plato begun to speak than they shouted from the back seats of the hall: "We can't hear you!" Plato raised his voice. Two minutes later, the boys again shouted, "We can't hear you!" Plato turned up the volume until he was almost shouting. The shouts were enough to satisfy the children, as the next day Plato was so hoarse that he was barely able to teach his regular class.

One day during a recess between classes, a few weeks before Passover, Yehiel played a game of cops and robbers with his friends that ended at the doctor's office. Yehiel tripped while pursuing one of his friends, falling heavily to the ground and cutting his leg under the left knee. The wound bled copiously. The teacher called the emergency service, and a horse-drawn cart came to the school. Yehiel was loaded into the cart, the driver raised his whip, and the horse was driven urgently to the Magen David Adom first aid station, where the wound was stitched.

After school was over, Yehiel went home. His mother was in the kitchen, and he went into another room without saying a word. A week or two passed, until on the night of the Seder, his mother noticed that he was sitting quietly in his chair, avoiding his usual running around. She leaned toward him, and noticed that his leg was bandaged. Only then did she discover what happened. Because the healing process had already begun, she was not particularly upset. After all, Yehiel was hardly an only child, but rather one of six.

CHAPTER 3

REPUTABLE REBBE

The Vershevsky Hotel operated until 1936, when it became a victim of the relative daring of the swimsuits worn by women who came to the beach. Although the style in those days was monastic by today's standards, the Chassidic Rebbes and the ultra-Orthodox guests from abroad who went out to the balcony to enjoy the sea air, or looked out of the windows in their rooms, were shocked at the sight. They searched for other hotels, to distance themselves from the disgrace. What saved the hotel from total bankruptcy was the fact that tourists in Eretz Israel in those days came to pamper themselves at the spa nearby, and then went to the Vershevsky to rest from their exertions.

Velvel thus reached the conclusion that the hotel would not become his source of pride and joy, not only because the profits were not particularly impressive, but mainly because he was concerned for the spiritual welfare of his three teenage daughters.

Hava, Yehiel's sister, recounted: "All kinds of elements began to come to the beach. They roamed around the promenade, smoked in public on Shabbat, did not wear head coverings, and did not behave appropriately. Father was afraid lest the slightest trace of this atmosphere cast a stain on his daughters' reputation and lead to disgrace."

So after thirteen years of managing the hotel, Velvel sold it for three hundred British pounds to a businessman named Landau, who was one of the owners of the *mikveh* on Mea Shearim Street (later Ha-Kovshim Street). Landau continued to manage it for several years. The family went to live one street away, in a rented apartment on Nahmani Street.

Yehiel's father continued to follow traditional Judaism and became active politically in the Poalei Agudat Yisrael movement, the ultra-Orthodox movement that split off from Agudat Yisrael. The new movement placed the settlement of Eretz Israel at the top of its social, political, and religious agenda. Over the years, it established fourteen settlements, including nine *moshavim* and two *kibbutzim*.

However, Velvel sorely felt his lack of a Rebbe. His previous Rebbes had remained in Poland, and he sought a religious authority, a mentor. He often visited Jerusalem, where, besides eagerly drinking in the atmosphere, he spent time in the courts of Chassidic Rebbes and other rabbis. There he met Noah Gad Weintraub, a Torah scholar, who printed small booklets with collections of commentaries on the weekly portion. On occasion, Weintraub came to Tel Aviv to sell his booklets for a few coins. Velvel began to assist him in this endeavor.

One day, in a small room in the Old City of Jerusalem, Velvel met a man of thirty-four with a hard-working wife and several children. He had red hair, a pale visage, and a penetrating gaze. Velvel sensed that this was a Rebbe in the making. He did not affect the manners of a Rebbe, however, and his financial situation was dire.

"Who is he?" Velvel asked the few individuals who were in the room.

"That's the Rebbe of Lelov, Rabbi Moshe Mordechai Biderman," they replied. "He's a sixth-generation descendant of Rabbi David, son of Rabbi Shlomo Zvi Biderman, founder of the Lelov Chassidic sect from Poland."

The second Rebbe in this dynasty, Rabbi Moshe Biderman, son of Rabbi David, made aliyah in 1852 with his children and grandchildren. The dynasty grew slowly but surely in Hebron and Jerusalem. The third Rebbe was Rabbi Elazar Menachem Mendel Biderman, while the fourth was his son, Rabbi David Zvi Shlomo Biderman, known as Reb Dudel. The fifth Rebbe was Reb Dudel's son, Rabbi Shimon Natan Nuta Biderman, and the sixth was Rabbi Moshe Mordechai Biderman, whom Velvel met that day in Jerusalem.

The Rebbe and Velvel began to discuss Talmudic matters, and Yehiel's father was astonished at the young Rebbe's breadth of knowledge. For his part, the Rebbe discovered that Velvel Kadishson was no simpleton. While still deep in conversation, Kadishson's brain cooked up an idea, and toward the end of their talk, he asked, "Rebbe, why doesn't Your Honor consider moving to Tel Aviv?"

"Tel Aviv?" the Rebbe responded in surprise. "Since the aliyah of my great-great-grandfather, Rabbi Moshe Biderman, may his memory be a blessing, whose name I bear, we have always lived in Jerusalem, the holy city. Why should we leave?"

"With all due respect to Jerusalem, the eternal city," Kadishson replied, "here there's a rabbi behind every other door."

"And what's wrong with that?" asked the Rebbe of Lelov.

"Nothing wrong with it, God forbid," said Kadishson. "But why should Tel Aviv get the bad end of the deal? Are there no observant Jews there? Are there no Chassidim there? There are plenty! But there are no Rebbes. There are sheep, but no shepherd."

While the Rebbe considered this, Kadishson continued: "Come to us, Rebbe, we'll organize a nice apartment for Your Honor. I'll bring you Chassidim who are looking for a Rebbe, and your court will blossom and grow."

The Rebbe asked for some time to think.

At the time, Nahmani Street, where the Kadishson family had moved after Velvel sold the hotel, was populated by the aristocratic society of Tel Aviv. For income, Velvel opened a store for writing implements called Writing Implements Center at 132 Allenby Street, next to the post office – once in the ink business, always in the ink business. The store earned a solid reputation for its quality products, which Velvel imported from Austria and England.

This step proved wise, and revenue was plentiful. Velvel did not sit on his money, but rather invested it in a field of twelve dunam (about three acres) in Gan Shlomo near Tel Mond, which he bought under excellent conditions through a project administered by the Mizrachi (Religious Zionist) movement. The burden of working the field fell on the shoulders of the oldest boy, Yehiel's oldest brother Yitzchak, who performed the job faithfully. The romance with the field ended in the bloody events of 1936, when Arab rioters entered the field in the dark of night and decimated it, uprooting everything up to the last tree. Eventually, after Velvel's death, his wife sold the field to the Yachin Hekel company and used the money to put a down payment on the apartment she was renting in Tel Aviv.

Velvel invested in more than material property – he also invested in the spiritual assets of Jewish heritage. During one of his visits to the Rebbe of Lelov in the 1930s, the Rebbe announced that he was willing to move to Tel Aviv. Velvel was prepared. He had already spoken with the owner of an apartment at the corner of Nachalat Binyamin Street and Lewinsky Street, which was then a central area of Tel Aviv that was in demand. Once he received the green light from the Rebbe of Lelov, he swiftly rented the apartment for him. Velvel also persuaded many of his friends and acquaintances to join the Rebbe's disciples, and the Lelover following grew. Before the arrival of the Rebbe of Lelov, other Chassidic sects had established roots in Tel Aviv, such as Amshinov, Modzits and Strikov, but they did not compete with each other, and there was plenty of room for the Chassidic groups to grow.

It turned out that the move to Tel Aviv was a smart one for the Lelov group. A few years after the move, a certain Chassid joined the Rebbe's following, and this man became quite wealthy. He bought the Rebbe a home on Mohaliver Street, a two-story house with a basement. The patron even built a *mikveh* in the basement. The Rebbe lived on the top floor, while his study was on the ground floor, which resonated with the sound of Torah learning. With the *mikveh* down below, what more could a Rebbe and his Chassidim want?

The Lelover Rebbe's reputation spread far and wide, and he was sought out by many. His Torah commentaries were published in the collection *Birkat Moshe*. He became known as a wonder-worker and immersed himself in the *mikveh* frequently. He also suffered from many illnesses. He prayed constantly for others, but he himself was not granted respite from his suffering.

Yehiel celebrated his bar mitzvah in the new home at 41 Nahmani Street, on the corner of Yehudah Ha-Levy Street. There is no comparison between twenty-first century bar mitzvah celebrations and those held in the early twentieth century. In those days, the main element of the celebration, in addition to the laying of tefillin for the first time on a weekday, was the aliyah to the Torah in the synagogue on Shabbat. Each week, Yehiel's father prayed in the Poalei Agudat Yisrael synagogue, located on the second floor of the "Blue Building," the nickname for the building of that color on Allenby Street across from the post office. It was one of the first apartment buildings in Eretz Israel. There were stores on the first floor and offices on the second, one of which contained the synagogue. On their bar mitzvah Shabbatot, some of Yehiel's friends went up to the Torah and read the entire *parashah* and *haftarah*, while others read portions from each. Yehiel did not push himself – he read only the *haftarah* of Parashat Yitro, but did so in a melodious voice that captured the hearts of the congregants – "In the year that King Uziyahu died…"(Is. 6:1).

After the service, Yehiel's family invited the congregants and extended family to a kiddush. As for gifts, at that time the accepted bar mitzvah gift was books, not checks as is common in Israel and many other places today, but books inscribed with a dedication. One relative of the Kadishson family, named Goldwasser, gave Yehiel a set of the Mishnah. Avraham Weinberg, Yehiel's cousin on his mother's side, who worked at the Ha-Po'el Ha-Mizrachi print shop at 109 Nachalat Binyamin Street, brought him a book of poetry by Uri Zvi Greenberg, *Sefer ha-Kitrug ve-ha-Emunah* (The Book of Indictment and Faith). It lacked a cover, because the print shop only did printing, and binding was done elsewhere.

Uri Zvi Greenberg and the Mishnah served as the paving stones of Yehiel's worldview, representing nationalism and tradition, respectively. These elements formed the foundation of his belief in the truth of his path, and throughout his life, he walked between them.

From a young age, Yehiel's life followed in the paths of the forefathers. The family home was strictly kosher, its ways founded on the pillars of the Jewish faith. As such, Yehiel was well acquainted with the byways that lead among the verses in Uri Zvi Greenberg's poems. Some of these became key phrases that described his life, such as the epigraph of Greenberg's collection of poetry, *Ezor Magen u-Ne'um Ben ha-Dam* (A Shield of Defense and the Word of the Son of Blood):

> Our God wants it, and the Messiah is here, too.
> There's a plow for the homeland, and ten thousand youths for
> the army.
> There's the gold, and there's the goldsmith waiting
> To strike the coin: For the freedom of Israel
> But who doesn't want it? – Evil Fate,

Dragging us forever through fire and blood:
From the teeth of Christianity to the teeth of Islam.

After one year in the apartment on Nahmani Street, the Kadishson family moved again, both due to the high cost of rent at four lirot per month, and also because of the apartment's relatively long distance from the store. The new apartment was at 81 Nachalat Binyamin Street, in a new building constructed by contractor Yisrael Habas, right behind their store. It was also cheaper – just three and a half lirot per month. They left that apartment after one year as well, this time moving to the building closest to the store at 83 Nachalat Binyamin, where the rent was just three lirot.

Yehiel's father was responsible for standing inside the store, praising the merchandise, and making an honest sale. In 1940, Yehiel's mother Faygele opened a corner grocery store on Yehudah Ha-Levy Street, at the corner of Allenby Street. Why? First of all, additional income never hurt anyone, and second – and this was the main reason – Faygele wanted his brother Yitzchak to settle down, get married and start his own family. After all, he was already an old man of twenty-eight. So she took action and prepared the ground for his eventual source of income.

But the problem was not just his age. Yitzchak had begun to spend time with the bohemians of Tel Aviv. He took the *kippah* off his head, abandoned the religious lifestyle, and carried a cigarette between his lips even on Shabbat. Faygele attempted to rehabilitate him, but it seemed she was trying to shut the stable door after the horse had already bolted.

Yitzchak had no interest whatsoever in the grocery store – instead, he entertained hopes of entering the arts. Although he didn't aspire to be an actor, he joined the Ha-Bimah youth theater group. He wrote passionate articles about plays, copying them and distributing them to the members. He became friends with Baruch Agadati, a bohemian Tel Aviv legend. Yitzchak became involved in organizing public balls on Purim and Hanukkah. Later he discovered Friday nights, when the movie theaters were closed due to Shabbat. He rented the Esther Theater in Tel Aviv and the Ramah in Ramat Gan, bringing performers that attracted large crowds to the stage. Later, he rented theaters in other cities as well. He produced shows with artists Yosef Goland, Mia Arbatova, Hasia Levi, and Tova

Piron. The pinnacle of his achievements was the discovery of Yemenite singer Shoshanna Damari. Later he met producer Yosef (Papo) Milo, and together they founded the Cameri Theater.

For Yehiel, like many youths of his generation, completion of junior high school was a sign that he was ready to go out to work to help support his family. His father's business was not the same as it had been in better times, and so Yehiel's work was truly a necessity. The family used his salary to help pay the rent.

At fifteen, Yehiel found a job as a distributor of pharmaceuticals for Salomon, Levin, & Elstein Ltd., a large commercial firm in Tel Aviv. This company, whose offices were at 85 Nachalat Binyamin Street, had a well-established reputation. The firm purchased medications and medical instruments from factories in Eretz Israel, and also imported from abroad, and sold them to pharmacies. Yehiel's work was not particularly complicated – he and three other youths who worked with him delivered orders to the pharmacies in the area by bicycle. Sometimes he delivered medicines to pharmacies in other areas, such as Ramle, but then he would take the bus.

"It was truly outrageous treatment," Yehiel recalled. "We started work at 7 a.m., and the company closed up shop at 6 p.m. But for some reason, at a quarter to six they always sent us out with urgent deliveries of medicines to pharmacies around town, or out of town, so we finished work at 6:30 or even 7 p.m., twelve hours after we had begun. These hours were possible because the pharmacies were open until 7 or even 8 p.m. I said to myself that it was not fair that we boys had to work many more hours than the managers and the rest of the employees."

Yehiel's socialistic nature took over, and he organized a strike. He recruited his three fellow delivery boys, who joined in enthusiastically. "One day, I went to the manager and said, 'This is not right. You should send us out on special deliveries at 5 p.m. or before, so that we can finish work at 6.'

"At first, he gave me a one-word answer: 'No!' Then he added, 'And don't bother showing up again for work.' 'Goodbye!' I retorted, and off I stormed. I told my fellow delivery boys what had happened, and they decided not to show up the next day for work either.

"On the day of our no-show demonstration, the manager, Yehudah Hazroni, came to my home, and said to my mother, 'Tell Yehiel he should come to work.' I ran to my three friends and said, 'Let's go, the strike's over.' We went back to work, and from that day on they sent us out on urgent deliveries before 5 p.m., and we went home at 5:30."

CHAPTER 4

FATEFUL DECISION

After finishing his elementary school studies, Yehiel continued at the Center for Qualified Teachers, a night school for clerks and commerce, on 12 Hess Street near Allenby Street. The teaching staff was small, and most of the classes were in math, English, and Hebrew. Tuition was thirty-five *grush* per month, and Yehiel's father paid each month in advance, as required.

Tel Aviv was still a small town of a few people, in the words of Nachum Gutman, who became the official painter of the first Hebrew city. On one of Yehiel's first days at the school, Yehiel's father met the principal as he was walking down the street.

"*Nu*," asked the proud father, "how is my son progressing in his studies?"

The principal glowered at him and replied, "How can he progress and where can he progress to, if he barely shows up?"

Velvel Kadishson lowered his glance and slunk away. Yehiel did attend class, but not always. As a matter of fact, his attendance was very irregular. At the time, he was fifteen. He had just discovered Betar, Ze'ev Jabotinsky's youth movement, and its activities quickly expanded to fill his entire world. Naturally, his attraction to the youth movement of the Revisionist Zionists originated in his parents' home, which was infused with love for the Land of Israel and the people of Israel.

"The house I grew up in," said Yehiel, "was a Jewish home filled with a combination of love for the family and love for the entire Jewish people. It was 1938–39, the outbreak of the Second World War, and every youth was involved in current events. There was no such thing as not being involved in something. I came to Betar as a result of my education at home, which instilled in me the desire to work toward the revival of the Jewish state that was not a dream, not a vision, but a reality. Many in the Yishuv did not consider this a given."

Yehiel felt comfortable with Betar's Zionist orientation, but even more so he was drawn to the movement because Betar connected action with interpretation. The "interpretation" was the poems of Uri Zvi Greenberg, while the "action" was Jabotinsky's pragmatic Zionism. In his novel *Samson*, Jabotinsky's main character articulated a well-known tripartite farewell message that mirrored the author's worldview: "iron, king, and laughter," acquire iron, choose a king, and learn to laugh.

Shmuel Topyol, a friend of Yehiel's from the Betar movement, later recounted that of Jabotinsky's principles, the ones that Yehiel embodied best were laughter and iron. Yehiel's speech was replete with witty comments, Jewish sayings, and jokes that had his friends doubled over with laughter. As for acquiring iron: "There was a small arms storage room in our backyard. One day, Yehiel appeared at our house on leave. He arrived straight from the train, rucksack on his back, dripping with sweat. He put down the rucksack and began to pull out personal items one after another. I thought to myself, what's he brought us in there? Who knows what kind of cannon he's hiding in the bag? Finally he pulled out five English rifle balls, including a bore snake for cleaning the barrel."

Yet Betar was not Yehiel's first stop. Initially, like most of the graduates of Tachkemoni school, he went to the local branch of Bnei Akiva, the youth movement of the Mizrachi, which held activities at the main offices of the organization at 108 Echad Ha-Am Street. Yehiel went there once and only once, for a Shabbat afternoon activity. He was not particularly impressed by the event, and decided to look elsewhere. Next he went to Brit Hashmona'im, the religious Zionist youth movement active in Eretz Israel mainly from 1937 to 1949, but his engagement with the movement lasted just one day. The third attempt was Betar, the movement he remained attached to his entire life.

Yehiel was attracted to Betar (and later the Irgun as well) because he identified with the movement's ideological principles, but more than that, he was practically pushed into this path by the events taking place both within Eretz Israel and outside it. Yehiel was fifteen in 1938, the harshest year yet for the Yishuv, at least in terms of loss of life, following the renewal of terrorist activities by Arab gangs in the fall of 1937. In the beginning of 1938, victims of Arab terror numbered between one and twelve per month. In July 1938, this number rose to seventeen, and in the last half of 1938, from July to September, the Jewish community suffered deep losses: sixty dead in July, forty-nine in August, fifty-three in September, forty-nine in October, and thirty-two over November and December combined. In total, 243 Jews were killed in that year, more than half of the number of all the victims in the three years of the Arab revolt. Terrorist incidents and attacks became daily occurrences. The Land burned.

In February, an Arab attack on Kibbutz Tirat Zvi was repelled. In April, the British arrested three members of the Betar recruitment arm in Rosh Pina who shot at an Arab bus in response to the murder of Jews in a taxi on the Acre-Safed road a short time earlier. (None of the Arab passengers were hurt, and the bus continued its route.) One of the three arrested, Shlomo Ben Yosef, was executed on June 29, 1938 (30 Sivan 5698); he became the first of the *olei ha-gardom*, the Jewish martyrs executed by the British. In July, legendary pioneer Alexander Zaid was murdered next to his home in Sheikh Abreik. The Arabs took control of the Old City in Jerusalem, except for the Jewish Quarter. The Jewish mayor of Tiberias, Zaki Alhadif, was murdered by Arabs. In Europe, the antisemitic winds of war began to blow: Kristallnacht, which took place in the German Reich in November 1938, was one of its lowest points.

Above all, Yehiel recalled the murder of two compassionate nurses, which took place in 1936. Nehama Zedek and Martha (Miriam) Fink worked in the hospital in Jaffa, treating Jews and Arabs together in the same rooms. They walked to work down the alleys of Jaffa in their white uniforms, heads held high, with a sense of mission. On that bitter day, at a bend in the road, they were ambushed by an Arab terrorist who riddled their bodies with pistol bullets.

New tragedies overlay the old, and because Israel has such a large number of terror victims, it is difficult to recall individual faces, and they are forgotten with time. But even Arab leaders were moved to denounce this murder of the two nurses by a savage Arab terrorist, as the nurses had cared for Arab patients as well as Jews. Yehiel did not know the nurses personally, but the shock affected the entire Jewish community and disturbed him deeply. He read about them and got to know them – after they were already dead.

Nehama was born in 1917 in Alexandria, Egypt. Her parents had been exiled from Palestine to Egypt by the Turks at the beginning of the First World War. When she was a year old, her family returned to Eretz Israel and became one of the first to settle in Ramat Gan. Nehama studied nursing at the government hospital in Jaffa, and then became a dedicated member of the staff there. She also served as a first aid instructor in the Haganah. After her murder, physicians and nurses spoke of her success at work despite the difficulties and harsh conditions, and the patients, Arabs as well as Jews, described her sensitivity and devotion to her work. Martha (Miriam) Fink was born in Vienna in 1919, and as a young woman she trained to be a kindergarten teacher before making aliyah. Once in Eretz Israel, she went through a difficult period of integration in her new country. Eventually she abandoned her Zionist dreams of being a simple laborer, and retrained to be a nurse. She had boundless love for her new profession.

On that terrible day, Monday, August 17, 1936 (29 Av 5696), the two nurses walked together to the hospital. The Arab murderer who shot the fatal bullets fled. News of the horrifying incident spread, shocking the entire country. During the funeral of the two women, all the businesses in the town closed. Tens of thousands participated in the tragic event, their lips pressed together and fists clenched, among them Mandate government representatives. The nurses, who had become blood sisters, were buried next to each other in the old cemetery on Trumpeldor Street in Tel Aviv. Nehama was nineteen and Martha was seventeen when they were murdered. Nehama was survived by her parents, two brothers, and two sisters. Martha was survived by one brother in Eretz Israel, and her mother and one sister in Vienna. A street in Jaffa was named Shetei Ha-Ahayot ("The Two Nurses") Street in their memory, and in Ramat Gan, the street where Nehama's family lived was named Nehama Avenue.

The terrible death of the two angels of mercy who treated both Jews and Arabs was a formative event for Yehiel, who was then thirteen. He was preoccupied by the murder. As a child, and even more so as a youth and a young man in the Irgun, he could not accept the term "restraint" that dominated the security concept of the Yishuv leadership. "Restraint" was the Haganah's policy toward Arab aggression against the Jewish community in Eretz Israel during the British Mandate, as well as toward the British forces, who stood fully behind the Arabs and took a hard line against the Jews. The Haganah policy called for the implementation of defensive maneuvers and fortifications, and restraint in response to attacks and other provocations. Mapai, the leftist workers' party, supported this policy, while the right opposed it vehemently. The chief rabbi of Israel at that time, Rabbi Yitzchak HaLevi Herzog, declared,

> We are now in an extremely difficult situation.... I told one individual who came to argue with me, I warn you that if God forbid I was shot and about to die, I would instruct the entire nation to be careful and refrain from acts of revenge. God forbid. We must not learn from the ways of evil gentiles.... We have achieved a major goal, sanctification of God's name before the entire gentile world, and the Jewish community here in Eretz Israel has demonstrated the spirit of purity and given expression to Jewish values that it practices. This is a great achievement.

Mapai leader Berl Katznelson said,

> Restraint means ethical tactics in battle.... We do not want our weapons to be tainted with innocent blood.... Restraint is a political and ethical policy derived from our history and our reality; it comes from our character and our battle conditions. If we were unfaithful to ourselves, if we adopt a different tactic – we would have lost the war long ago.

The Jewish National Council was the executive branch of Jewish elected officials during the period of the British Mandate, and it served as the governing council of the nascent state. The Council published a statement on this issue:

> The spilled blood of our sacrificed victims will not be redeemed by spilling more blood, but rather by renewed

efforts to promote our project and ceaseless striving toward new conquests on the road to our liberation. To our deep distress, in Jerusalem we have been witness to acts of revenge against Arabs, which have stained the honor of the Jewish community and endangered the peace in Jerusalem. The National Council…expresses its horror at these crimes, which undermine the ethical principles of Judaism and Zionism, sow hatred among the peoples of this land, and are liable to bring disaster on the Jewish community and the entire Land of Israel.

Mapai leader David Ben-Gurion said that the policy of restraint would lead to improved relations with Great Britain and positive feelings toward Zionism in world opinion, which would prove beneficial toward the Jewish community. "For political reasons, we cannot follow in the Arabs' footsteps," he said.

On the other hand, Ze'ev Jabotinsky's stance was in complete opposition:

I mentioned the word *havlagah*, "restraint." An unusual word. We have never heard this word before in modern, everyday Hebrew, in Eretz Israel.… Apparently this has become the most frequently used and the most hated word in the country.… Jews should not distort the facts or make accusations. In Eretz Israel, youths on both the left and the right are not afraid of confrontation with British soldiers, but they are being forced to play the role of cowards.… A native people will fight settlers as long as there is a flicker of hope that the foreign settlement may be excised. This is how the Arabs in the Land of Israel behave, and they will continue to behave in this manner as long as they maintain a spark of hope that they will succeed in preventing the conversion of Palestine into the Land of Israel.… Therefore our settlement can [only] grow… behind a wall of iron that the local population will not be able to breach.

David Raziel, commander of the Irgun, was decisive:

> Arab terror and its faithful partner, Jewish restraint, have created a situation in Eretz Israel in which a Jew must avoid particular jobs because he faces mortal danger on the roads, while an Arab can go anywhere he likes and do any job he pleases, even in a purely Jewish area.... If the goal of the war is to break the will of the enemy, we cannot achieve this without breaking its strength, and clearly we cannot to be satisfied with actions of pure defense.... Whoever does not want to defeated has no choice but to attack.... He must strike his enemy and break its strength and its will; before the enemy can attack him, he must neutralize his enemy's ability to attack.

In the middle of the night, anonymous hands pasted Irgun posters on city walls, in the spirit of this one:

> Do not be tempted by the argument of a war for and against fascism. Today fascism will not help us, nor will socialism. They are stealing our eternal and unique hope for Israel with the spilled blood of Jews. The only real answer is – blood for blood! Do not hide anymore at the sight of the rioters among us! Destroy the enemy, before it raises its hand! Go out to the front and do not flee from the trenches! Our front is in the center of the Arab community, and that is where our hand must be outstretched. The path forged by the bombs in the markets of Haifa, the Old City of Jerusalem, and Jaffa – this will save us. There are no innocents among the Arabs! There is no naiveté among the Arabs! Hebrew youth, enlist to destroy the enemy with courage!

The argument over whether or not to practice restraint continued for many years, and was never decisively won. Another Irgun poster was printed just five months before the declaration of Israel's independence, with the following statement:

> Put an end to the passive method of defense! Let's go out to the murderers' nests and wipe them out! We have no argument

with the Arab world. We want peace with the neighboring people, but we will mercilessly destroy the murderers. The murderers are not just the incited Arab rioters. They are also, or mainly, the representatives of the Nazi-British enslaver. They are also responsible for pushing the Land of Israel into a cycle of blood. They arm and encourage the rioters. They forbid Jewish defenders and dismantle their arms. They murder them in cold blood.… We will smite the Nazi-British enslaver. We will not permit them to calmly regard the bloody attacks, which are the results of their incitement, and the attrition of our forces. We will force and push them to leave the Land – as opposed to their satanic tactics. Put an end to the bloody turmoil in Eretz Israel!

The concept of restraint was recycled in the latter half of the twentieth century and renamed "containment," and it caused Yehiel's blood to boil. He could not accept it, not as a child in the 1930s and 1940s, and not as an adult.

The Betar movement became Yehiel's entire world. He began to neglect his studies in favor of activities for the movement. At the time, there were three branches of Betar in Tel Aviv: Kerem Ha-Teimanim, Florentine neighborhood, and 38 King George V Street. Eventually, the movement headquarters was built at King George Street. It was called Metzudat Ze'ev ("Ze'ev Fortress"), and later Jabotinsky House.

Gideon Abramowitz (Baruch Zakin), a member of the Betar youth movement, noticed an unknown youth eyeing the local branch building longingly from outside. "I approached him," he related, "and said, 'Why don't you come in?' He went in – and stayed there for the rest of his life."

"I went in," Yehiel recounted, "and it was hardly impressive. It was a small sandstone building, and later we learned that it was built in a field where cement had been poured for a basement, but the work hadn't been finished. The little branch building was built on this cement platform. It was about the size of a table, no more. I walked around the building surprised, but suddenly someone came out and banished me: 'Get out of here, kid.' I walked away.

"The next Shabbat at four in the afternoon, I returned. A young man approached me – later I learned that this was Baruch Giladi. Years afterward, I found out that his original name was "Burkeh" – Baruch Zakin. His father, Dov Zakin, was a member of Kibbutz Lehavot Ha-Bashan and a Knesset member representing Mapam [the United Workers' Party]. 'What are you doing here?' he asked. 'What do you want?' I want to come in, I said. He grabbed me by the ear and dragged me into the basement. On the way down there was a stairwell that led to the Perchick Bakery. Under the stairs sat a group of about ten teenage boys and girls, all high school students, most of whom were killed later in wars. One of them was Yehuda (Avidan) Lampert, who was killed in Ramle; another was Shimon (Sioma) Layzerovitch, who died during the occupation of Jaffa. Others present were Aharon Dagan (Dagovitch), Moshe Lichtenstein, Masha Herzig, Yona Reznitzky, and Yona Eichenbaum.

"Also sitting under the stairs that day was Hadassah Tel-Vardi (Rosenberg-Giladi), who taught us songs. That first Shabbat, she taught a song whose words Jabotinsky wrote, inspired by the story of a Betar youth from Poland named Simcha Plotnitzky. Simcha had wanted to make aliyah, but he could not obtain a certificate because the Jewish Agency limited the number of certificates granted to Betar members. So he went to Danzig (Gdansk) port and sneaked onto a coal ship that was sailing to Palestine. During the journey, the crew discovered him in the ship's hold – but he was no longer alive. In his memory, Jabotinsky wrote the poem *"Kula Sheli"* ("It's all mine," Betar song of 1937/5697):

> From the day I was chosen as the icon
> Of Betar, Zion, and Sinai
> I was imprisoned by brothers
> And my mother's home was locked to me.
> Betar fellows, the homeland is not ours
> For the likes of us, it's eternal exile.
> God, You have chosen us for grief
> And my brother for the hangman.
> Not by revenge, nor with weapons
> Will a Jew's sin against a Jew be punished.
> The entire nation will repay you, Cain

When it recites my songs and my speeches.
On our path, in our name, with us
He will lift my flag to the treetops as witness
For God, You have chosen us for this
And ordered our hearts to become stone.

"Another song we learned that Shabbat was a humorous one, inspired by the concept of partition. The idea was to turn Mandate Palestine into a confederation of cantons, like Switzerland. The words to the song were, 'Canton-ization, concretization… Who is shrinking you, homeland?' After Shabbat was over, they gave us copies of the newspaper *Masua*, which published Betar articles and poems – we had to sell them for one *grush* each. I was teamed up with a girl name Ziona Levi, and we went from door to door on Rothschild Avenue to try to sell the newspaper. Some of the people who opened the door for us agreed to buy, others shooed us away, and still others stared at us in apathy. When the evening was over, we returned to the branch with ten *grush* that we donated to the miniscule Betar budget."

Over time, Yehiel became more involved in movement life. Activity in the youth movement included endless, heated arguments over differences in viewpoints between the Irgun and Mapai, and the resultant differences in their activities. They also debated the internal state of the Irgun. They debated with sharp rhetoric, sincere youthful enthusiasm, and lucid ideological awareness. Yehiel's counselors identified him as highly motivated and deeply connected ideologically. He took the counselor training course at the branch, the seventh course given by Betar Tel Aviv.

During the course, he was thrown out of the movement – briefly.

Yehiel tells the story: "People always have differences of opinion on issues, some important, others less so. One day, an argument broke out among the branch leaders over a minor issue, and apparently most supported one particular position. I, the *shaygetz*, was chosen to represent the opposition. I went to the branch chief and said that we wouldn't listen to his orders any more, something like that. Of course, I stood at attention and said [the salute], 'Tel Hai,' according to official procedure. Then we were told that we were no longer welcome at the branch."

This story took place during the stormy period of controversy between Irgun leaders David Raziel and Avraham (Yair) Stern. The debate centered on several main issues: Raziel considered the Irgun an organized army, while Stern considered it an underground paramilitary group. Raziel thought the movement leaders, headed by Ze'ev Jabotinsky, should be responsible for outlining the political policy, and that Irgun members should bow to their authority. In contrast, Stern argued that the Irgun should break free from its dependence on Jabotinsky's Revisionist Zionist party, and decide its political strategy for itself. Another issue was the question of how to fight the British. Stern asserted that the Jews should not end their battle against the British, even if the British were at war with Germany. He thought that as long as the British ruled Palestine, they were the Irgun's number one enemy, and the group should fight them until they succeeded in banishing them from the country.

Raziel, on the other hand, considered the Germans to be the Jews' number one enemy, and that the Jews should not make life difficult for the British while the latter were fighting Hitler. Furthermore, recruitment of Betar members into the British army to fight the Germans was a number one priority for Raziel. On this point, his views were in line with Jabotinsky's. Despite the White Paper policy of 1939, which restricted Jewish immigration to Palestine and was mocked as the "Black Paper," or "Betrayal Paper," Jabotinsky viewed the British as allies in the war against Nazi Germany. These problems between Stern and Raziel were exacerbated by differences of personality and style, which added fuel to the fire, and the ultimate result was a schism.

Yehiel and his comrades were not involved in the dramatic debate taking place among the top leadership of the movement, but they did debate the issues among themselves. In retrospect, they identified with one side without realizing that this provoked the anger of the other, resulting in their expulsion.

"Luckily, the counselors' training course was not held at the branch, but rather at the private apartment of Dr. Hallelson [who was also the mother of Yoel Tabor, the assistant director of the training course] on Ehad Ha-Am Street next to Herzliya Gymnasia. This site was chosen because her apartment had a large number of empty rooms. The classes were held for seven or eight months. By the time we finished the course, the conflict at the branch was resolved and we returned to Metzudat Ze'ev. At the end of the course, we were inducted as Betar counselors."

In the meantime, Yehiel played an active role in volatile demonstrations against the British, some organized by the Haganah. Whenever a demonstration was held, Yehiel was there. One of these, organized by the Haganah in 1939, was against the White Paper issued that same year. Yehiel, sixteen at the time, joined the demonstration at November 2nd Square (Mugrabi Square). The demonstrators marched toward the British government offices at 138 Allenby Street. When the demonstrators reached Lilienblum Street, British policemen rushed forward in an attempt to scatter them. One policeman set his sights on Yehiel, ran straight toward him, and beat him on the back of his neck with a baton. Yehiel began to run home, which was not far away, but after a few strides, he fainted and collapsed on the sidewalk. When he came to, he brushed off the sand that had stuck to his clothing and walked home. He told no one what had happened. Why should he talk about it? Everything was fine. But he never forgot that baton beating.

Another demonstration was held after the Irgun broke into the British government's offices in Tel Aviv. They upended furniture, scattered documents, and set the offices on fire. Many participants were put in prison. Yehiel came through without a scratch. On a different occasion – and "this is not an important story," as he said – he participated in a demonstration against the British on a certain issue. When the policemen began to run toward the demonstrators, Yehiel escaped over the train tracks on Mikveh Yisrael Street. He climbed a barbed wire fence and lost a shoe. He feared that the shoe would lead the police to his home, but luckily, this did not happen.

At the same time, Yehiel became more lax in his adherence to the religious lifestyle, as did many of his comrades. One day, the beret that adorned his head disappeared, and he began to go out in public with his head bare, the ultimate sign of conversion to the secular lifestyle. His cousin Rachel, who was very close to his mother, saw him one Shabbat outside the neighborhood, bareheaded, with not even a hat peeking out from his pocket. His cousin feared for her family's reputation. Shocked, she rushed to Yehiel's home to relate what she had seen to Yehiel's mother, Zipporah Feige.

"Rachel," Zipporah Feige replied to Rachel slowly, "Don't come tell me stories about what my children are doing. Okay?"

Rachel thought that she had misheard. But Zipporah, who had been well aware of Yehiel's abandonment of tradition for some time, nodded her head at the cousin, as if to say, That's exactly what I said, and that's exactly what I meant.

"It's not that I had anything against religion," Yehiel mused much later. "But the Betar activities took place on Shabbat. For example, two or three months after I began to go to the branch regularly to participate in programs, our counselor, Meir Sternik, asked me to join in a special activity. He was working in the British Ministry of Health, and as part of his job he had a hunting rifle, perhaps in order to hunt diseased foxes. One day Meir announced that on the coming Shabbat, he would teach our group to shoot. On that Shabbat, we went out to a field, and he explained the assembly of the hunting rifle. We hung up paper targets with circles, tacked them to trees, and shot. I was nearsighted, so I couldn't see the circles – I could barely see the tree. I fired a shot, and the bullet went up to the sky. I realized that shooting on Shabbat was not exactly a big mitzvah. At age fifteen, I was not afraid that a lightning bolt would come down from the sky and hit me for desecrating Shabbat. The only thing I was really afraid of was that Father would see me. What reassured me was that usually on Shabbat I was in places he never went."

Indeed, the issue of religion was very important to Yehiel's father, but he was very aware of the reality of their environment, and he realized that rebukes and bans would prevent neither Yehiel nor his two brothers from taking a different path than the one he and his forefathers had followed for generations. He felt he had no choice but to accept things as they were. With time, Yehiel gradually understood how important this issue was to his father. Evidence of Velvel's feelings was his comment about the young man who married Hava, one of Yehiel's sisters.

One day, Hava came home with a handsome young man named Ludwig Sheige, who had made aliyah from Germany with the Aliyat Ha-Noar (Youth Aliyah) movement. He was fluent in spoken Hebrew, but did not know how to write the language, and he made his living in construction. Hava and Ludwig became friendly, and began to see each other. When the connection became serious and they began to consider marriage, she decided to introduce him to her parents.

Yehiel's father spoke with Ludwig, to take his measure and see what he was like. The youth was very open, and did not hide anything about his parents or his background. Eventually, Yehiel's father said to one of his friends, "I have three sons, and now Hava brings home a boyfriend. I am now teaching this boy to lay tefillin, and he has become dearer to me than my own sons."

Seeing his friend's shock at these harsh words, Velvel continued, "You have to understand – I invested all my energy in my sons so that they would be God-fearing observant Jews, but I was not very successful. This boy is an innocent who was raised among non-Jews. It's not his fault that he knows nothing about Judaism, and he's thirsty to learn."

Velvel suggested to Ludwig that he change his name to Yair, and the youth agreed. But what made Velvel particularly happy was the fact that Yair began to observe the religious lifestyle. Soon after, Yair and Hava married.

As for Betar, Yehiel lived from one activity to the next. For a long period, he participated in activities at the branch on King George Street. Later, when he became a counselor, he helped found the Neve Zedek branch, called by its abbreviation, Netz. The branch was established on Ha-Besht Street, in a location which had originally housed the Dubek cigarette factory before it moved to Bnei Brak. Betar activists concluded that the abandoned Dubek building, which was half ruin, half cave, was certainly appropriate for its needs, and they took it over and did some minor remodeling, inside and out. Menachem Yedid, who eventually became a member of Knesset representing Herut, Gahal, and the Likud, was branch leader. Yehiel, who by this time had completed the counselors' course, served as a counselor at this branch, which offered a wide variety of activities, including training young members and teaching history, Zionism, and Jewish philosophy. These activities, although diverse, did not quench Yehiel's thirst, and he continued attending the older, more established King George branch.

The movement reached a turning point in late 1940. The debates that had been brewing between David Raziel and Yair Stern came to a head. On July 17, 1940, Stern resigned from the Irgun to found his own organization, which at first was called Ha-Irgun ha-Zva'i ha-Leumi be-Yisrael (National Military Organization in Israel), as opposed to Ha-Irgun ha-Zva'i ha-Leumi be-Eretz Yisrael (National Military Organization in the Land of Israel), now headed by David Raziel. Stern's organization later became known as Lohamei Herut Yisrael – Lehi (or the "Stern Gang").

Less than three weeks later, on August 3, 1940 (29 Tammuz 5700), Ze'ev Jabotinsky passed away in New York, after an honorable career as leader of Betar, chairman of the Revisionist movement, president of the New Zionist Federation (NZF), and military leader of the Irgun.

And a few months later, in 1940, Yehiel joined the Irgun.

CHAPTER 5

FOR AND AGAINST THE BRITISH

Yehiel's road to the Irgun was not easy, especially after the schism. Yehiel knew that Yehuda Lampert, a fellow Betar member, was also a member of the Irgun. One day, Yehiel asked Yehuda to put him in touch with the organization. Lampert agreed.

Two days later, Yehuda informed Yehiel, "Go on Tuesday at 9 p.m. to the Yemenite Talmud Torah school on Kalischer Street. Someone will wait for you at the entrance."

On the appointed day and time, Yehiel, then seventeen, was at the meeting place. He waited patiently for something to happen. He didn't have to wait for long. The door opened, and a young man of about twenty examined his face carefully. The young man asked, "Who are you?"

"Yehiel Kadishai," he answered.

"Follow me," the youth said in a controlled voice.

Yehiel went in, and the youth shut the door quickly behind him, indicating with a nod for Yehiel to follow him. Silently, he led Yehiel into a classroom with darkened windows.

"Sit down," someone said.

Yehiel sat on a chair that was before him. In front of him stood two tall teacher's desks turned on their sides and placed parallel and almost touching each other, so that between the two desks was a small crack. A powerful spotlight was directed straight at Yehiel. Two or three people were sitting behind the lamp, next to the chalkboard – apparently Irgun members from the admission committee. They could see Yehiel's face, but he could not see them. Yehiel noticed an unusual detail: among those who questioned him, he could hear the voice of an unidentified woman.

The committee members asked him a variety of questions in cross-examination: Did he know what the Irgun was? What was its goal? What were the obligations of an Irgun member? And so forth. Yehiel replied to the best of his knowledge. Then came time for the question that seemed trivial: "Who sent you?"

"Betar sent me," he replied. He gave this answer because no one individual had really sent him – it was his Betar education that led him naturally to volunteer for the Irgun.

But he did not know that the repercussions of the schism had reached the admissions committee, and apparently relations between the Irgun and Betar Tel Aviv were somewhat problematic. "Relations between them were strained," he later said, as is often the case with underground movements.

"You're free to go," they told him. "We'll be in touch." The same Irgun representative who had escorted Yehiel inside now led him out, where he stood half-dazed from the bright light.

A week passed, then two or three – no one called him, no one contacted him. No contact. Quiet. "Quiet is mire," Yehiel chuckled to himself, citing a verse from Jabotinsky's "Betar song." He went to visit his friend Yehuda Lampert.

"Why don't they contact me?" he asked. "Maybe I don't belong in the Irgun?"

"I'll check," Yehuda replied.

He returned with the answer: "They'll contact you."

As promised, a week later he was called to meet with the admissions committee again. Again the same procedure, including the trick question, "Who sent you?"

Yehiel's answer remained the same: "Betar sent me."

The response was also the same: "We'll be in touch."

Once again, a few weeks passed, and he was called to meet with the committee for the third time. Again he was asked why he wanted to join the Irgun. They were interested in discovering the extent of his willingness to serve and his goals, and they asked him if he was aware that he might be imprisoned by the British enemy and that they might use torture to force him to reveal information. This time, surprisingly, they did not ask the problematic question. This time, at the end of the interview he was sworn into the Irgun.

"There was a table nearby, draped in the national flag, with a Bible and a pistol lying on top," Yehiel recalled. "I took the oath of loyalty, which included a declaration of my allegiance to the Irgun Zva'i Leumi, and to the Jewish state, including willingness to sacrifice my life for these lofty goals."

"We'll contact you," he was finally told. This time he was sure that it would happen faster than previously. He still could not see the faces of the individuals who swore him in, and their identities remained a mystery for him. A few years later, in a chance conversation with Esther Raziel-Naor, an Irgun leader who later became a Knesset member representing Herut, Gahal, and the Likud, she revealed that she had been one of the interviewers.

Yehiel left the meeting with a special feeling. He was no longer just another Betar member – now he was an Irgun man. He studied the faces of the passersby: did they know? Did they notice the change in him? He was very excited, but he couldn't share his feelings with anyone, since his membership in the Irgun was a well-guarded secret.

Ten days after his swearing-in, Yehiel was called up for his first operation. The meeting point was a hut belonging to a Yemenite family named Levi, on 15 Pines Street in Tel Aviv, in the Kerem Ha-Teimanim neighborhood near the *mikveh*. One of the family members, Yoav, nicknamed "Kushi," was an Irgun member. This house served as an Irgun weapons cache, from which the members went out to various operations. Before they left, Yoav's mother would give each one her personal blessing for a safe return. If someone did not return from battle, she would mourn for many days, as if mourning her own son or daughter.

Yehiel met eight other youths at the house. They dug up a clay jug buried in a small garden in the corner of the yard. From it, they pulled out a pistol and a hand grenade. An instructor gave them their first lesson in how to use a pistol: its structure, parts, assembling and dismantling. After that, they learned firing theory. During lessons, Yoav's mother sat outside the house, and if she saw anyone suspicious approach, she would throw stones on the tin roof, the loud noise signaling the trainees to hide the weapons and themselves. When there were no disturbances, each lesson lasted for forty-five minutes, and then they had a ten-minute recess. Break time was not wasted – one of the members would teach history, such as the story of Bar Kochba according to the ancient legends of the Sages.

After the motivational speech, it was time for grenades. They used a grenade constructed specially for teaching. Later, during his service in the British army, Yehiel would throw the live version of this armament. The British had no idea where he had gotten his first lesson in the use of grenades, but his second lesson was mainly trial and error.

After the Second World War began, the Parliament in London held a fierce debate over whether to establish a Jewish military force as part of the British army to help battle the common German enemy. Additional troops could help safeguard their interests in the Middle East, and the Jews would certainly be enthusiastic and dedicated to the defense of the region and defeat of the Nazis. But on the other hand, the British worried that training Jews would enrage the Arab population at a time when Britain sought to appease them. They feared that the establishment of a Jewish army would lead to renewal of the demand to establish a Jewish state after peace was achieved. Members of the Jewish leadership in Palestine were of one mind, with even the two sworn enemies Dr. Chaim Weizmann and Ze'ev Jabotinsky both supporting the inclusion of Jewish troops. On the British side, Henry Ludwig Mond, the second Baron Melchett (1898–1949), a Jew and a member of the Conservative Party, was completely opposed to the concept. By contrast, Labor representative Josiah Clement Wedgwood (1872–1942), who was not Jewish, invested great energy in advancing the Zionist issue, and lent his support to the idea.

Irgun members wanted to voice their opinion on the issue. One night, they raided Melchett Street in Tel Aviv, tore down all the street signs with the name Melchett, and hung up new signs in their place: "Wedgwood Street." Wedgwood, in – Melchett, out. The operation succeeded and was publicized. Many years later, Yehiel learned that the street had been named after Henry Mond's father, Alfred Moritz Mond, the first Lord Melchett (1868–1930). He was an industrialist, capitalist, and politician, at first a member of the Conservative Party and later the Liberal Party, and also a leader of British Jewry and a generous and active Zionist who made his mark throughout the Land of Israel.

Another night, Yehiel and his friends went out to hang posters around the city that showed a portrait of the British High Commissioner, Harold McMichael, with the word "Wanted" written in large letters underneath. The Irgun blamed McMichael for the mysterious sinking of the *Struma* in the Black Sea. The ship was carrying Jews who hoped to immigrate to Palestine, which was officially closed to them under British rule. The tattered ship had saved hundreds of Jews from Romania, six months after the slaughter of the Jews in Bukovina and Serbia had begun. After a voyage full of mishaps, they reached Istanbul, where they hoped to obtain entry permits into Palestine. For ten weeks, the passengers were trapped in the ship because they did not have permits. The British stubbornly refused to grant even one. The Turks, for their part, refused to accept the Jews for even a short time. On February 23, 1942, the Turkish coast guard dragged the boat into the open sea, despite the objections of the would-be immigrants, who had no food, water, or fuel. Within a few hours, the *Struma* was sunk, apparently in error, by a torpedo from a Soviet submarine. She sank into the depths, along with almost all her passengers. In this disaster, 768 would-be immigrants drowned, and only one survived. The feeling among many in the Yishuv was that the British bore responsibility for the deaths of the lost passengers, and this was the motivation for the protest.

This is how the activists put up the posters: Two youths slipped among the houses carrying the posters, while after them another youth ran silently, carrying a bucket, brush, and glue. Behind them a guard stood watch, constantly surveying the territory so that they would not be surprised by an unwanted British guard or policeman. They worked swiftly and smoothly. First they decided on a site to post, either spontaneously or after a reconnaissance mission the previous day. The bucket-carrier spread glue on the wall, the others hung the poster – and the operation was complete.

"My group was never caught, not even once!" said Yehiel proudly, decades later.

But demonstrations were not moneymakers, so Yehiel began working in a diamond-polishing factory. He and many other workers sat at long tables facing big polishing wheels. He learned the secrets of the trade from one of the factory's experienced polishers. For the first two months, he was still considered a trainee and did not earn anything. In the third month he earned thirty lira, a respectable sum in those days, which he turned over to his family to help pay for rent and food. His brothers and sisters also contributed their salaries to help support the family. In his fourth month of working in diamonds, he took home forty lira, a sizable sum. But in late 1942, just as he began to earn more, the diamond workers called a strike. Forced to stay home from work, one morning Yehiel told his parents that he was going swimming in the ocean but went instead to the enlistment office.

It was late 1942. The British had debated the question of permitting Jewish battalions to join their army in the battle against Nazi Germany for many months. In the end, the advance of the Germans toward the Egyptian border under the command of Field Marshal Erwin Rommel decided the issue. The British began to feel the Nazis' breath on their necks. Viscount Cranborne, the new secretary of state for the colonies, who replaced the anti-Zionist Lord Moyne, agreed to establish a "Palestinian Regiment" with an equal number of Jews and Arabs, in separate battalions. The idea began to take shape, and Jews enlisted in the British army, filling one battalion after another, while the Arabs avoided it completely. To many of the volunteers, it was clear that aside from the concept of fighting the Germans to ward off the danger that threatened Palestine, volunteering for the British army would also serve their interest of establishing a Jewish army, which many believed would soon arise.

After obtaining special permission from their commanders, Irgun and Betar members signed up. The situation was complex, as commanders and members of these groups became soldiers in the very army they had been bent on crushing.

The largest group of Betar volunteers chose to enlist on a symbolic Hebrew date: 29 Tammuz, the anniversary of the death of their leader Ze'ev Jabotinsky, who had died two years earlier.

Yehiel did not tell his parents that he had enlisted with the British, nor did he ask for their advice. At age eighteen and a half, he felt himself mature, independent, and responsible enough to make his own decisions. He did not tell them goodbye, nor did he ask for their blessing. "We didn't ask our parents," he related, "and we didn't ask anyone else. We simply got up and went."

Yet Yehiel's parents were well aware that he had enlisted. On the morning of July 14, 1942, the new recruits were paraded from the British army enlistment office on Allenby Street at the corner of Nachalat Binyamin, next to the well-known Pil (Elephant) shoe store, to south Tel Aviv, where trucks that would take them to the big base at Sarafand Garrison (now Zrifin) awaited them.

That day, a Mr. Reiber, Yehiel's neighbor on nearby Ha-Gesher Street, was standing on the balcony of his apartment when he saw Yehiel's mother walking down the street below. He shouted to her, "This morning we saw your Yehiel in the parade of new recruits for the British army!"

Yehiel's mother stopped in her tracks and digested the thought. Then, without a word, she continued on her way.

Yehiel and the others reached the Brits' main training camp at Sarafand, where they began basic training. Yehiel received his service number, 17596. They went through full-fledged basic training for three months, during which they practiced night maneuvers, obstacle courses, light weaponry, hand grenades, and endless discipline drills. Division between officers and subordinates was the name of the game. Unit officers shot out orders in sharp English, using Hebrew translators to help those who needed explanation. Very few of the volunteers knew English well.

The British attitude was that transforming citizens into soldiers was like changing a bulb into a flower. First the bulb has to rot and disintegrate, and only then can a magnificent flower grow out of it.

The summer was burning hot, but the British did not consider giving any leniencies to the new recruits. "The army is not a convalescent home," they said.

After a month, the new soldiers received their first leave. Yehiel went home. His father, who was officially unaware of his service, studied his uniformed son and asked him how he was, but did not mention the army. Apparently, he thought that if his son had not involved him before his enlistment, there was no reason to discuss it afterward.

The weekend ended all too quickly, like all army leave, but there was no choice, and on Sunday Yehiel returned to the base for the continuation of basic training. He had two more strenuous months, this time without any leave, and at the end, he and his friends swore their allegiance to the British crown. This act seemed completely bizarre to them, but they knew that the end justified the means. Swearing allegiance to the British? They did what they had to. But Yehiel and his friends knew that their allegiance was first and foremost to Eretz Israel, and everything they confronted had to be tested on the basis of this standard.

In this spirit, Yehiel was contacted at that point by one of his fellow Betar members who had served at Sarafand, Menachem Lickerman, who whispered a deep secret into his ear: "After basic training, you'll be taken to guard Italian prisoners who were brought over from the African front and who are being held in a large camp at Latrun. Under the guard room is an underground bunker, which holds a sizable quantity of explosives. You can get some good stuff there for us, but I can't tell you how to do it. I only know that the site is easy to penetrate covertly and enables a quick getaway. When you get there, keep your eyes open."

Their Irgun commander, Tanchum Rabinowitz, decided that they must take the supplies. This was not the first Irgun mission to seize weapons from the British. In early 1942, underground fighters broke into a large weapons warehouse that belonged to the Royal Air Force, located among the olive groves between Ramle and Rehovot. They took forty-two crates containing forty-two thousand bullets. After taking possession of the crates, Irgun fighters discovered that these bullets only fit the Browning heavy machine guns used by British aircraft, not the British rifles that the Irgun possessed. It would be six years before the Irgun was able to use the bullets, after seizing a Browning machine gun in one of its operations against the Arabs.

As expected, after basic training was over, the British commanders informed the troops that their first mission was to guard the Italian prisoners who had been brought over from the African front and transferred to the prisoners of war camp in Latrun.

A thought passed through Yehiel's head: "This is exactly what they told me about."

In order to lodge the thousands of Italian prisoners, the British built a large camp surrounded with rolls of barbed wire and guard towers. Yehiel and his friends from the Royal East Kent Regiment ("Buffs") 22 were sent there. Their role was to stand in the guard towers, armed with heavy machine guns, and see which of the Italians wished to take a spontaneous vacation. Of course, they didn't have to shoot, as none of the Italians ever tried to flee.

Yehiel and his comrades knew that they had to wait for the right moment to complete their extracurricular mission, but it was not long in coming. The unit, most of whose soldiers were Irgun and Betar members, was stationed at the prisoners' camp near the main Tel Aviv-Jerusalem road. One of Yehiel's duties was to check the rosters that showed which guards were stationed at the storerooms. Ideally, both the watch captain and his second-in-command would be Buffs, and at least two Buffs would be on watch at a certain time of night, with a few others guarding. According to the British procedure, every day at twelve noon the duty roster was posted. Each day, the soldiers rushed to see who was on guard and at which position. Then one day, Yehiel noticed that the roster for that night showed an ideal list of guards. The watch captain was Menachem Likerman, the second-in-command was Aryeh Melnick, and the guard was Menachem Dardikman.

"As soon as we realized this," said Mordechai Schweitzer (Shani), a soldier in the regiment, "Yehiel grabbed me and said, 'Mordechai, you have to go to Tel Aviv and let them know what's going on. I'll write you a message.' In the British army, it wasn't easy to just get up and go. I had no choice – suddenly I was overcome with a terrible toothache and I had to get the permission of the staff sergeant to leave the base for treatment. Luckily our staff sergeant was a Jew from Jerusalem – Hillel Pfefferman. I went to him and said I had to go see a dentist. Pfefferman looked down at me from his sizable height and said, 'Be back here at five sharp.' Yes, sir, I said, and got a travel slip to Zrifin, but instead I went to Tel Aviv.

"I went to Eitan Livni, the Irgun operations officer, who was then working as a dispatcher for a taxi company on Ben Yehuda Street. I gave him Yehiel's message – later, I learned it said that they could take out all kinds of 'good things' that night. I waited for the reply. In half an hour, after making the necessary arrangements, Livni came back and said, 'Go back to the base, everything's fine.' I went back by way of Zrifin, of course, so that I could have my sick leave form signed, and when I returned to the base Yehiel told me what was going on, and more importantly, what was going to happen."

The operation to take over the weapons supply began. On a stormy, rainy night in December 1942, around eleven p.m., Livni arrived at the Trappist monastery at Latrun with two trucks and fourteen fighters. The vehicles stopped and the porters jumped down. While one of the guards opened the storeroom door, the porters worked skillfully and rapidly. In a short time, they loaded 150 jerry cans filled with about three tons of valuable explosives onto the trucks. Maneuvering quickly, the vehicles rapidly left the camp without arousing any curiosity and drove to the secret unloading destination. Before leaving, the fighters changed the lock on the storeroom door and eliminated all signs of their break-in. They replaced the crates they had removed from the storeroom with empty ones, so that during the weekly inspection, the British would not discover what had happened. It took six months for the British to find out about the seizure, and by that time, Yehiel's unit was in Egypt supporting the British at El Alamein. When the discovery was made, the Brits dismissed the unit commander from his position.

During the operation, Yehiel remained in his tent, awake and alert. He watched the dim lights as they reached the location, and then saw the trucks as they departed. Only then was he was able to fall asleep.

"All in all, it was quite a simple operation," Yehiel later related. "All I had to do was to note the guard roster and inform Eitan in Tel Aviv when the ideal moment arrived. They sent trucks and porters to the explosives storeroom and emptied it out. A very simple but very important operation."

The Irgun used these explosives in sabotage operations from the beginning of the Jewish rebellion against the British in February 1944 until the Saison ("Hunting Season") of October 1944–October 1945, when Haganah and Palmach forces kidnapped Irgun fighters and turned them over to the British. The Haganah and Palmach took over some of these explosives when they seized a central Irgun weapons depot in Petah Tikva.

Chapter 6

Flag and Insignia

The flag incident, and then the symbol incident, were central events that took place afterward in the lives of the Jewish soldiers in the British army. These incidents triggered a great storm in the Yishuv and dragged the soldiers along with the entire Jewish community into an emotional and political maelstrom.

"The event took place in late 1942," Yehiel recalled. "It was before winter arrived. At the time, we were camped at Latrun. We all lived in tents, including our major, the regiment commander, who lived in an Indian-style tent. The only small hut there served as mess hall and canteen. After news of the horrors of the Holocaust began to reach Palestine, the Yishuv declared a national day of commemoration of the slaughter of European Jewry. They made it a day of fasting and national mourning, and everyone participated – from the highest echelon of the leadership down to the lowliest citizens."

The Jewish battalions in the British army also wanted to participate in this national day of mourning. On the appointed day, they planned to fast and to hold a special assembly at which they would hoist the Jewish national flag at half-mast and wrap it in black. The commander of their Jewish regiment, Major Simpson, permitted the fast, but not the assembly, and certainly not the hoisting of the Jewish national flag.

"We Betar and Irgun members did not accept this decree," Yehiel related. "We decided that not only would we hoist the national flag – we would do so on the flagpole that stood outside Major Simpson's tent. We had to go all the way."

The decision was made inside the canteen, where the soldiers were resting after a day of training exercises. The conversation focused on the Yishuv initiative. Mordechai (Moti) Ya'akobi, a Betar member from Hadera, said, "We should hang up the flag as well."

Sharon Weitz, son of Yosef Weitz of the Jewish National Fund, replied, "We have to get the commanding officer's permission."

This statement instigated a stormy dispute between right and left, until finally one member's logic decided the issue: "Even if we don't get permission, we'll raise the flag anyway – so why do we need to ask permission? That will just make our disobedience worse!"

The next morning, Mordechai Schweitzer (Shani) traveled to Tel Aviv on some excuse and brought back the blue and white flag. Because they didn't have black ribbons with which to decorate it, they cut out the rubber linings of their helmets and used these to make black bands.

The flag was ready, the flagpole waiting. But then, for some reason Major Simpson decided it was time to paint the flagpole – or at least that was what he said. He ordered two chance passersby to pull it out of the ground and lay it down. Did he know something? Had a rumor reached his ears? The two, who happened to be in on the secret, had no choice but to follow orders. But Yehiel and his friends did not give up. They gathered to discuss what to do about the new situation, and to find a solution. When morning came, they decided to transfer the mission to an electric pole that stood straight as a mast next to a tree. Responsibility for the operation was given to the guards on the last watch, just before dawn. When the world was still enveloped in darkness, the men of the last watch silently retrieved the flag, which had a rope strung through the hoist.

The three fighters involved were Yoel Eilenberg, Menachem Lipsky, and Yehiel. Yoel was a muscular sportsman and flexible as a cat. He climbed up the electric pole with Lipsky supporting him from below and pushing him upward, while Yehiel held the flag and pulled the rope taut. In a flash, they affixed the flag at the top of the pole and it began to wave merrily and, more importantly, with Jewish pride.

After the operation, the three returned to their tent and went back to sleep, as if nothing had happened.

At 6 a.m. sharp, reveille sounded. The soldiers jumped from their beds as the order passed among them: "Roll call in two minutes!"

The major's face was purple with anger. Gesturing to the flag, he barked, "Take it down now!"

Two of the soldiers volunteered. Sharon Weitz, who was standing beside Yehiel, muttered, "What a rag…"

True, the flag was hardly new. It was wrinkled and faded. But it was the national flag – how could he call it a rag? Sharon was tall and strong, while Yehiel was thin, no Samson.

"But the second he called it a rag, I couldn't hold back – I slapped him with all my might," said Yehiel.

Sharon was shocked by the blow, and even more so by the aggressor. He examined Yehiel as if trying to determine the weakest point at which he would begin to tear him apart, or at least to pay him back double. Yehiel thought that his judgment day had come, but it was not to be.

Sharon leaned toward him and said, "Sorry, I didn't mean to upset you."

"Who hung up the flag?" the major demanded.

No reply. No one hung it. What flag was he talking about?

"Whoever hung up the flag, take one step forward," ordered the major.

He asked the same question at three or four more special roll calls that were held afterward. As the major did not receive a satisfactory reply – in fact he did not receive any reply – all leaves were canceled. What's more important than leave for a soldier? This was the worst possible blow.

At that point, two soldiers went to the camp commandant, Yehoshua Brandes Hacohen, a Haganah member and a good friend of the Irgun fighters, and David Mashiach, a young *oleh* from Bulgaria. "We raised the flag," they announced.

The major glared at them, asked for their names, and said, "Get out of here. You didn't do it."

Over the next four days, the major called in anyone whom he suspected of being the "criminal" under the pretense of minor infractions of discipline, such as late arrival to roll call and dirty rifle butts, and gave him a dressing-down. No one admitted responsibility for the crime, and the detention on base remained in force. But after a while, it was eased.

The two sentries who had stood guard that night around the officers' quarters, Simcha Rais (Raz) and Mordechai Ya'akobi, kept their mouths shut and refused to reveal the guilty parties to the commanding officer.

They were placed on trial, and the major sentenced them to twenty-eight days of incarceration and forced labor in the Jerusalem military prison.

Two months after hoisting the flag, Yoel Solomon, a soldier in the regiment who was from a well-known Jerusalem family, was sent to Cairo to attend an administrative course. While in Cairo, as he later revealed to Yehiel, he saw a document that listed the names of the ten soldiers who were questioned by Major Simpson in the flag incident. The paper was signed by one of the regiment soldiers, a Haganah man. That was when Yehiel realized why the major had decided "all of a sudden" to paint the flagpole.

Yehiel kept the news about the informant to himself. Over twenty years later, in 1968, he went to the Knesset to serve as Minister Menachem Begin's chief of staff. One day, in the Knesset corridors, he met the man who had handed over the list of names.

"He looked at me," Yehiel related, "and I said right away: 'You told them.'"

The man's face turned white, but he tried to buy time. He asked, "What exactly did I say, and who is 'them'?"

"You know exactly who I mean," said Yehiel, and he walked off.

The informant never again set foot in the Knesset.

Raising the blue and white flag as a sign of identification with the destruction of European Jewry crossed the lines of all the Jewish battalions in the British army – the three Jewish battalions of the Palestinian regiment did so, as well as units of the engineering corps and artillery in Palestine, Egypt, and Libya.

***

The echoes of the flag incident had barely begun to fade when the insignia incident occurred and caused another upheaval. The Buffs Regiment 22 was once again at its center.

A symbol or insignia has great significance, not just in civilian life, but also, and perhaps most importantly, in the army. All of the twenty thousand Jewish soldiers in the British army, regardless of their political beliefs, wanted the Jewish brigades to be decorated with Jewish symbols. They felt that maintaining their national identity within the British framework was essential. The Brits were informed of this desire, and the upper echelons of the Haganah and Irgun believed the matter would be resolved. But nothing happened.

In summer 1942, the Betar and Irgun soldiers in the various military camps took the initiative, and began to wear ribbons on their shoulders with the Hebrew words "Eretz Yisrael." Some battalions even went so far as to draw the Star of David on their helmets. Wearing these marks of recognition gave them pride in their battalions as well as in their nation. The Revisionist soldiers proposed expanding this act of Jewish identification to all the regiments. But the national institutions in Eretz Israel rejected the proposal, and instructed those soldiers who had defied protocol to remove the ribbons and other signs of identification. They were told that the order was only temporary, and that they should wait for another order that would come soon.

In fall 1943, the British decided to establish a new insignia for the Palestine regiment instead of the traditional Buffs symbol (a dragon spitting fire). The new insignia was similar to a 100 *mil* coin (10 *grush*), with an olive branch in the middle and the word "Palestine" in English, Hebrew, and Arabic. In Hebrew, it read "Palestine (E. Y.) [the initials of Eretz Yisrael]". News of the decision leaked out long before the insignia was actually introduced, causing uproar among the soldiers and the public. They viewed it negatively as a reflection of the intent of the British regime in Palestine to blur the national character of the three Jewish battalions, which formed the lion's share of the regiment, and to emphasize their "Palestinian" character. The Jewish Agency instructed the soldiers to wear it. At a roll call at Zrifin in November 1943, the insignia was given to the volunteers with a direct order to wear it, and most obeyed.

But some refused outright: sixty-nine soldiers who were members of Betar and the Irgun. They predicted that if the British refused to give the Jews their own insignia, they certainly would not make it easy for the Jews to obtain independence in the future. Further, many of the soldiers remembered that the Jewish battalions in the First World War, who were smaller and less important than the Jewish Brigade, had their own uniquely Jewish insignia, and that this time, clearly, the decision had been made intentionally.

Members of the minority nationalist movement decided to speak out for thousands who also opposed the decision but lacked the courage to act. Four Haganah members joined the others in this fundamental and emotionally charged struggle. They soon joined the Irgun officially, acting admirably as commanders during the rebellion of 1944. In the military camps, meetings of the battalion committees were held, and an anti-insignia protest rapidly spread among the soldiers. The resolute decision was not to wear the Palestinian insignia, nor to even accept it when it was distributed at roll call. Slogans distributed in various towns informed the Jewish community in Palestine about events taking place among the Jewish battalions in the British army.

The sixty-nine Betar and Irgun soldiers stood firm in their refusal to wear the insignia. In response, they were arrested and tried in military court under the most severe accusations: organizing an insurgency and refusing to obey orders. One of the sixty-nine was Yehiel.

The trials began on December 2, 1942, in the military court at Zrifin and continued for a week. Each of the accused was tried separately. Top lawyers came to their defense, including the "two Maxes," Max Seligman and his partner, Max Kritzman. Seligman was in England before the trial, and after receiving an urgent telegram from Kritzman, he packed his suitcase and returned to Palestine, enthusiastic to pursue the legal challenge.

Seligman requested an urgent meeting with the military prosecutors, who informed him that the punishment for organizing an insurgency was no less than death by firing squad.

Seligman knew how to handle the British, and he asked the prosecutors: "Are you prepared to shoot sixty-nine people for refusing to wear an insignia that conflicts with their beliefs?"

The British squirmed. They knew that public opinion would turn against them if they pursued the issue. In the end, they accepted Seligman's sophisticated legal proposal to try one soldier, who as an individual could not be accused of "organizing." The verdict for that soldier would serve as precedent for the others, who would be tried before several military judges.

When the first trial began on December 2, 1942, the accused enjoyed broad public support. Many leaders, including religious representatives, spoke out on their behalf. The two chief rabbis, Rabbi Ben-Zion Hai Uziel and Rabbi Yitzchak HaLevi Herzog, published an outspoken article in support of the soldiers. They also sent a letter to the military court in which they praised the willingness of the accused to endanger their lives for shared goals. "This was a moment of truth that could not be ignored, both religiously and nationally," they wrote, "the moment they were ordered to don an insignia in which the name Eretz Yisrael was obscured behind the abbreviation E.Y. – that holy, precious name, honored by all, with which all our souls are connected inseparably for all time."

On the other hand, the Jewish institutions reacted coolly, and to a certain extent even acted against the accused, whom they considered delinquents. A lead article in *Davar* newspaper, written by Moshe Shertok (Sharett), called the act "unacceptable" and harshly criticized the insubordinate soldiers. The article said that "slandering this insignia is equivalent to slandering the struggles of the Jewish soldiers and their gradual achievements."

One of the central arguments of the British judges was that the Jewish soldiers should accept the insignia since it included the abbreviation E.Y., for Eretz Yisrael. Yosef Gedalia Klausner, a professor of history and literature, argued that in the Talmud the same letters stood for *eino yehudi*, "not Jewish." Jewish soldiers could not be forced to wear insignia declaring that they were not Jews! Furthermore, over twenty years previously, following the First World War, Jabotinsky's brigades (the Judean Regiment) were awarded a special insignia: a menorah, with the word *kadimah* (forward; eastward) underneath.

One of the accused pointed out that the translation of the word "Palestine" into Hebrew should not be the abbreviation E.Y., but the words "Eretz Yisrael" written out in full, and if those words had appeared on the insignia, he would not have refused to wear it.

On the day of the trial, poet Shlomo Skolsky published a poem that serves as a powerful expression of the upheaval caused by this event:

> We went to spill our blood,
> To roll the wheel of liberty forward.
> The groaning nation in ruins

Was rescued from the bullet by solid chests.
The blood of the Maccabees and of Bar Kochba
Boiled anew in burning veins.
The eye – saw a vision unfolding
The heart – the Lord of Hosts built the Temple there.
The nations desecrated our Temple.
They placed idols in God's holy abode.
We prepared our altar in trembling,
But they brought swine to us instead.
Like the wall in Jerusalem of yore –
The fortress of honor in the heart was shaken.
With the barrel of rebellion in hand
We tried to ignite the flames of the Maccabees.
Let us remove "E.Y.–Palestine"
Onward – instead, the yellow patch;
We'll yet sing "Nicanor Day"
We'll face lion and elephant, to the end!

News of Yehiel's arrest reached his parents through one of his friends, Mina. Yehiel's sister Hava was frightened by the news that her brother was under arrest in Sarafand and would likely stand trial. Without a second thought, she ran to see him. She asked passersby at the central bus station how to get to Sarafand. She was told that the bus to Jerusalem passed by the military camp; she took the bus, and the other passengers showed her where to get off. Hava saw an army base and walked until she reached a barrier and a gate manned by a British soldier, a military policeman. Teary eyed, Hava pleaded with him in her schoolgirl English: "My brother's here, I would like to see him!"

The soldier stood poker-faced. Hava's tears and weeping made no impression on him – he did not even bother to reply. She attempted to go through the gate, but he took a half step forward and with a terrifying expression told her that should she continue, the consequences would be dire. Frustrated, Hava decided to go home without seeing her brother. The problem was, how would she get home?

"Then a military jeep stopped beside the gate," Hava related. "In it sat a handsome British major. He stared at me for several long moments, and asked, 'Who are you waiting for, madam?' I burst into tears again, and told him that my brother was under arrest in the prison on the base, and that I had come to see him. 'Wait here a few minutes,' he said, 'I'll get you an entry permit.'"

With that, the officer pressed hard on the gas pedal and the jeep lurched forward. His eyes were glued to the mirror, keeping the tearful but attractive young Jewish woman in sight. He returned a few minutes later and handed her a permit. He accompanied her to an outbuilding, where a British officer sat, decorated with gold insignia and rank markings.

"Yes," said the officer who received her. "I understand you're Yehiel Kadishai's sister."

"I am," Hava answered, her eyes on the floor.

"I have to tell you," he announced, "that we're planning on giving him a hard time. He'll never get out of here."

He glanced at one of his assistants and nodded his head. The door opened and in walked Yehiel and his close friend Simcha Raz. They were flanked by two severe-faced military police guards carrying heavy batons. Shaken by the sight, Hava burst into tears once again.

"I was embarrassed by my tears," she recounted. "But what amazed me was their positive mood. Yehiel and Simcha whispered to me, 'Bring us something good. Make sure they bring us something good.' I nodded, but my heart ached at the sight of them. They looked terrible – but their mood was amazing. To my astonishment, they laughed – simply stood there and laughed, while I sobbed. I went home, and a few days later I had a surprise: the British officer came to our home to take Yehiel and Simcha a package filled with candy, cake, and chocolate, to sweeten their jail time. My parents were not afraid of the Brit – what was important was for Yehiel to receive the package."

The British officer, it was evident, was polite, but he was hardly one of the righteous gentiles. What interested him was not Yehiel's chocolate, but to catch another glimpse of Hava.

Yehiel's trial took place on December 4, 1943. He was tried along with Menachem Lickerman, Gunther Marenstein, Dov Peleg, Max Koren, and Ze'ev Kempler. They all admitted to refusing orders outright, based on nationalist, Zionist, and religious motives. They were certain they would be found guilty.

On December 11, the sentences were passed for the first four accused, and then for their sixty-five comrades: sixty days of forced labor. Yehiel and his friends were sent to the military prison at Zrifin army base, which later became IDF Prison No. 4. Yehiel arrived at the prison with a duffel bag.

"Here we do everything at a run!" The sergeant major greeted him in a roar. "We run all the time. Even when we shave. Now run to the barber! Move it!"

A military barber shaved Yehiel's head. When he left, he saw his friends with shaved heads as well – they looked like a group of criminals. The conditions in prison were hardly luxurious, and he and his comrades found themselves sleeping on a bare cement floor. *It's only for two months*, Yehiel consoled himself, with the robust optimism that was an integral part of his character.

The forced labor they had to perform was comprised of two projects: dirt and mess tins. The dirt was make-work. Every day, the inmates were ordered to dig up dirt. Then they had to pack the dirt into buckets, filling them to the brim, run with the buckets to another site about fifty meters away, and dump the dirt onto a growing pile. After they had created a small hill, they were ordered to move it another fifty meters. The job was purposely designed to punish these soldiers, whom the Brits considered rebellious. The British military warden was a severe bloke who railed at them when they were unable to meet his quota.

In the evenings, Yehiel and several of his fellow prisoners had to work together to scrub twenty-five mess tins, which were encrusted with rust. In the morning they had to present the mess tins to the sergeant, polished to a high shine. The mess tins were not meant to be reused, but rather served to highlight the forced labor. But for this project, the Jewish prisoners prepared a surprise for the British jailers. One of Yehiel's friends discovered a supply of new mess tins and dishes in a nearby storage room. The laborers jumped on the discovery as if they had found a valuable treasure. They buried the old, rusty mess tins in the ground, and presented the new ones in their stead. The British were left speechless at the high quality of the Jewish labor.

CHAPTER 7

THE FIRST MEETING

In the end, the achievement was somewhat of a hollow victory. After serving their sentence, all of the Jewish soldiers who had refused orders returned to their battalions and were received with respect and esteem by their comrades-in-arms. However, the Jewish military liaison office instructed them, as per the orders of the Irgun and Betar headquarters, to discontinue their rebellion and wear the British insignia. They had passed the test of national pride, but the fact was that they had to wear the loathsome insignia, and this proved, as Yehiel realized, that "we could not trust the British – just as Jabotinsky had believed, and he was also disappointed."

Another conclusion that Yehiel reached in the wake of this incident is reflected in the well-known saying of the sage Hillel in Ethics of Our Fathers: "If I am not for myself, who will be for me?" (1:13). After his release from prison, Yehiel said, "I truly understood the deep logic of this statement by Hillel, one of the great peacemakers of our people. After that, during my service in the British army, I used every free moment to help the Irgun as much as possible."

After being released, Yehiel was given a short leave. He arrived home with a shaven head, as was the rule for every British army prisoner. He did not talk much about what he had undergone. Neither did he make any mention of another issue, about which his parents had heard from acquaintances, parents of other soldiers, and which calmed them significantly – Yehiel and his friends were making serious efforts to create a kosher kitchen in their unit.

The standard British breakfast, for Jews and non-Jews alike, was comprised of bacon and eggs. The Jewish soldiers protested, and requested a kosher kitchen. Their major's response was dry: "I'm sorry, we have no budget for that."

Yehiel's father told him that his first priority should be to eat well so that he would have strength, especially when in the field. Strength was important in the military, and Yehiel was not a particularly strong physical specimen.

"If you must eat their meat," his father said, "just don't suck the bones in pleasure."

But the Jewish soldiers did not give up their dream of a kosher kitchen on base, no matter the lack of budget. "Each of us will pay half a lira per month from his salary," Yehiel and his comrades suggested to the British officer. "That way we'll have a budget."

This time, their request fell on willing ears, and the kosher kitchen became a reality.

Service in the British army was intensive and left Yehiel and his comrades almost no free time. Still, he took advantage of what little time he did find to assist the Irgun as much as possible.

For example, when the Irgun decided to launch a simultaneous attack on the British tax offices in the three main cities – Jerusalem, Tel Aviv, and Haifa – Yehiel joined the mission. The Irgun viewed the tax offices as representative of the financial arm of British rule in Palestine. During those years, the British government levied an income tax on the inhabitants of Palestine of 5–12 percent. Most of the burden fell on the shoulders of the Jewish population, as the Arab population did not pay taxes for various and sundry reasons. Thus, the Jews were the primary financial supporters of the activities of the British against them.

Yehiel's unit was then stationed in Atlit and its easy access to Haifa facilitated his participation in the operation there, which took place on February 27, 1944. Eitan Livni, the Irgun operations officer, reported that the target was not an easy one. The tax offices in Haifa were located in a small house on Jaffa Street, on the corner of one of the alleys leading to today's Carmel Avenue. The main entrance to the building was from Jaffa Street. The front of the building was protected by a broad cement fence, about five feet (1.5 m) from the entrance. A hexagonal fence surrounded the building. Although the area was dark at night, military guards patrolled it twenty-four hours a day. A much more dangerous threat was the British military base that stood fifty-five yards (50 m) from the building. The base was manned by African soldiers, mostly from Kenya and South Africa, who were hired to secure the British army bases.

Following surveillance of activity in the region, the Irgun operatives discovered that the patrol around the nearby buildings lasted for about ten minutes. The Irgun bomb squad thus had only a short time at their disposal, and they decided to place a large quantity of explosives beside the building, so that it would be destroyed by the shock wave. First they had to bring the explosives to the area. Luckily, as it turned out, Irgun member Yehudit Mozar (Ben-Amitai) lived nearby in a former German colony home. Yehiel, along with his colleague Bela Hermoni, discreetly brought the explosives to her house. They pushed a baby carriage down the street, acting like a couple hurrying home with their infant. But instead of a baby, the carriage held a charming doll covered with a blue blanket. Under the doll lay hidden two packages of explosives that they had picked up from the home of Zalman Zemmelman (Beit Halachmi), an Irgun fighter, on 42 Masada Street in the Hadar Ha-Carmel neighborhood of Haifa. The weight of the first package was forty-four pounds (20 kg) while the second, smaller package was twenty-six pounds (12 kg), combined to form a very healthy "baby" weighing seventy pounds (32 kg).

Suddenly a wheel fell off the baby carriage and rolled down Herzl Sreet. Yehiel's heart stopped. Bela tried to hold the carriage straight so it wouldn't fall, while Yehiel ran after the stray wheel. A passerby laughed raucously at the sight of the youth pursuing the runaway wheel. Had he known what was in the carriage, surely he wouldn't have laughed so hard. Finally, Yehiel managed to catch the wheel and put it back in place in an improvised fashion. The "walk with the baby" ended in the kitchen of Yehudit Mozar's home, where they hid the explosives under the counter, among the pots and packages of flour and rice.

The operation was carried out by a group of seven or eight fighters, including a guard unit. One of the unit members cut the barbed wire, while three others entered with the explosives. Working hastily, they placed the explosives between the cement fence and the barrier wall. They retreated, then activated the explosives. The barrier wall exploded, and files scattered everywhere. Giant holes gaped in the side of the building. The explosion shattered windows in the nearby area, blanketing the streets with a layer of glass shards.

The Irgun fighters did not stop at actions against the British institutions that symbolized the regime's adversarial immigration policy, nor at actions against its financial arm. They stepped up their operations. A month after bombing the tax offices, on March 23, 1944, they carried out another multi-city operation, this time against the intelligence services of the Palestine Police Criminal Investigation Department (CID) – a symbol of the repressive British regime in Eretz Israel. Yehiel took an active part in the Haifa operation.

The Haifa headquarters of the intelligence service was located in a building known as Moussaieff House, on Hassan Shukri Street, on the border between the Jewish neighborhood of Hadar Ha-Carmel and the Arab neighborhoods. The fighters had to transport the explosives near the time of the operation without awakening the suspicion of the British or the passersby.

The building was empty at night. The private offices inside it were closed, and the only wing that was occupied was the one that housed the intelligence services. Four people carried the explosives – Yehiel, Yoel Eilenberg, David Giladi, and Ya'akov Shulgasser. They approached two at a time, carrying backpacks with eighty-eight pounds (40 kg) of explosives each. Working in the dark, they placed the explosives in the adjoining open field, beside the stone fence, and dashed off the same way they had come. Their appearance was innocuous, since their British army uniforms would arouse no suspicion.

Eleven sappers participated in the operation. Later that night, they collected the backpacks that had been left beside the fence and surreptitiously brought the explosives into a small wooden booth that served as a storage room, which stood under the British offices and living quarters. The explosion was designed to take place twenty minutes later, in order to enable the occupants to evacuate the building and the bomb squad to retreat safely. But the delay mechanism malfunctioned, and the explosion took place earlier than expected. There was no time to call and warn all the people who were endangered. As a result, the building was not evacuated. The bomb squad retreated as planned, and then they heard a powerful explosion. The building was severely damaged, especially the intelligence archives. Four British intelligence officers were killed, and three wounded.

After completing their tour of duty guarding the Italian prisoners at Latrun, Yehiel's unit was transferred to Egypt, where they were given the job of guarding the Suez refineries, which supplied the fuel for the planes of the American air force in Tunisia.

At one point, Yehiel's unit was stationed in the western desert near Alexandria. Their tasks were not particularly interesting, and mainly routine. Yehiel tried to spice up the monotony by driving for the first – and only – time in his life.

"It was in December 1942," Yehiel related. "I drove a big, heavy truck, fifteen tons. The British army never bothered to check driver's licenses. What did it involve, anyway? You press the gas pedal and you go, press the brake and you stop. Big deal. I got into the truck. Turning the thing on wasn't complicated either. I drove for a quarter mile [400 m.] through a big empty lot on the base, turned around and went back. The problem was that just before the turnaround, there was a flagpole stuck in the ground. It had been left there by one of the battalions that had been based there previously. I ran into it and pushed it over.

"Aryeh Melnick, who was in charge of the trucks, was watching me carefully as I drove. When I returned to the parking lot, I opened the door on the driver's side and climbed down from the cabin. Aryeh awaited me down below. His expression serious, he asked me, 'Why did you run into the flagpole?' I replied with a laugh, 'No real reason, I just wanted to see what would happen to it.' Melnick's expression became even more serious, and he continued, 'Yehiel, take some advice from someone who knows about driving: you must never, ever drive a car.' What was he talking about? I was surprised. I'd been riding a bike for years. I had made my living from distributing medicines to pharmacies, and I had ridden my bike for all those kilometers between them. I knew how to drive. Melnick was not interested in arguing with me, and said again, with the utmost solemnity: 'If you want to stay alive, you must never, ever hold a steering wheel in your hands.' With that, my driving career came to an end, and

I've never again driven since. And you know what? It's never bothered me. I've gone everywhere I ever wanted, without driving. What's more, I had a good friend named Marco who was a driving teacher. He offered to teach me how to drive, but I refused. He was quite surprised, but I stood my ground. Instead, he taught my wife Bambi, and she passed the driving test on the first try, with no difficulties. So we have a driver in the family, and it's hardly a disaster if I can't drive."

Another memory Yehiel had from Egypt is a conversation he had in a tent in Suez with a youth named Dudai from Kibbutz Sha'ar Ha-Golan. Dudai expressed his disappointment at the fact that in those times, it was impossible to realize the principles of socialism. Yehiel, by contrast, was full of optimism, and said he was certain that a state would be established on Jewish principles. Eventually, even after the State of Israel was founded and Begin became prime minister, Yehiel remarked that, "Decades passed, but for Dudai, nothing changed. He continued to be disappointed that we could not implement socialist principles."

After their stay in Egypt, Yehiel and his comrades were sent back to Palestine to guard British installations. Guard duty was monotonous. Day followed day, night followed night. For Yehiel and his comrades, the only things that broke the tedium of routine were the Irgun operations in which they participated, although each stage involved extreme personal danger.

In early 1945, Yehiel found himself at the British training base at Ismailia, where the last groups of recruits to the Jewish brigade arrived. The British called the base the Palestine Regiment Training Depot, but it was known in Arabic as Mu'asker.

"Max Khodorovsky, later called Menachem Savidor, who became Speaker of the Eighth Knesset," Yehiel related, "was a top dog in Ismailia. He was the chief translator of the Allied Forces in the advanced training center for sabotage. Savidor ruled his little empire from an office on the base that the British army put at his disposal. One day, I went to him and said, 'Max, here's your opportunity for fame and glory – the opportunity of a lifetime.'"

"What do I have to do?" Savidor queried.

"The Irgun needs detonators," replied Yehiel, "and they're like candies to you."

"Don't exaggerate," said Savidor. "I wouldn't exactly say candy."

"Look," said Yehiel. "There are more detonators around you than around me."

Savidor agreed to this statement, but continued, "I'm sorry, I'm really sorry, but I can't."

Yehiel did not give up.

"Max," he said, "your best friend, Tanchum Rabinowitz (Irgun's commander of Irgun soldiers in the British army), asked me to speak to you about it."

Savidor scratched his forehead, then said, "Okay, come back in a week. I won't be at this base, I'll be at another one, but the door will be open. Take whatever's under this cabinet, opposite the entrance on the right."

One week later, Yehiel came to the empty office along with Aryeh Melnick of Haifa, who helped in removing the explosives from Latrun. Yehiel and Melnick rushed to the office cabinet. Underneath it, in a wooden chest, they discovered two boxes, each one containing twenty-five detonators. This was a much-needed shot in the arm for the Irgun.

Beforehand, Yehiel and Melnick had requested a few days' leave. In Ismailia, they boarded a train through Kuneitra to Lod, where they gave the explosive material to the appropriate people. These detonators proved highly useful in the Irgun's attacks on the British during that time.

On May 13, 1945, while still stationed with the brigade in Egypt, Yehiel sent a letter to his sister Hava. The letter was written on the back of a menu, which was proclaimed on the front side, "Victory Dinner 1939–1945." The menu included cream of tomato soup; a choice of lung of mutton, cold roast beef, or mutton; Russian salad and mashed potatoes; as well as beer. This is what he wrote:

> Somewhere in the middle of this lousy river country still…
> Warm greetings to you, Hava. Yesterday I received your letter, the scent of victory already wafting from it. My letter will probably bear the same scent… I'm writing to you on the blank side of the "Victory Menu" in the stupid camp where I'm posted.
> What can I tell you – I wasn't joyful on [victory] day, nor did I celebrate it with drums and dancing. It was just the end of

the sum total of my thirty-four months of service in the British army, which I fell into during the El Alamein period. At this time, I happen to be near the same place. "Near" in more than one sense – in location and in status. "Status" – also in more than one sense, meaning my mood and also the political situation.… You know, exactly as we all do, the reason for this horrible war, and the results of our work on behalf of the general effort of all the world powers. In fact, I wanted to send you a letter with no words at all, just a drawing by one of my friends that symbolizes our "victory." Here is the content of the drawing. Scene 1 – the gas chamber at Maidanek. Scene 2 – the gates of Eretz Israel locked, in the shadow of perfidious Albion's spear. Scene 3 – our brothers in Mauritius and Sudan behind exposed points of barbed wire. But this artist-friend is not present here at the moment, because he left yesterday. So I am forced by necessity to resort to a description of this tragic-comic drawing. Don't be angry at me if I ruined your good mood, because there were two paths before me. One was not to write at all; the other was the one I chose. I preferred the second to the first. Physically I am quite fit, couldn't be better. From my writing you realize that I'm still at loose ends somewhere not far from the borders of our homeland.
Yehiel

The strongest memory Yehiel retained all his life from the early 1940s is of his first meeting with Menachem Begin, the person who would go on to have the greatest influence on his life. In early 1943, Yehiel's unit was posted in Egypt, performing boring, monotonous labor. In that parched desert, he and his fellow Betar and Irgun members were thirsty not for water, but rather for sustenance for the soul. An opportunity came their way when they returned to Tel Aviv for a short leave, traveling by train from Egypt. When they arrived in the city, they were informed that the next morning, they and other Betar and Irgun members serving in British army battalions would meet with an "interesting speaker" whose name was not disclosed.

Accordingly, in the morning Yehiel and his comrades went to the basement of Metzudat Ze'ev, where they met fellow Betar and Irgun members – fifteen youths in total. They sat tense in anticipation of the arrival of the mysterious speaker. At first they conversed among themselves about issues at the top of the agenda in those days. They wondered if any news had arrived from Europe, because in the Jewish community in Palestine, rumors were flying that horrifying things were happening over there. They speculated over the fate of the battalions in which they were serving, and questioned whether a Jewish army would ever be possible. Throughout the discussion, they kept glancing toward the door, which was constructed of wooden planks held together with wire and hanging on loose, rusty hinges. Half an hour went by. The rickety door slowly swung open to reveal a very thin man. On his nose he wore round eyeglasses that would fit under a gas mask if needed. Decades later, in a new time and place, this style would be known as "John Lennon" eyeglasses. The man wore a Polish army uniform, a khaki shirt and three-quarter length pants, the hems tucked into long leggings. On his head he wore a boater with the symbol of an eagle, the insignia of the Polish army.

"Menachem Begin–" the man's name flew like lightning through the waiting audience.

Yehiel had not the faintest idea who this man was. This was the first time in his life he had ever heard the name.

Without delay, the man began to deliver a fascinating lecture on politics that lasted about half an hour. Yehiel was all ears, and was fascinated by Begin's words – weighty content delivered in an enthralling manner.

The title of the lecture was, "Yes, They Can Be Saved." This was also the title of an article with the same aim that Begin published in the *Herut* newspaper, the newspaper of the Revisionist party, on 26 Shvat 5703 (February 1, 1943).

Begin began his speech as follows:

> The destruction of contemporary European Jewry is actually the same destruction of Diaspora Jewry that was predicted by the major leaders of Zionism. The only difference is in the thoroughness and cruelty of the annihilation – not economic

damage and immigration, but robbery and mass murder. In addition, the destruction is taking place during a total world war, and thus the disaster is engulfed and the need to save [the Jews] is obscured. Because the question of the destruction of Diaspora Jewry was never solved in the past, despite the danger that hung over our heads for decades, this question has now taken on the form of realization, according to the interests and motivations of the current European rulers.

In addition, Begin emphasized, the remedy for the catastrophe, if it was at all possible to speak of such, was the very same remedy that would also encourage the end of the Diaspora – the identical solution, and no other. For in order to "temporarily" rescue those remnants who could be saved, the Jews had to rely on their own land. This was obvious to every thinking individual. Said Begin:

If we demand from the neutral countries, and from Great Britain and the US, that they admit our persecuted brethren, we will be like beggars asking for charity – and we will achieve nothing but pennies. But if we realize that we are not beggars, that we have the right to live in our homeland no less than all other human beings, then we will not hesitate to demand our rights to our land. Then it will be clear to all that the annihilation of European Jewry is not just a consequence of the Germans' evil, but also of the closure of the gates of our homeland by the British, thereby preventing rescue and redemption.

He continued:

Even before the war, the Jews of Europe begged to be saved from the danger threatening them. They boarded ships and sailed to their homeland without asking for permission. During wartime as well, they did the same. The names *Struma* and *Salvador* symbolize the path of suffering and anguish that accompanied the longing for redemption expressed by the masses of our brethren in the Diaspora. But the "enlightened" nations prevent this from them with cruelty and force, and thus they – particularly Great Britain – bear direct responsibility for the destruction of European Jewry.

Begin raised his voice:

> It is not our role to ask for mercy, for the foreign nations to absorb Jews, but rather to remove the artificial political barriers that England places on the path leading to Eretz Israel. If we succeed in removing them, the other means by which we can save an additional number of Jews will become freely available, and other possibilities that have the power to save the murder of the Jews will immediately become more tangible and real.

In a voice that revealed a hint of desperation, Begin said that the leadership faction of the Jewish community in Eretz Israel was in denial as to the urgent need to begin a serious, persistent battle to open the gates of the Land immediately. They made all kinds of demands – even that Poland commit to permitting reentry after the war for those Jews who fled its borders for neutral countries. Otherwise, they expected a miracle to happen, that a Jewish or Zionist organization would arise to implement the miracle of rescue. But one thing they did not do: they did not organize a real battle for the rights of Jews to their homeland!

Begin asked,

> Can they still be rescued? Is it too late? Yes, it is possible! The Jews of Bulgaria and Hungary and the survivors of Romanian Jewry are waiting anxiously to get out from under the revolving sword and to immigrate to their national homeland. Their exit depends only on whether we succeed in annulling the decree that forbids Jews from returning to their homeland. This is something that can be achieved – if we truly fight, and draw all the [proper] conclusions from England's opposition to rescue.

He emphasized that

> if we save the Jews of Bulgaria, Hungary, and Romania, the situation of the other Jewish communities in Europe will change on its own. Once the Jews are given true assistance by the allied nations, they will no longer be considered abandoned – especially by the Germans and their allies. Then the neutral nations will agree to provide temporary shelter to a larger number of Jews.

Begin concluded,

> Therefore, the rescue of European Jewry is first and foremost a political act in the spirit of redemptive Zionism, whose goal is political fulfillment, and not an issue of any Va'ad Hatzalah [Rescue Committee] or working committee attached to any particular institution. Nor is it especially important who initiates this battle – it is not the official authority that counts, but rather the moral authority that derives from a just demand. Every non-Jew will understand that those who demand the opening of the homeland's gates to the Jews at a time when the threat of slaughter hangs over their heads – they and no others truly represent the will of the people.

He concluded with the punch line: "They can be saved, but there is no one to save them."

CHAPTER 8

WITH THE SURVIVORS OF THE HORRORS

In September 1944, after complex struggles and deliberations, the Jewish Infantry Brigade Group, better known as the "Jewish Brigade," was established. The Brigade absorbed the Jewish volunteer battalions, including the one in which Yehiel was serving. This time there was no need for any flag "exercises," as the blue and white flag flew proudly over the bases of the Jewish soldiers. The three battalions of the brigade gathered at bases near Alexandria, and in early November 1944 sailed to Italy. Some of the soldiers were able to participate in the early stages of the last Allied attack on the Germans in April 1945.

Yehiel was not one of these fighters. Instead, he served in a rear unit that was left behind in Egypt, and most of his efforts were focused on establishing an additional recruitment base near Ismailia. In the middle of 1945, Yehiel's unit weighed anchor and sailed to the bleeding continent of Europe. They first sailed to Toulon, France, then continued to Ghent, Belgium. They guarded a small air force base near Antwerp, and continued to Holland, where they guarded storehouses and military installations at Eindhoven.

Some eighteen months earlier, in January 1944, representatives of the Jewish Brigade who were released from duty established a body called the Refugee Center. After some time, the name was changed to the Diaspora Center, and it was headed by Ze'ev (Zigmund) Herring, a Haganah member who had served in the Brigade, and who later became a Labor Party Knesset representative.

The Diaspora Center was staffed by representatives of all the major streams and movements in Palestine. Its goal was to serve the hundreds of thousands of Jewish refugees who wandered Europe after the end of the Second World War. To this end, it worked to provide the refugees with shelter and employment, as far as possible; to establish clinics for the ill and frail following the terrible trauma of the concentration and death camps; and to assist in organizing the youth and establishing educational and training institutions that would prepare them for aliyah to Eretz Israel – no easy job, as the British had closed the gates to Jewish immigrants. Diaspora Center staff members were responsible for sending Brigade soldiers to operate among the Jewish refugees. One of the Center leaders was Zalman Levinberg, who was responsible for the Betar members. He had previously served together with Yehiel in the same battalion in the Jewish Brigade and sat together with him in prison following the insignia incident. Levinberg recommended Yehiel to the Diaspora Center administrators as capable of successfully assisting the survivors in Europe, and his recommendation was accepted.

One day in September 1945, Yehiel was sent to Antwerp to meet with Ze'ev Herring. When he reached his destination, Herring handed him a travel permit and instructed him to go to Bergen-Belsen in Germany, then serving as a displaced persons camp in the British occupied zone. On his travel permit, the section marked "occupation" was filled in with the abbreviation TTG. Abbreviations were the routine in British military documents, as they are in any army. But this abbreviation, used exclusively by the Palestinian soldiers, was unique. They had neither the time nor the desire to find an exact definition for their jobs, and then boil it down to an abbreviation. Instead, they used a unique contraction of the popular Arabic expression *tilhas tizi* ("licking rear ends," to be blunt), and the Yiddish word *Gesheften* (business). TTG thus meant "business of licking rear ends." The expression had no relation to their actual jobs, but at least it fulfilled the requirement for an abbreviation. This abbreviation was often used to refer to underground activities abroad, mainly smuggling weapons abroad and operations for the Mossad le-Aliyah Bet, a branch of the Haganah that facilitated the clandestine emigration of Holocaust survivors to Palestine.

Yehiel went in uniform to Bergen-Belsen together with a Haganah representative. To reach their destination, Yehiel and his comrade hitched rides, mainly on British military trucks. In Bergen-Belsen, Yehiel was directly exposed for the first time to the horrors experienced by European Jewry.

"There were thousands of liberated prisoners in Bergen-Belsen," he related, "most in terrible condition. Whoever was capable of speaking, and wanted to do so, related things that were hard for me to believe. But it was all true. The camp was organized. The living quarters were in the German barracks – some were large stone buildings, others were just one story. The kitchens were run by the camp committee. There were cultural activities, and they even published a camp newspaper."

He had just barely managed to get organized in Bergen-Belsen, when he received the order to depart hastily for the DP camp on the edge of the city of Braunschweig. The report he received was of thousands of Polish refugees in the camp, along with one hundred Jewish women, survivors of labor and concentration camps, who were the target of harsh antisemitic attacks. Yehiel made his way to Braunschweig on his bicycle, through towns and villages, on roads and dirt paths, up hills and down valleys.

"How did I get to the bicycle, or how did the bike get to me?" Yehiel related. "Two brothers named Olevsky survived the Holocaust. One was in Bergen-Belsen, the other was a rabbi living in Celle, a town nearby, at the time of liberation. I met Rabbi Olevsky when I was wearing my British army uniform. He told me what was happening with the women – he had heard it from his brother. He gave me the address of the camp at Braunschweig. I wondered how I would get there, and then the rabbi offered me his bicycle, which I used to get there."

Yehiel rode through the destroyed roads of Braunschweig, which had been a large industrial city before the war but was then completely devastated. It was hard for him to believe the sea of destruction before his eyes. When he reached the DP camp, located in a suburb in a military barracks called Siegfried Kaserne, he asked one of the camp directors to gather the hundred women in a small hall on the site. He proceeded to speak with them, to hear their stories. He learned that in the last months of the war, they had been forced laborers in German ammunition factories, and had been given food that was better than the usual fare given to camp prisoners. They told him about the antisemitic barbs hurled at them by the non-Jewish survivors, who were mostly rude, uneducated Poles and

Italians, and they expressed concern for their safety. The oldest, who was around forty years old, named Burstein, said that out of fear of the Poles, the women locked themselves in their rooms in the evenings. They worried about what might happen to them should they go out. After hearing their descriptions, Yehiel promised, "I'll do my best to get you out of here."

The first idea he proposed was to send the women on buses to the Bergen-Belsen DP camp, where they would be in an environment with more Jews, more secure. He had not yet implemented the idea when he met a Polish Jew named Yeshayahu Goldfinger, who had served as a chaplain in the French army. He had been taken prisoner by the Germans, survived the camps, and then joined the London-based Jewish Relief Unit (the British version of the Joint Distribution Committee). Yehiel told him that he was looking for a way to get one hundred women out of the camp in Braunschweig, where they were in danger.

Rabbi Goldfinger promised to help. He contacted the local authorities, and they agreed to transfer the women to a two-story building of generous size that had belonged to the Jewish community of Braunschweig before the war. The building, located at 4 Steinstrasse, had survived the heavy bombing of the city and was left almost completely erect, except for some light damage.

Rabbi Goldfinger told Yehiel that the authorities were willing to carry out renovations on the building immediately in order to convert it into temporary living quarters, suitable perhaps even for several months. The authorities contacted a German remodeling company, which worked day and night, and within a week they had completed the necessary renovations at a high level.

"We put two bunk beds in each room," Yehiel recalled, "so that four young women could sleep there. They had cupboards, so that they could preserve some privacy within the group. The building had a spacious study hall, which also served as a cafeteria and synagogue, and we built a kitchen with all the necessary equipment. Two young men helped run the center: Hanek Videvsky, and another named Rottenberg. A couple who got married there also became part of the staff – Marik and Helena Lipke, whose son became an attorney in Ramat Gan and worked in the Knesset."

Yehiel taught the women classes in Hebrew, Jewish history, and Zionism

– subjects which for some were completely new. He told them about Eretz Israel. The center rapidly became a kibbutz under the direction of the No'ar Halutzi Me'uhad (United Pioneer Youth) movement, preparing hopeful emigrants for aliyah. More survivors came to the Braunschweig women's center, and Jewish life there began to flourish. The women conducted community life, published a newspaper, advanced in their Hebrew studies, and held discussions – some very serious – on their difficult pasts and cloudy futures, on hope and despair. Most decided that they belonged in Eretz Israel. They had already tasted enough of the Diaspora.

Yehiel's activities, there and in other locations throughout the smoldering ruins of Europe, filled his days. His parents and siblings had very little knowledge of his whereabouts and what he was doing, as he had no time to write, and even if he had found time, he was hardly a dedicated correspondent. Still, in one of his rare letters, sent to his parents on the eve of Rosh Hashanah 5707 (1947), he wrote on a greeting card drawn for him by his good friend Yoel Eilenberg: "I'm still among the ruins of Europe that I mourn, still among the survivors for whom I feel pain. For the coming year, may we all be free from the burden of foreign rule in our eternal homeland." He signed it with one of his aliases: Reuven.

On Purim, Yehiel read the Scroll of Esther to the women in Braunschweig. Some were familiar with the story, but a significant number had no knowledge of it, or had only a foggy notion of what it was about. During the reading, his eyes sought out another Esther – who eventually became his own.

Esther Brown was a refined and charming young woman, with a nickname that fit her character: "Bambi" (or "Little Bambi"). She did not come from a home that was Zionist or religiously observant. Aside from the fact of her Jewishness, she did not know much about her religion, nor did she have knowledge of any of the topics Yehiel introduced. She knew only Polish, not even Yiddish – and Yehiel helped her learn her first Hebrew letter. Still, his lectures began to awaken something within her, perhaps primeval, something that lit the Jewish spark within her.

Eventually, Bambi became Yehiel's wife.

Meanwhile, Yehiel learned that each night a train would arrive in Braunschweig, transporting Jews from Poznan, Poland, to the British-controlled zone of Germany, from where the Jews would pass to the American zone. The trains stopped in Braunschweig for several hours.

"We arranged a kitchen for them in the communal building," Yehiel related, "so that they would have a hot, kosher meal. News of the opening of the kitchen spread rapidly. It was open all night long, as Jews often arrived in the wee hours of the morning. A hot meal always awaited them. Henyek and Sala Goldstein, a married couple, operated the kitchen with efficiency and skill. The meat was from tin cans brought over from England."

About two months later, Yehiel was asked to go to other DP camps to continue in the same line of activity. This he did while keeping up with the Braunschweig camp and the fate of the women there. He even sent one of them, Bambi of course, a valuable gift through a friend who was going there: a watch that Yehiel bought from someone who was selling at a bargain price. The small watch was a lovely gift, and it would have been even more attractive had it reached Bambi. Unfortunately, the watch fell out of his friend's pocket on the way, and was lost forever.

"I began to take an active role in the various camps," Yehiel recounted. "I met hundreds, even thousands of Holocaust survivors. They no longer looked like *muselmanner*, the walking dead. After they recuperated from the horrors they had experienced and recovered their strength in the survivor camps, some even looked like Jews from Palestine.

"The memories of their recent experiences were very fresh. The terrible past was still present in their minds – some talked about it, while others kept silent. But they certainly wanted to continue forward, to rebuild their lives, to begin again from the point where they had been forced to abandon their normal course of existence. On the first day of my arrival at one camp, I was approached by two Latvian Jews. I was wearing the uniform of the Jewish Brigade. They asked me, 'When can we go to Eretz Israel?' I replied, 'It depends. If we remove the British from Palestine tomorrow, you can come within the week. If not, it will take a bit longer.' They were middle-aged – I was only twenty-three."

One of the inmates in another DP camp was Zehava Immerglick, then seventeen years old. A native of Budapest, she went by the Hungarian name of Kato, while Russian, Polish, and Lithuanian friends called her

Katya. Later, after she came to Eretz Israel, she took the name Zehava, the Hebrew version of her Jewish name, Golda. She, like countless other European Jews, had drunk the cup of Nazi troubles down to the dregs. In Hungary, in October 1944, she was recruited for "labor for the public benefit" – forced labor digging trenches. Finally, after forced marches and journeys in train cars meant for animals, she reached Kaufering concentration camp, near Dachau.

"On April 30, 1945, I was liberated from the camps, along with my father," she related. "He was then ill with typhus, but he managed to survive. After liberation, we returned to Hungary to see if anyone from my family had survived. We quickly learned that my mother and two older brothers had been killed. Of a family of six, only three of us remained – my father, my younger brother, and me. I left my birthplace forever, and forged my new path toward the old-new homeland that I barely knew."

The group that Zehava joined, a Betar unit, stayed in a DP camp in Feldafing, Germany, near Starnberg Lake, in a building that had served as a dormitory for the Hitlerjugend (Hitler Youth). Just after arriving, she was astonished to see young people wearing the uniforms of the Hitler Youth. She later learned that these were actually Jewish youth. They had come to Feldafing from the camps before any adults arrived, broke into the storerooms, and donned the clothes they found there.

When the Betar movement chose candidates for a Betar and Irgun instructors' course, Zehava was among them. The course, which was named after Irgun leader David Raziel, was held in the town of Heidenheim, and Yehiel was the director. The instructors gave the novices basic training in weaponry as well as in subjects that bolstered their emotional resilience: history and Judaism.

Heidenheim showed no signs of the terrible war in Europe. This corner of Germany had been spared the bombing, and never became a front for the battles. Its houses stood intact, as did its roads. The post office and the stores enjoyed an atmosphere of peacetime and German punctuality. Zehava was the only participant whose native language was Hungarian. The others spoke Yiddish, or else they understood Yiddish, and all the lectures were given in this language. They even published a newspaper, which was also in Yiddish, of course. Its editor was Shlomo Kor, who eventually became a founder of the Herut and Likud parties, and who was the second-in-command of the Israel Broadcasting Authority in the 1980s.

Zehava recounted, "Most of the Jewish organizations and movements grew on the soil of defeated Germany, in institutions designed for rehabilitation, recuperation, and education. Each movement attempted to publicize the political positions of the party behind it. The same applied to us: Betar, which operated our camp, tried to mold the youth under its care in accordance with its worldview on national issues. Our instructors' course was led by a youth of about twenty. His name was Reuven. He had light-colored hair, blonde or light brown. He wore the clothes typical of Eretz Israel – in summer, a khaki shirt and shorts above the knee. Sometimes he wore the uniform of the Jewish Brigade, which operated as part of the British army. We trainees, natives of cities in Eastern Europe with long histories of Jewish tradition, were deeply impressed by a simple detail from Reuven's biography: he was born in Eretz Israel. Only decades later did I discover that he was really born in Warsaw, and had arrived in Palestine at three months – so he was almost a Sabra [native Israeli]. His spectacles were the only part of his appearance that had any resemblance to the old-style European Jewish youth, who were often highly educated. In addition, Reuven was also well versed in topics he taught. He was only a few years older than most of us, but in the knowledge he displayed, this quiet, solid young man easily surpassed us. It was many decades before I learned that that his name was not really Reuven, but something else altogether. At the time, we knew only this about him: he was a member of the Irgun, a freedom fighter on the soil of Eretz Israel. Some of our group even said that the British had put a price of three thousand pounds on his head. This sounded exciting, but was completely untrue."

Zehava added that "only some of our group knew Hebrew, and if they did, they knew only a smattering. In general," she said, "they remembered only texts of prayers and blessings. The only one who knew Hebrew fluently was Reuven, and he tried to ply our ears with the language of our forefathers and of our future, yet-unborn children. There in the DP camp, we danced the hora and sang Hebrew songs. Reuven was an enthusiastic Betar member. He considered himself obligated to the noble values of the Jabotinsky movement – especially the ideal of *hadar*.[1] Reuven expressed this ideal of the ultimate Hebrew gentleman more in his behavior and personality than in his mode of dress. He was a responsible and understanding commander. He did not recite slogans, but rather educated us on principles and values – the love of Eretz Israel and our state, even though it had not yet been established. He gave us a vision that helped me educate my children in the future. I completed the instructors' course successfully, and became an instructor for a group of twenty-three children."

Zehava and her friends sailed for Palestine on a boat as part of the Ma'apilim (clandestine immigration) movement, but the British caught the boat and deported the passengers to Cyprus. She had to wait for a while before she immigrated to Israel, married, and established a family.

"Years went by," she said, "years filled with struggles, work, and studies. I became a registered nurse. In the early sixties I went to Tel Aviv with my husband, who was then my fiancé, to see a performance of the popular theater club quartet. To our disappointment, we were greeted at the box office by a sign that read, 'Sold out.' Disappointed, we wandered around, in search of something to do in Tel Aviv. Suddenly we heard a voice calling, 'Katya!' The voice sounded very familiar. I wondered, after so many years, who was it that knew me by the nickname I had been given in the instructors' course? I turned toward the voice, and I was astonished to see that it was Reuven. He ran toward me and peppered me with questions – What are you doing now? Where do you live? Why don't I see you at Ze'ev Fortress, the Betar headquarters? After introducing my fiancé, I answered his questions one by one. As for the headquarters, I said, 'To me, the whole country is a fortress.' Reuven shook hands with us, and escorted us into the theater, which was already dark. He whispered to the ticket-taker, 'They're my guests!' Then I learned that he was the box office manager of the movie theater and performance hall."

There was another chance meeting that surprised Zehava even more. "Decades passed," she continued. "One evening, I was watching

---

1   Translator's note: Literally, this word means "splendor" or "glory," but Jabotinsky used it to define his model for behavior: a combination of chivalrous attitude, respectable outward appearance, honor, self-esteem, politeness, and faithfulness.

television, Amos Ettinger's program *What a Life* was on, with the prime minister's office chief of staff – Yehiel Kadishai. When I saw the face of the show's guest, I jumped out of my chair and cried, 'That's Reuven!' Only then, after almost half a lifetime, did I learn who Reuven really was. 'Commander Reuven!' I exclaimed in excitement, 'Yehiel!'"

***

Yehiel remained in Heidenheim for one month. From there he went on to other DP camps to organize similar activities. One of the camps he reached was in Dusseldorf, where, as opposed to his past experiences, he wore his British uniform.

In July 1946, the Jewish Brigade returned to Palestine. Yehiel was ordered by the Irgun to remain in Europe to work with the survivors, along with ten other Betar and Irgun members and 120 other natives of Palestine, mostly Haganah members. They had all served in the British army and been exposed to the horrors of the Holocaust. They went AWOL from the British army to avoid returning to Eretz Israel with their brigade. Yehiel did not like using this expression; as he put it, "I did not return to the British army." Had he been caught, "then I would have served ten days in jail – not so terrible."

For these individuals, their new positions were one volunteer job on top of another – first they volunteered for the British army and served in the war, and then they volunteered to remain in Europe, which meant they were away from Eretz Israel for several years. In addition, they endangered themselves by living under borrowed identities and using falsified documents, and then after the job was finished they would have to return to Palestine by illegal methods.

At this stage, in cooperation with the Diaspora Center and its directors in the DP camps, Yehiel himself became a refugee. He was ordered to get rid of his uniform and to go only by his alias, Reuven.

Yehiel took off his uniform and buried it in the forest near a bunker in Dusseldorf. He donned a secondhand suit and became a civilian. He turned over his official documents to Ze'ev Herring of the Diaspora Center. Yehiel's documents and those of his comrades underwent the necessary conversions. Subsequently, others disguised themselves as Yehiel and his comrades. They were then officially "released" from the British army, and used these documents to "return" to Palestine. They even received release payments and clothing – khaki shirts and shorts – and more importantly, identity cards.

The soldiers' job demanded precise preparation, and the job of the double was just as challenging. For the most part, the meetings between the original Brigade soldiers and their doubles took place in the DP camps, where the doubles were trained and the soldiers underwent the transformation to their new identity. The double had to learn the real soldier's identity: his birthplace, where he grew up, the names of his parents and siblings, the date of his induction into the Brigade, and where he had served. The doubles also learned basic principles of military behavior, mainly salutes and basic orders in English, as well as the proper way to wear a uniform. After all, the double was about to be inducted into the Brigade... In return, the double taught the soldier his life story, so that the soldier could play the part perfectly. They could not know what part of the story might be used to trip them up. But unlike the other pairs, Yehiel and his double had no time to conduct a proper briefing. One of the only details that the double knew about Yehiel was his home address in Palestine. Yehiel knew nothing about his double.

When Yehiel's double reached Palestine, he rushed to Yehiel's parents' home and announced in Yiddish, "I'm your son." Yehiel's mother took one look at him and laughed. "I know Yehiel. You're not Yehiel!" Then the new immigrant told her about the trick that led to his carrying Yehiel's identity card and his biography, at least temporarily.

Meanwhile, Yehiel was carrying an identity card that noted his birthplace as Trakai, a Jewish town near Vilna. An appropriate biography was compiled for him, including dates, so that he could use it when needed.

His first activity in the Dusseldorf DP camp was to organize the release of a group of some five hundred Jewish refugees who were caught at the Belgium-France border, as they did not possess entrance visas. It was later discovered that because appropriate arrangements had not been made, the group did not meet up with its contact people, the representatives of the Bricha (the underground movement for illegal immigration to Palestine) who were responsible for escorting them smoothly through the border.

Yehiel remained with the group for a while. At first, they thought arrangements would be made quickly and they would soon be able to reach France, as had been originally planned, and from there board a boat sailing to Eretz Israel. While with them, he wasted no time – neither his nor theirs – but taught classes and gave lectures. The refugees stayed in Dusseldorf for several weeks, during which they stayed in a giant bunker and in the nearby forest, until they were dispersed among other DP camps. Finally, they joined other immigration groups, which had greater success.

One day, Yehiel planned to go to the train station, bound for Munich, where he would receive new orders for his next activity. When he arrived at the camp gate, a jeep pulled up alongside him. Its driver asked him where he was going, and offered him a ride. Yehiel replied willingly. The driver was an elderly man with white hair, neatly attired in the UNRRA uniform. He began to speak to Yehiel in German. Yehiel replied in Yiddish, distorting his accent to something approaching German, or so he thought. He did not know, however, that this strange accent aroused the UNRWA representative's distrust. The man became even more suspicious when Yehiel said that he was from the town of Trakai, near Vilna – but he clearly knew no Russian or Polish. What could all this mean? He was obviously a dangerous spy. At the time, tension between East and West had begun to flare, and suspicions about spies were a common occurrence.

In vain, Yehiel attempted to explain that he was the son of a fanatic rabbi who had insisted that his family speak only Hebrew or Yiddish in their home. When they reached the train station, the UNWRA man stopped the jeep next to an American military police patrol, and demanded, "Take this guy and keep an eye on him. He's a Russian spy!"

Yehiel barely had time to figure out what kind of mess he had gotten himself into, when he found himself before the American military commander. He was then taken to a prison camp outside the city. The camp was tidy and freshly painted, surrounded by a fence, and adorned with well-kept gardens. Yehiel was taken into a small room with a table and bed. His escorts locked the door behind him, after warning him that any attempt to leave would endanger his safety. In the afternoon, a military policeman arrived and accompanied him to lunch in the camp canteen. This happened again in the evening. "I hadn't eaten such good food in a long time," Yehiel recalled. "After all, this was the American army…"

Late at night, they began to interrogate him about what had happened. Yehiel stuck to his story that he was a refugee from Trakai who wanted to go to Eretz Israel by boat. Yehiel had with him a schoolboy's satchel containing cans of kosher meat from Kassel in Germany, tefillin, a map, and a small spiral notebook with topics for lectures, important addresses, and other information.

The interrogation lasted for several nights, but did not lift the cloud of suspicion from Yehiel. When they had finished with him, the Americans handed him over to the German Ministry of the Interior in Kassel, so that they would decide what to do with him. The interrogators released him after apparently concluding that this strange young man had been adversely affected by the Holocaust.

"I sat alone in one of the rooms in the German office, waiting for a travel permit so that I could go to Munich," Yehiel recounted. "In the meantime, out of boredom I began to flip through the spiral notebook that was in my bag. Suddenly I noticed that I had written something in code, a combination of abbreviations that the British used to write on travel permits. They represented passes for leave or for a certain job. This code permitted free transfer from Germany to Belgium. It wouldn't be good for me to possess such a code, I said to myself, as ordinary citizens were not allowed to know such things, and it could reawaken and strengthen the suspicion that I was a Russian spy or some such.

"Slowly, I ripped the page from my notebook, rolled it between my fingers, and threw it under the table. Someone saw what I had done, probably through the cameras that were hidden on the wall. No sooner had the wrinkled slip of paper landed on the floor than a clerk burst into the room like a storm. He picked up the paper from under the table, reattached it into the notebook, and demanded, 'What is this?' I said that a British soldier had given me these abbreviations so that I could cross the border, get to France, and from there go to Palestine. This explanation was perhaps enough to convince me, but not them. They decided to detain me until they checked into the matter thoroughly.

"They took me to a prison cell. My cellmate was a drunken Pole. One night he would ask me questions in Polish, the next night in Russian. I didn't know either of these languages, so I didn't reply. In retrospect, I realized that the Pole was planted' in the cell to try to make me talk and reveal once and for all that I was definitely a dangerous spy. But this attempt didn't succeed either.

"In the meantime, my friends in Munich were waiting for me to arrive – but I did not appear. The problem was solved by a completely unexpected source. At the American intelligence headquarters in Stuttgart, there was a Jew named Gorby. My interrogators, who were convinced that I really was a spy, and a particularly hard nut to crack at that, sent him a message that they were holding someone named Reuven Rabin. They asked him to check for my name on his lists, to find out if I was a fat fish from the lake or just a little sardine. Who was Gorby? Gorby was a Jew from Vienna who had also been a Betar member. My name seemed very Jewish, and apparently he asked my comrades if the name meant anything to them. Indeed, the name meant a great deal to them. Gorby informed the interrogators in Kassel that I was okay, and they released me."

CHAPTER 9

EXPLOSION IN ROME

Yehiel's next stop was Rome. He traveled on orders from Eli Tavin, then head of underground intelligence for the Irgun, which was operating in Europe following a decision by Irgun commander Begin to open a second front against the British. In France, negotiations had just been successfully completed with the French authorities for the establishment of an Irgun political and organization center there, under one clear condition: within French borders, no military operations would be carried out which might harm French relations with other states.

Thus, Tavin decided that the first Irgun operations outside the borders of Palestine would take place in Italy.

The mission given to Yehiel was to participate in an operation to bomb the British embassy in Rome, on 20 September Street (Via XX Settembre). The goal was not to harm the embassy employees or passersby, but to cause maximum damage to the embassy building. The secondary targets were the British consulates in Naples, Bari, and Milano, on which they decided to paint swastikas.

They decided to bomb the embassies so that the results would reverberate, in more than one sense, far beyond the borders of Rome. The British had extended their war against illegal immigration to the European field. Not only had they surrounded the shores of Eretz Israel with guard boats and radar stations in order to prevent the boats filled with immigrants from illegal entry into Palestine; they also tried to prevent the boats from even setting sail. According to the information held by the Irgun in Europe, the orders for operations against illegal immigration came from the British embassy in Rome.

When Eli Tavin arrived in the Italian capital, he found a significant number of Irgun and Betar members there. Some were refugees from the

Holocaust. The others were former British army soldiers who had been released, or who had released themselves. The ones who weren't in Rome were organized into Irgun cells in other cities and countries at a reasonable travel distance from Rome.

In his book *The Second Front* (Hebrew. Tel Aviv: Ron, 1973), Eli Tavin reveals that the big question was not who would carry out this operation, because the number of enthusiastic volunteers exceeded the number of roles required. The real question was who *wouldn't* participate. So the participants were chosen by lottery. At the same time, the organizers maintained the highest level of secrecy so that news of the planned operation would not leak.

Yehiel was appointed as a member of the mission, along with Abba Klurman, a partisan leader from Wolin, Poland; Menachem Benor, a Polish officer who had studied at the Soviet training school for saboteurs; and Yehiel's good friend Yoel Eilenberg, who had also served in the British military, and who, like Yehiel, did not return to Palestine with the unit. Before the operation, they collected valuable intelligence, without which the operation could not have proceeded. Chaya Lazar and Nayusya Dalugi, who had fought in the Jewish unit of the Lithuanian partisan brigade, were sent to spy on the building and map it. They visited the embassy in various disguises and obtained information on the arrangement of the rooms inside. Extensive surveillance from hidden positions documented the arrangements of the building's guards, who were Italian policemen and British soldiers. Reconnaissance missions around the building gave them an idea of the extent of activity late at night and movement of passersby. Menachem Benor, who was on Yehiel's team, checked the width of the outside walls and gates, and decided that 110 pounds (50 kg) of explosives was enough to collapse them. Preparations for the operation continued for three months. They obtained the explosives from Italian fishermen, who used them for fishing purposes, and used detonators smuggled into Italy by the Irgun headquarters in Austria.

The final list of participants in this operation was determined just one week before implementation. The date was set for October 31, 1946, and the wheels of operation began to roll. At 9 p.m., two pairs of fighters left Grottaferrata, a town on the outskirts of Rome. Ya'akov Havel went with

Shraga Shapira, while Aryeh Stern was teamed with Huna Steingarten. They rode the electric streetcar to its final stop. Each pair carried a leather briefcase stuffed full of explosives. When the streetcar reached the last stop, they placed the briefcases on the sidewalk where Dov Shilansky, the Irgun commander in Rome, awaited them. He took the briefcases and ordered the men to return to Grottaferrata immediately, in order to reduce the number of people involved at the site. Yehiel was already at the embassy, along with Yoel Eilenberg and Menachem Benor. Without wasting a moment, the briefcases were placed inside a taxi that took them to a small hotel at 94 Via Montebello, a short walk from the embassy building. If the taxi driver had known what was in the suitcases, he would not have been so happy to find clients.

Years later, Shilansky related that "My admiration for the Irgun members who fought in Palestine was so great that I imagined that they banished the British with a mere glance, that the entire British Empire was petrified by them. When I met Yehiel, I suddenly saw a man who looked like a typical intellectual, polite and wearing spectacles."

At the same time, Tavin himself was waiting anxiously in the home of Dr. Gershon Dalugi at 120 Via Cavour. At 11 p.m., the communications expert Klorman arrived and informed him that while placing the explosives they discovered that a hand on one of the two timer clocks was broken. Klorman feared that the detonators were also faulty. Tavin instructed him to try one of the detonators they had in stock to check whether they were operative and live. Then Tavin went to his apartment to bring his own alarm clock, which could be set to function as a timer in an emergency.

By the time Tavin returned, Menachem Benor had already managed to repair the broken timer. Yehiel and Klorman accompanied Tavin back to his apartment. They then went to the monumental Colosseum, the famous symbol of Rome, which was packed with visitors throughout the day but completely empty at night, in order to check the detonator. Yehiel blessed his good fortune for having finished a training course on explosives and mine-clearing in the British army, so that he could attend to the detonator suspected of being troublesome. The test was simple: the two quickly dug a furrow in the ground with their hands, buried the detonator, and operated it with an electric battery. The muffled explosion was audible, but there was no else present who might hear. The working detonator was the green light to finish executing the last stages of the plan.

Around 2:30 a.m., all was ready and prepared for action. Tavin went out for a final inspection of the area a few minutes prior to the explosion, in order to give the orders for the operation. One of the operatives, Utchi Rench, arrived in a taxi at the hotel where the suitcases were located, and three "guests" – Yehiel, Yoel Eilenberg, and Menachem Benor – loaded them inside. They drove to an alley alongside the embassy. Rench continued in the taxi for another quarter mile (400 m.) so as not to arouse suspicion, and in the meantime, the three others secretly carried the suitcases into the hallway of the house at 7 Via Bezzecca. Benor opened them and set the timers attached to the explosive device for precisely ten minutes later. A light rain began to fall.

To distract the embassy guards, Feigele Kuperberg (Zippora Milstein) and Klorman walked down the road embracing each other like a romantic couple. One of the guards did indeed leave the guard booth. He looked at the sky, then at the pair of "lovers," and then returned to the booth. The couple continued walking as they scanned the surrounding area. Then Yehiel left his hiding place, and set up small red flags on both sides of the embassy with warning signs, "Caution – mines!" so that no innocent passersby would accidentally be harmed. Benor and Eilenberg went out after him and placed the suitcases at the embassy's main entrance. The countdown began.

No one saw them coming, and no one saw them leaving – the entire group fled the site and returned to the apartment where they were supposed to sleep, if it was even possible for them to close an eye with all the excitement.

On the morning of November 1, at 2:46 a.m., a powerful explosion shook Rome. As a result of the explosion of the two suitcases, the entire central wing of the embassy collapsed. Reverberations were heard throughout the city. Houses shook and the windshields in a one kilometer radius exploded. Two Italians were mildly wounded, as they had left a nightclub next to the embassy and happened to be at the site. Firefighters and police were summoned. Foreign Minister Pietro Nenni was awakened from his bed and rushed to the site, followed by a train of senior civil servants in the interior and foreign ministries. Under cover of the confusion, Irgun operatives completed the second stage of the operation: painting swastikas on the British consuls in Bari, Naples, and Milan. At dawn, Foreign Minister Nenni made an announcement condemning the act and promising British Ambassador Noel Charles that he would catch and punish the perpetrators. Nenni's only problem was that he had no clue as to who had carried out the deed.

Italy speculated – who was behind the explosion? A broad range of possibilities was suggested in the local and international news: neo-Fascists, Yugoslavians, communists, and more. Only two newspapers blamed "terrorists from Palestine."

At Irgun headquarters in Palestine, the success of the operation and the wide-ranging reverberations it caused were received with great satisfaction. The organization's leaders sent a congratulatory telegram to the operatives, which read: "We congratulate you, fellow fighters. For the sake of our afflicted people, for the sake of our plundered land, smite the enemy, and do not waver!"

The British secret service placed investigation of the explosion at the top of its list of priorities. Two days after the event, on November 3, 1946, two senior investigators of the CID arrived in Rome: Richard Catling, then number two in the Criminal Investigation Division; and John O'Sullivan, who worked alongside Catling on Jewish issues. Their goal was to investigate the explosion and find the perpetrators. They collected preliminary information at the destroyed embassy, reviewed the media reports, and rapidly concluded that the Irgun was responsible for the explosion.

They did not need special investigative abilities nor did they need to work particularly hard to find those responsible, because the Irgun itself came to their aid. In a letter sent by the Irgun to the Italian prime minister, Alcide De Gasperi, and Foreign Minister Nenni, the Irgun took responsibility for the act and gave a detailed explanation for the reasons behind it. To avoid any possibility of mistake, copies of the letter to the senior Italian leaders were sent to the local and international media.

The first result was that sixteen Italian, Yugoslavian, and Polish suspects were released from arrest. The second result was that the two experienced British investigators concluded that the Irgun branch operating in Italy was likely to be planning similar operations against British institutions in other European locations.

The problem of the Jewish people – mainly, the closure of the gates of Eretz Israel to refugees who had escaped by the skin of their teeth from the horrors of the Nazi beast – became an urgent topic of discussion in the pages of newspapers throughout Europe. Many reporters debated it. Journalists in Britain competed in their shocking descriptions of what was expected to happen to the Parliament buildings, airports, and ports, if and when the Irgun should decide to attack them as it had the embassy in Rome. The British public was furious – which proved useful, as it led to stormy debates in Parliament and the House of Lords. Security for heads of state and senior military officers was fortified due to fear for attempts on their lives. Fear of the Irgun reached unprecedented levels.

History relates that the British secret service was not exactly surprised at the event, as it had already been expecting such an act of terrorism in Europe. A secret British report that was publicized many years later stated that "in early 1946, the Irgun decided to attack British embassies and consulates in every possible location. The possibilities were France, Italy, Egypt, and Syria. Irgun members left Palestine and organized groups. One was formed in France, but it was not as powerful as the one in Italy."

Meanwhile in Rome, O'Sullivan received information from the CID about three senior Irgun leaders who had recently arrived in Italy. Although they were not suspects in the explosion, the papers found in their possession permitted the investigators to arrest them: Moshe Galili, a leader of the *Af Al Pi* illegal immigration project; Hananiah Yekutieli (Deitel), a former officer in the Italian military who came to Europe with Eli Tavin to help establish Irgun headquarters abroad; and Israel Epstein (Gundar Aviel) of the Betar unit in Rosh Pina, who eventually became a senior Irgun officer and, simultaneously, a member of the inner circle of Menachem Begin's advisors. Two other Irgun members were arrested on suspicion of distributing leaflets: Michael Brown and Dov (Uzbek) Gurwitz. Then, in early December 1946, the British pursued and arrested Eli Tavin himself, and he was imprisoned.

Some three weeks later, a plan was hatched to smuggle Israel Epstein out of prison in Rome. Undoubtedly, this attempt was motivated by the fact that the Italians were about to turn him over to the British, who would deport him to Eritrea. Irgun activists in Rome were prepared to endanger themselves in order to aid in his escape.

Moreover, the escape plan did not seem particularly complicated or dangerous. Epstein was held on the second floor of the police station, and its windows faced a side alley that was left unguarded at night. Supplies were smuggled into his cell, slipped into food packages that were brought to him daily from the outside: candies filled with sleeping powder to put the guards to sleep, and a rope with which to climb out of the narrow window to freedom.

On the night of December 27, zero hour arrived. Epstein offered the candies to the two guards outside his cell. Around midnight, when he thought that the guards were deeply asleep, he removed the rope from its hiding place. Without a sound, he tied one end to the central heating pipes that were attached under the windowsill, slipped the other end outside, and crawled onto the sill in order to climb down the rope on the outside wall. A pair of Irgun scouts watched from the ground in tense anticipation, ready to whisk him away in a car to the train station, where a young woman awaited them with tickets to the north in her pocket.

A chain of mishaps then began, which eventually led to tragedy. Apparently the opening of the window made some noise, and then the blind squeaked. The sleeping powder in the candies proved too weak, and one of the guards awoke and noticed what was going on. He rapidly regained his alertness, woke his comrade, and shouted at Epstein, "Stop!" But the escapee was already outside the window, slowly climbing down the rope to the ground. Only one step separated him from freedom. But the guard pulled out his pistol, raced to the window, and shot at Epstein from above. Epstein was hit hard in the stomach. The rope slipped out of his hand, and he fell to the ground, fatally wounded. At the sound of the shot, guards rushed to the site, and Epstein was caught and transferred to the hospital, where he died the next day. He was buried in Milan. Seven years later, his body was exhumed and brought to Israel for final burial in the cemetery at Nachalat Yitzchak.

Not long afterward Yehiel was also arrested, this time not by non-Jews, but by fellow Jews – members of the Haganah operating in Europe.

Like a mirror image, the fierce battles between Haganah and the Irgun in Palestine influenced the relationship between the two organizations on European soil. In his book on the Saison ("the Hunting Season"), Yehudah Lapidot notes that prior to the war, the Irgun operated intensively in Eastern Europe, winning over the masses and accumulating not only supporters but a large store of weapons. After the war, in early 1946, Irgun cells reorganized in Europe, with its main base established in Italy. The Irgun in Europe collected explosives with one hand, while its other hand was outstretched toward illegal immigration to Palestine.

During the first months of the Bricha movement, Gnadenwald camp near Innsbruck, Austria, was administrated by Betar. But because of the strategic importance of the location as a border crossing to Italy, Haganah signed an agreement with Betar that the two groups would cooperate on Bricha activities throughout Austria; Haganah's intention was to eliminate Betar's complete control over Innsbruck and the Italian border. Despite the cooperation agreement, Haganah members shortchanged Betar for immigration candidates, so Irgun and Betar began their own independent operation for smuggling refugees from Austria to Italy. The open hostility between Haganah and Irgun led to a series of serious incidents.

In September 1947, Haganah members involved in Bricha activities in Europe had Yehiel and two of his Irgun comrades, Menachem Spiegler and Elchanan Telerant, arrested.

"In September 1947, when I was in Italy," Yehiel related, "we received an order from the command center in Paris to sneak across the Italian-Austrian border and go to Munich. We didn't ask why, but we assumed this was a training mission, to exchange commanders, a consequence of friction between Irgun and Betar, or other such issues. Regular activity. We started off. There were three of us: Menachem Spiegler, Elchanan Telerant, and myself. We traveled by train and bus, and hitched rides until we reached the Italian-Austrian border near Merano (at Hof Finster Minz). A young Jew who was an expert in illegal border crossings took us over the border safely. We reached the Austrian border and crossed it. It was night, and the snow was heavy. At that very moment, a group of

Jews arrived, who had come to Italy on their way south to the ports for immigration to Palestine."

Some of these Jews, whom they happened to know, warned Yehiel and his comrades that because they were not Haganah members, they should be careful. The warning did not fall on deaf ears, but the three were still identified by Haganah representatives of Bricha.

"Suddenly Haganah people appeared," Yehiel recounted. "They grabbed the three of us and handed us over to the Austrian gendarmerie, instructing them to send us back to Italy to the border police there, with the accusation of illegally crossing the border."

The Haganah members turned in the Irgun men because they did not want the Irgun Bricha to bring its supporters to Eretz Israel, certainly not at that point in time.

"The Austrians didn't ask too many questions. They handed us over to the Italian border police in Merano, and we sat in jail there for ten days. Then the Italian police sent us to Bolzano, where we sat in jail for another ten days. On the way from one jail to the other, Spiegler managed to disappear somehow, so that only two of us remained in jail, Telerant and myself. Afterward we learned that our border smuggler had also disappeared. The jail term was very easy. There were two other illegal border crossers with us, of other nationalities. One thing I will never forget was the delicious Italian food that was served to us prisoners.

"When our people found out about our arrest, they contacted an Italian lawyer who knew about our activities, and he released us after a total of twenty days in jail. After we were released, we returned to our unit in Villa Faraggiana, near the picturesque Lake Maggiore."

The betrayal was malicious, but its severity was dwarfed in comparison to what happened soon afterward. Strained relations deteriorated to the point of bloodshed. The terrible mishap took place in the Wiesenhof DP camp, near Innsbruck. A large group of Betar activists infiltrated the camp in order to exercise the rights of Betar members there to immigrate to Palestine. But due to the long political rivalry between the Jewish groups, the Haganah representatives wanted to stop them. A bitter argument broke out, which developed into a fight between Betar members and several representatives from Eretz Israel. At one point, one of the Betar men pulled out a pistol, and a bullet was discharged, fatally wounding Eitan Avidov of Nahalal, a Haganah member who had just arrived in the camp from Palestine. Three others were wounded.

The French military police were called to the site, and they proceeded to confiscate weapons and make arrests. Eighteen of those arrested were sentenced to prison for differing lengths of time. A Jewish Agency investigative committee determined that "The infiltrators did not intend to take the life of Eitan, of blessed memory, and thus there is no reason to speak of premeditated murder, but rather manslaughter." But the legal definitions made no difference to the victim, whose terrible tragedy became a symbol of what blind hatred can breed.

After Yehiel's mission to Germany hit the shoals, he remained in Italy and continued his routine activities – mainly training and operations, teaching classes and giving lectures to refugees and Betar members, and preparing them to perform their missions when they reached Palestine. At the same time, he also aided in the distribution of leaflet bombs. Leaflets were attached together at the bottom with a small amount of explosives, not enough to cause serious injury. When the small explosive detonated and the operator had moved away from the site, the leaflets flew all around – transmitting the message with a thunderous boom that was relatively contained, but quite effective. The leaflets clarified that while the world war was over, the Irgun's war against the British had not yet ended, and that it would end only when the last British soldier left Palestine.

"What was our method with those leaflets?" Yehiel recalled. "We decided that just to paste the leaflets on the walls would not arouse any interest, and no one would know we even existed. We decided that we would distribute them by exploding them – simultaneously, in eight central cities, several dozens of leaflets in each city. It would make noise and be in the papers, and maybe they would even print a photo of the leaflet. So we sent pairs of young men to Padua, Venice, Milan, Rome, Florence, Bari, Naples, and Turin. There was also a symbolic angle: we decided to blow up the leaflets in the central squares of each city – Independence Square, Garibaldi Square, and so forth. In fact, the media did document the operation in large headlines. Major articles reported that two of the individuals responsible were arrested: Yosef Rosenfeld and Aryeh Latz."

One operation followed the next. Yehiel was informed of the plan to kidnap and murder British general Evelyn Barker, commander of the British forces in Palestine, who had aroused the enmity of the Jewish community after signing the death sentences of Irgun fighters Dov Gruner, Yehiel Dov Dresner, Eliezer Kashani, and Mordechai Elkachi. An Irgun military court declared their condemnation of Barker, an avowed antisemite and hater of the Jewish community in Palestine, for what they saw as the murder of Jewish prisoners of war. They sentenced him to death and whisked him out of Palestine on the day after his condemnation of the Irgun fighters. Irgun headquarters in Palestine ordered one of its European units to carry out the sentence, but the plan was discovered and foiled by the British secret service.

Years later, Barker, who was married and had a son, was revealed to have had an affair with a Christian Arab, Katy Antonius, daughter of a socially prominent family from eastern Jerusalem. After leaving Palestine, Barker continued the relationship in passionate correspondence; some one hundred letters were found by Jewish fighters during the battle over Jerusalem. In one of his letters to her, he wrote: "Yesterday they hung my four Jews. I hope the Arabs won't continue to think that we're afraid of hanging Jews." In another letter, he wrote about the Jews: "Yes I loathe the lot – whether they be Zionists or not. Why should we be afraid of saying we hate them. It's time this damned race knew what we think of them – loathsome people."

After this incident, Yehiel participated in the purchase of explosives from weapons caches held by partisans, for whom the war was then over.

At one point, in late 1946 or early 1947, a senior Italian partisan officer, a member of the Italian partisan organization ANPI, contacted Irgun members and made them a very appealing offer. He called himself an Irgun supporter who identified with the struggle for freedom. He said he had information about a weapons cache in a village in Tuscany that they no longer needed. Since the Irgun was still at the height of its war, he offered to transfer the weapons to them for free. When Irgun representatives showed great interest, the Italian pulled from his pocket a list of weapons held by his organization: 217 rifles and machine guns, 350 hand grenades, hundreds of pistols, thousands of bullets for various types of weapons, and more. He added that he would inform the villager responsible for the cache that Irgun people would be contacting him to transfer the weapons.

"Dan Nimrod, one of our best people, and myself and two other young men took the lists," Yehiel recounted. "We drove a truck to the village. The driver was from Eretz Israel, he worked for the American Joint [Distribution Committee]. We hired him and his truck for the night, in order to load the weapons and unload them in Faraggiana. I don't think his employers knew exactly what their truck was doing at night. We drove to Tuscany, went to the villager, and gave him the lists. After scanning them, the villager said, 'Yes, we have all the weapons listed here, but we have to collect them because they're scattered around the villages nearby.'

"Before we left, he added, 'I have something special here for you, really special.' He took us into his home and started to take apart the parquet floor. Underneath was a staircase that led down to a basement. We followed him down, and we couldn't believe our eyes: dozens of bombs! Bombs of different sizes and weights – fifty-five pounds [25 kg], forty-four pounds [20 kg]. We loaded the bombs onto the truck and took them to our camp at Villa Faraggiana. I couldn't recall such backbreaking labor. The four of us loaded the bombs onto the truck – a total of about two tons! Then we took the highway to Faraggiana, full of fear, which dissipated after no one stopped us on the way and no one asked any questions. A smooth job.

"When we reached the base, we unloaded the bombs into the basement, which served as our target practice range, and from then on, as our explosives storeroom. What did we do? We cut into the metal cover of the bomb, removed the explosive material inside, and wrapped it in paper that did not absorb moisture. It was arduous. Avraham Menker (Buma) even got a severe infection on his hands from contact with the explosives. We took him to a doctor who checked his hand from all sides, and asked with concern what had happened to him. Of course, we couldn't explain the source of the infection, so Menker fed him a few stories that were completely fictitious. Then we packed up all that explosive material and sent it to Eretz Israel in a shipment of agricultural tools and supplies. The shipment reached its destination on the eve of the establishment of the state, and to the best of my knowledge, the explosives went to the army."

After this weapons operation, Yehiel continued training and organizing survivors in the DP camps, fields in which he had gathered broad experience. He also participated in the training of some three hundred young men and women who were members of the Irgun branch in Italy.

One of these was Penina (Fini) Horowitz. Penina was a child of the war. She was born in Austria and escaped to Italy, but two weeks before the war's end she was caught by the Germans and sent to jail. Italian partisans, led by Vito Volterra, a Jew who had fled from Switzerland, released her along with other prisoners. After the war, she was sent to a DP camp established and run by the UNRRA in Santa Maria al Bagno in southern Italy, in the heart of a breathtakingly beautiful area. Her parents, whose lives were destroyed, were with her as well. There she heard for the first time of what had transpired in the death camps.

Penina, who was from an Orthodox family, had known the names of Jerusalem and Eretz Israel as abstract concepts, dreams, but not realities. Suddenly, in Santa Maria, she met youths who had survived the Holocaust, whose faces were turned toward Eretz Israel. Everyone organized in groups to make aliyah, and she debated which group she should join. She went to the Mizrachi, and Ha-Shomer Ha-Tzair, but she found she was drawn to the philosophy of the Irgun. But before she made up her mind, her parents decided to leave the camp and move to Milan.

"We came to a transit camp in northern Italy, run by Americans," Penina recollected. "I went to the Scuola Cadorna school. That's where I met Yehiel. He gave classes in topics like Hebrew and history. Then I moved to a little town called Casino Nova, where the Irgun held its first weapons course. Yehiel was very active there as well – he organized the courses and also taught. For example, he taught us to put together explosive devices, use a pistol, throw hand grenades, conduct organizational exercises and roll calls. Besides all this, Yehiel made a strong impression on me. This was the first time I had ever met a positive, normal person. He knew how to laugh naturally, not like someone who was frightened of every moment. It wasn't cynical laughter, it was laughter with all his heart. We sat in a circle and he taught us songs, songs from Eretz Israel, Chassidic tunes like 'When God brought us back to Zion, we were like dreamers' [Psalms 126], and Betar songs. He told us about the Irgun activities in Eretz Israel: operations, attacks, and shootings.

"At one point, they recruited me for operations in Europe. Before the bombing of the British embassy in Rome, in which Yehiel played a part, I was sent to scout the area to see who arrived, who walked around, whether there were regular visitors. Every bit of information was vital. I even wrote down on slips of paper the license numbers of the cars that went into the compound. I gave all this information to my commanders. No one suspected me, that thin girl. Then I moved to Villa Faraggiana, where the Irgun organized activity in Europe and maintained a weapons cache. Yehiel was an active presence there. Because I knew how to type, I also typed the leaflets that the Irgun distributed, in several European languages I knew well. Yehiel also sent me on another mission – to scout the port near Venice. I did this riding a bike, which I didn't know how to do previously."

Fini made aliyah on the *Altalena* at age seventeen, already married. During the battles for the State of Israel her husband was severely wounded twice, first in the Galilee and then in the south. They lived in Jaffa, on the edge of Bat Yam. Their financial situation was precarious, not only due to her husband's wounds, but also because he was an Irgun member, and so he lacked the precious "red book" of the Histadrut, the proof of party membership that opened doors. One day, Penina met Yehiel by chance. She told him about their difficult situation, and he immediately offered her a job with Shikum Lohamei Hofesh (Shelah – "Rehabilitation for Freedom Fighters"), the organization that took care of former underground fighters and their families. Penina took the job on the spot. One of her responsibilities was to administrate the list of the many needy that Shelah assisted. Yehiel even arranged meals for her at a restaurant whose owners he knew. "I ate lunch there," she related, "and I even got leftovers for the little dog I had picked up along the way."

In 1952, Penina's father died in Milan, leaving her mother with two younger daughters. Penina and her husband decided they had to move there temporarily in order to help her mother adjust to the new situation. So they moved to Milan, and remained there until 1970 under the stigma of being *yordim*, those who emigrate from Eretz Israel.[2] In August 1964, they went

---

2 Translator's note: *Yordim* literally means "those who descend," in contrast to those who immigrate to Eretz Israel, who make aliya ("ascend").

to Israel for a visit, and met with Yehiel and other friends at Pontabello restaurant in Tel Aviv. For all these years, Fini has kept a memento of this occasion, a menu on which Yehiel wrote her a short poem entitled, "To the *Yordim*": "Over red wine and zucchini, over pickled calf's feet and stuffed chicken, we've had an enjoyable evening, without moon or stars." Everyone signed: Yehudit and Meir, Lonia and Fini, Yehiel and Bambi.

In the meantime, in Milan, Penina's family managed a chemical factory. In 1969, her husband died, and she was left with three children, her mother, and a business she could not manage alone. Penina decided to sell the business, and a year later she returned to Israel with her family. She invested the money from the sale of the factory in businesses that were unsuccessful and a store that hobbled until she finally closed it in 1978. Discouraged, she picked up the phone to Yehiel and shared her distress with him. Yehiel offered her a solution: "Call Kotlovitz at the Jewish Agency. He needs an office manager." Raphael Kotlovitz was the head of the Immigration and Absorption department of the Jewish Agency. She called him, and she started work the next day. She worked there for two and a half years, and then she left when Ya'akov Meridor, a member of the Knesset and a founder of Herut, offered her a job as his office manager. She worked for him for a while, and then when Prime Minister Begin's public inquiries manager left her job, Yehiel offered Penina the open position. She accepted without hesitation. She then continued to work with Foreign Minister and Deputy Prime Minister Yitzhak Shamir until the rotation agreement with Shimon Peres in 1984.

CHAPTER 10

PROFOUND HATRED

Yehiel left Italy and went to Marseille to wait for a ship that would carry him back to Eretz Israel. There a surprise awaited him. One day he noticed Esther (Bambi) Brown, walking along the beach, carrying a heavy suitcase. His comrades had brought her over from France, illegally, of course.

Years later, Bambi related that she reached Marseille only after she had learned definitively that her brother Mordechai Brown had survived the Holocaust. What does "definitively" mean? In those days, even a tiny scrap of information was like a breath of fresh air. This is the story of what happened when Bambi was still in Braunschweig DP camp, which naturally became a center for survivors searching for relatives.

One day, three youths arrived in Braunschweig. They were traveling from one place to another, searching for relatives. They stayed overnight in the camp in order to continue their desperate searches the next day, as sometimes their efforts bore fruit. Some of the refugees sat with the youths and talked about what had happened and what might still be. Then one of the youths pulled out a pack of cards from his pocket and said he was an expert in reading fortunes in cards. He began to read the womens' fortunes in the cards, basing his predictions on true personal details. When Esther's turn arrived, she refused to participate in the game, saying she didn't believe in it. He worked to convince her until she agreed. After examining the cards, he said: "A long voyage awaits you." This was true, because she was about to travel to Eretz Israel. Then he continued: "You had two brothers, right?" This was also correct. Bambi replied affirmatively. She had two brothers: her twin brother Mordechai, and another, older brother named Yanek, or Gedalia.

"One of the brothers is no longer alive," said the fortune teller.

"Right," Esther replied. "Yanek died while we were still in the ghetto."

"But one brother is alive," the man announced with complete assurance.

Bambi needed no more proof in order to accept this as completely true. She knew that she had to find him, the last remnant of her family, after her parents – her mother, Rivka and her father, Yosef – had died in the Holocaust.

One of Bambi's three roommates, who was corresponding with Yehiel, sent him the name of Mordechai Brown and a few details about Bambi's brother, and asked Yehiel to try to locate him during the course of his travels to DP camps throughout Europe. Wherever he went Yehiel made inquiries, but to no avail.

One day, Yehiel went to the Eretz Israel representational office in Rome. He studied the list of survivors who had been to the office, and to his surprise, he discovered among them the name of Mordechai Brown. His heart skipped a beat. He knew something that Esther didn't know, something she desperately wanted to know.

"Where is he?" Yehiel asked one of the head activists in the office.

"Here, in Italy," came the reply.

"But where in Italy?" Yehiel persisted.

"He joined the Dror kibbutz in Bari," came the more detailed answer.

Yehiel's route took him through Bari. He arrived at the Dror refugee kibbutz, and was just about to enter the main living quarters when he saw a washtub at the entrance. Inside it was a baby, and beside it stood its young mother, wearing a housecoat.

"Who are you looking for?" she asked in Yiddish.

"Mordechai Brown," Yehiel replied.

"He's my husband," the woman stated, to Yehiel's astonishment. This was Dula, Esther's brother's wife. Mordechai was not at home at the time, as he was putting all his energy into forging documents for the Bricha. He worked in a small house near Milan that the Bricha rented for this purpose, and he had transformed it into an expert forgery workshop. Soon after, Yehiel met with him in his home.

"We met a few times," Yehiel related. "At our first meeting, I told him that his sister was alive. He was thunderstruck, and then he jumped for joy. Mordechai had been certain that his sister had died. There in Milan, after we finished our urgent business, we sat and drank cognac and talked about

Esther." Yehiel wrote the news to Bambi's friend, and Bambi received final confirmation that the fortune teller had not erred. Then the siblings began to correspond, and they finally met up in Eretz Israel.

Meanwhile, back on the beach in Marseille, on the way to Eretz Israel, Yehiel hid his feelings on seeing Bambi. He approached her, and she remembered him. He took the suitcase from her hand, and together they walked to Port-de-Bouc. At the dock they met the *Altalena*, the boat that would take to Eretz Israel 930 Holocaust refugees, along with Jews from Eretz Israel returning home and Jewish volunteers from various countries who wanted to take part in the nascent state's battle for independence. It also carried a large store of weapons.

Yehiel and Bambi boarded the *Altalena* for the voyage that ended in a violent and tragic confrontation between the Irgun and the IDF, which remained a subject of debate for dozens of years afterward. This was in June 1948, some five weeks after the establishment of the State of Israel.

In Italian, *Altalena* means "lever" or "swing." Perhaps the ship served as a lever, a driving force for full resolution of the relationship between the two ideological camps that had been at odds in Eretz Israel and abroad. The Jewish paramilitary groups shared an identical goal – establishment of a Jewish state – but a tragic conflict developed between them over the method of attainment. Or from a different point of view, perhaps the incident acted more as a swing, reflecting the tumultuous relationship between the two groups, which continued well into the years after establishment of the state.

Either way, the ship was not named with these images in mind. *Altalena* was also the pen name of Ze'ev Jabotinsky. In 1947, it became the name of this ship, which served as an American landing craft in the Second World War and was purchased for $131 by the Emergency Committee to Save the Jewish People of Europe, the political and public relations arm of the Irgun in the United States. The landing craft was converted into a passenger ship, with the goal of bringing to Palestine armed immigrants who were ready for the battle for independence.

The arms had been received from various sources – from Spanish anarchists to French communists. The Irgun had established excellent connections in the top echelons of the French government. French secretary of state for foreign affairs Georges Bidault instructed the French chief of staff to supply weapons to the Irgun. An impressive stream of arms flowed to the ship, which was docked in Port-de-Bouc: five thousand Lee-Enfield rifles, 250 Bren machine guns, 250 Sten submachine guns, 150 Spandau machine guns, three million rounds of ammunitions for the guns, fifty eight-inch mortars, five thousand shells for these mortars, and an impressive quantity of explosive material.

The immigrants watched as the weapons were loaded onto the boat, their hearts swelling with pride. They were about to take part in the liberation of their homeland and the defeat of the Arab enemy. Most had undergone weapons training in their DP camps by Irgun instructors. On the evening of June 11, 1948, the *Altalena* weighed anchor, with young immigrants from fifteen countries crowding her decks. Among them were young Holocaust survivor Esther Brown (Bambi), and Yehiel. They got to know each other on the ship. Bambi told him tidbits about herself, while Yehiel unburdened himself to her.

"Even then," Yehiel recalled, "Bambi had no idea of my intentions toward her. Later she said that she had heard rumors about 'Yehiel's bride,' but she had absolutely no idea that they were directed at her – that she was the bride…"

The commander of the ship was Irgun officer Eliyahu Lankin, while Monroe (Emmanuel) Fein, an American Jew who had served in the US navy during World War II, served as the captain. The ship was actually not full – it could have held at least another thousand passengers. The Irgun central command had submitted a request to board additional passengers to Shaul Avigor, head of the Haganah arms purchasing agency in Europe, but the response was negative. In retrospect, perhaps many lives were saved because of this.

While the ship was making its way to the shores of Palestine, a ten-day trip, the political and military leadership in Israel was busily fomenting the possibility that its arrival signaled a putsch. What became known as the Altalena Affair took place during the first truce of the War of Independence. At the time, the Jewish community in the nascent State of Israel found itself in a nearly impossible defense situation, threatened on all borders by Arab armies. The IDF, which was newly established and still in its first organizational stages, suffered a severe shortage of fighters and weapons. The *Altalena* had plenty of each.

On the other hand, many feared that the arrival of the ship, packed as it was with Irgun fighters and weapons, would undermine Prime Minister David Ben-Gurion's aspirations to establish statehood and minimize the split between Zionist factions. He had already ordered the Haganah, Irgun, and Lehi forces to join the newly formed IDF for the sake of uniting the Jewish fighting forces under one framework. Irgun and Lehi eventually agreed to integrate their fighters, but they also wanted to preserve some of their independence from Ben-Gurion. The dynamic between the government's push toward centrality and the movements' preference for independence provided a fertile bed for conflict. The Altalena Affair represented the pinnacle – or the rock bottom – of these tensions, depending on one's point of view.

In any case, the Irgun command worked to integrate their fighters into the state's new army. On April 12, 1948, before independence was declared, the Irgun signed an agreement with Haganah leaders over incorporation of separate Irgun units into the Jewish army. The day after independence, on May 15, 1948, in a speech broadcast to all citizens of the new state, Menachem Begin announced that "The Irgun Zva'i Leumi is leaving the underground inside the boundaries of the independent Hebrew state." He continued, "In the State of Israel, we shall be soldiers and builders. We shall respect its government, for it is our government."

After the ten-day voyage, in the early hours of the morning, the ship approached the beach at Kfar Vitkin. "That was my second meeting with Menachem Begin," Yehiel said. "Dawn was about to break. We were all on board the ship. Suddenly, we heard Begin's voice on the loudspeaker. He asked Commander Eliyahu Lankin and Captain Monroe Fein to return to sea, as per the request of the government of the State of Israel. This was because they couldn't unload the weapons under the watchful eye of the UN inspectors [who were in place to ensure that no rearming took place during the truce]. The boat sailed back out to sea, and returned to shore after dark."

There, on the beach of Kfar Vitkin, the first battle broke out as described in chapter 1. Six Irgun fighters and two IDF soldiers were killed during the volleys, while both sides suffered injuries. The decision was made for Begin to board the ship. Fewer than one hundred passengers remained on board, mostly Irgun fighters along with some immigrants. The *Altalena* then sailed down the coast to Tel Aviv, where she ran aground. After futile negotiations between the two sides, shots were fired from shore, and the ship began to burn.

The *Altalena* was a national tragedy. Jews shot at fellow Jews for many hours. Jews were shot at and killed by the bullets of other Jews – all in a truce during the War of Independence. At the end of the tragic struggle, three IDF soldiers and sixteen Irgun fighters lay dead – among them, several immigrants.

Yehiel carried the memory of the heartbreaking battle with him for his entire lifetime.

When he returned home, his family gave him an emotional reception. They had no idea of his doings throughout the three years – from 1945 to June 1948 – of his stay in Europe. His scarce letters had merely served to whet their curiosity, and now that he had returned, they hardly had time to listen to his recollections, as the need for an income demanded they spend long hours at work.

In the meantime, Bambi and her friends were taken from the beach to a small tent camp set up near the adjacent town of Netanya. The next morning, the women were driven by truck to an immigrant camp in Ra'anana. Residents of the camp treated the *Altalena* immigrants like lepers, due to their connection with Betar and Irgun. They were even housed in a separate building. The situation became intolerable, even more so after the *Altalena* went up in flames and the entire Yishuv was drawn into the passionate controversy. One evening, Esther and two other women decided to flee. They had not immigrated to Israel to face hostility and maltreatment; they had already undergone enough, though the situations were vastly different.

Where would they go, since they knew no one in their new country? They decided that the closest thing they had to family was the Irgun. So they secretly went out to the main road to Tel Aviv to try to hitch a ride. One of the three, Hannah Shein of Kovno, knew Hebrew well. The two others barely even knew Yiddish. A car stopped to pick up the three women around 11 p.m. Where to? Tel Aviv. Where in Tel Aviv? Hannah replied: "Near the central post office on Allenby Street." Hannah knew that the post office was near Yehudah Ha-Levy Street, where Freud Hospital, which served not only as a maternity ward and a clinic for Irgun wounded but also as Irgun headquarters, was located.

They reached the hospital and approached one of the managers. He sent them to the Alliance school (Kol Yisrael Haverim) in Jaffa, which was also an Irgun base. There they met another group of women who had arrived on the *Altalena* and who had also been the targets of antagonism. What facilities were inside the school? None; they slept on the floor. Every once in a while, Alliance school representatives hostile to the underground organizations asked them to vacate the site, and then they would walk to the beach and return in the evening so that they would have a roof over their heads.

In the meantime, the men who had arrived with them were drafted into the army and went to fight on the fronts. The Irgun was in its last days, winding down its missions and beginning to break up. It was not organized enough to offer the women regular living arrangements. Instead, the Irgun began to build an immigrant camp in Ha-Tikvah neighborhood. Until the camp was built, which was expected to take only a short time, the Irgun asked their members' families to host immigrants in their homes (for sleeping arrangements only). Many of these families were still mourning the precious souls they had lost in the war. Yehiel knew about this plan, and he asked his mother to host two or three young women. The task was turned over to Yehiel's sister, Hava.

Yehiel told Hava about a certain young woman by the name of Esther Brown, and he asked his sister to try to bring Esther to their home. To his last day, Yehiel had no idea how Hava discovered that Bambi was staying the Alliance school, but sure enough Esther and two other women eventually came to stay with Yehiel's sister. Then, when the temporary lodgings carried on past the planned deadline, the young women moved to his parents' home.

Bambi was given a narrow daybed in the front hallway. She did not waste her days, but began to work as a seamstress in a dress workshop on Allenby Street. After the day's work, Yehiel accompanied her to Hebrew classes at an evening school on Balfour Street. The classes cost thirty *grush* per month, while Bambi earned four *lirot* per month.

Bambi became part of the family. She began to talk about her background. She spoke of her home in Lodz, and of her parents Rivka and Yosef. Her father had a metal factory for manufacturing faucets. Her parents were not religious. Her father attended synagogue only during the High Holidays. They held a Passover Seder in their home, including a second Seder on the second night of the holiday, as is customary outside Eretz Israel. But the grandparents on both sides did not participate, because they were observant and they did not trust her parents' standards of kashrut. When the grandparents came to visit, they would not eat anything in Esther's parents' home, only drink a glass of tea.

Their home was in a heavily Polish area on 11th of November Street. It had two bedrooms, a kitchen, and a large balcony – then considered spacious. Once, a competition was held in the city for the most beautiful courtyard, and theirs won a prize. There were no Jews in the neighborhood. The Brown children's friends were non-Jewish Polish boys and girls. They spoke Polish in the home, and the children did not know Yiddish or Hebrew. The children were not members in any Zionist youth movement, and they heard nothing about Eretz Israel at home. They were three siblings: Bambi, her twin brother Mordechai, and her brother Yanek, who was two years older than the twins.

They noticed almost no antisemitism. Once, a friend of Bambi's brother Mordechai exclaimed to him, "Go to Palestine!" – but he had no idea what he was talking about. Another antisemitic incident occurred when the streetcar ran over a man in the street. Everyone rushed to see what had happened. A passerby who was walking on the sidewalk in the opposite direction said, "Why are you running? Nothing happened, it's only a Jew."

In 1939, when Poland was occupied by the Germans, Yanek was fifteen, while Bambi and her twin brother were thirteen. When the Germans began to bomb Lodz, the Brown family went to Esther's aunt, her mother's sister, who also lived with her family in town, but on the ground floor, which was considered safer. They stayed with this aunt for two days, and then returned home. When the Germans entered the city, they burst into the apartment with shouts of "*Raus!*" They gave the family ten minutes to pack their belongings, and then threw the Browns out of their home. Within a mere three days, their entire world fell apart. They had barely managed to flee their home when a German family moved in, pleased as punch. The Germans took over their factory at once.

Distressed, they contacted a friend of Esther's mother, who agreed to take them into their small apartment. They lived there until they were sent to the ghetto. They were given an address, and they shared the apartment with another family. A Polish neighbor from their original home who was a good friend of Esther's mother kept in contact with the Browns and brought supplies to them in the ghetto on occasion.

In the ghetto, despite the harsh conditions, the Jews tried to organize a daily routine. They established a school and held classes. Every adult had to work, because whoever didn't work was ineligible for food rations. Esther's father worked in a large metal factory; Yanek and Mordechai soon went to work there as well. Esther's mother worked in a shoe factory. Then Esther began work in Kreitsky's textile factory. Work began at 6 a.m., with only a short break at midday for soup. The family was paid with ghetto coupons, which had value inside the ghetto, but were worthless everywhere else. The ghetto also had its own coins.

Later, Yanek was appointed to guard the metal factory. Standing outside at the gate in the freezing cold, he fell ill with pneumonia that developed into tuberculosis, and shortly afterward he died. He was sixteen.

Esther was on the first transport from Lodz to the death camps in 1943. One day, Mordechai lay sick in bed, and Esther was at home as well. Suddenly, without any warning, the Germans invaded the ghetto, with shouts of "*Alle raus!*" (Everyone outside!). They collected the Jews in a central area of the ghetto. Esther's parents were at work, and were taken later from the factories. Mordechai and Esther were loaded into a cattle car with over a hundred others; the SS kicked the doors shut, and a tortuous journey began. Several people died inside the suffocating, foul-smelling car. The passengers had no idea where they were being sent. Eventually, the train arrived – at Auschwitz. The doors opened, and the Jews spilled out onto a ramp. The SS separated the men from the women, so Mordechai and Esther were forced to go their separate ways. No one knew that they were twins – this proved to be a stroke of luck, as they avoided the unspeakable trials of Josef Mengele.

Until Yehiel's chance meeting with Dula, Mordechai's wife, Mordechai had no idea that his sister had survived. They were reunited in Israel, and shortly afterward, the same Yehiel who had informed him that his sister was alive became his brother-in-law.

As for Yehiel, he filed away his memories and reacclimated to life in Israel. But this was at the height of the War of Independence, and so before he began to look for work, he presented himself at the draft office to make his contribution to the war effort. At first, the army refused to take him, as they discovered he had a lung disease.

"After the UN decision of November 29, 1947 [the Partition Plan for Palestine]," Yehiel related, "I was still in Faraggiana. We planned to return to Eretz Israel. We had trained our new members in military exercises for this purpose. There were some 250 young men and women at the site, who had lived there for about eighteen months. There was a Betar command center there, with a rifle range and weapons. The training course included crawling, jumping, and other physical preparation. One night we crawled for hours, until we were sweating like horses. Apparently, the combination of perspiration and the bitter cold weather did damage to my lungs. In addition, I still smoked in those days, and this made matters even worse.

"The examinations in preparation for the draft revealed something irregular, and they sent me to the office of the League for the Battle against Tuberculosis at 16 Hovevei Zion Street. In those days, this organization was both active and efficient. League members sent me to a convalescent home in Gadera, but I left after a short while. Poor health notwithstanding, I went to the draft office in Jaffa. I had a certificate documenting my position in the Irgun as a company lieutenant commander, but the army rejected me once again. The rejection continued for a few months, until they finally decided that I was not fit for regular, active service, but could serve in the reserves. Reserves? I took it. My reserves unit was one of the foot soldier battalions, and most of my posts were for guard duty. Later I took an explosives course at Beit Nabala, and in the Sinai War I dismantled mines at El Arish in northern Sinai. In the Six-Day War, I guarded Hawk missiles at the airport in Lod (which became Ben-Gurion Airport)."

In the meantime, the air in the Kadishson home was filled with the possibility that Yehiel's and Bambi's futures might be connected, but nothing happened until the day Yehiel's father asked Bambi point-blank, "Why don't you get married?"

Bambi blushed at the directness of his question, and replied, "Because no one has asked me to marry him!"

But although the wedding march began to play in the background for Esther and Yehiel, the opening bars sounded off-key. While Yehiel was still working in Italy, he had made the acquaintance of a couple by the name of Steingarten, parents of one of his friends. They saw each other several times in Rome. At one of their meetings, like all good Jews at the sight of a young man who has reached marriageable age, they began to inquire whether he had a girlfriend, and if he was thinking of getting married. "Just to get them off my back," Yehiel later related, "I told them in my usual jesting style that they had nothing to worry about, because I already had a wife in Germany. It worked, and they stopped pressuring me." When they made aliyah, Yehiel asked them to go to his parents' home and give them his greetings.

Accordingly, when they reached Eretz Israel, the Steingartens visited his parents. They said that they had met Yehiel, that he was a very nice young man, and sent them his best wishes. His parents continued to ask about him, and one of the answers surprised them: "He's in Italy now, but we haven't met his wife, because she's in Germany."

His wife? His parents were astonished. Yehiel was married? To whom? When? Why hadn't he informed them? Why hadn't he written? Ah, they surmised, she's probably not Jewish, a German gentile!

When Yehiel arrived in Israel, his parents wondered about his "gentile wife." But they didn't ask him anything. Later, when the young immigrant women came to live in their home, his parents saw that their son and Esther were acquainted. They assumed that this must be the mysterious wife… His father never asked him whether Esther was the anonymous wife. His mother never asked either, and their speculations remained unverified.

Bambi never imagined that anyone would connect her with Yehiel. First of all, after they first met in Germany, she did not see him again for the two years during which he worked in Italy. Secondly, she considered him a representative of another world entirely. He was from Eretz Israel, wore an army uniform – that of the British army. He was full of self-confidence, active, constantly organizing things, and didn't rest for a moment. She, on the other hand, had never even dreamed of making aliyah, because in her childhood home Eretz Israel was not part of her parents' aspirations. Only later did she begin to develop an interest in Eretz Israel. At first, it was the Germans who pushed her toward aliyah – not because of what they had done to the Jews during the war, but because of their situation after it was over. After the war, Germany was a wasteland of destruction. Everywhere she went Esther saw the Germans picking up the pieces, sweeping the streets, clearing away the ruins. She looked at them and said to herself, *They have a home. Whether ruined or still standing, they have something to rebuild. I have nothing. I have no home, and no country to live in.* When she reached the DP camp in Kassel, she began to learn Yiddish. Others told her about Eretz Israel – that place where people were fighting so that the Jews would have their own state. The idea fascinated her. Gradually, the plan of living in Eretz Israel, in her own homeland, without non-Jews, took root in her consciousness. She heard nothing about the Arabs who also wanted that same small piece of land.

In the meantime, Esther's aunt in Toronto discovered her name on a list of survivors. Malka Soberman was Esther's father's sister and had immigrated to Canada before World War I. Malka sent a letter to Esther in the DP camp, and asked her to send by return post the names of her parents and where she had lived before the catastrophe. Esther did so, and Malka realized beyond any doubt that this was indeed her niece, who had survived the Holocaust. In another letter, the aunt invited Esther to Canada to live with her and her family. She would send her a flight ticket and pay for her studies. Esther had only to agree.

However, Esther replied that she had no desire to exchange one Diaspora for another and that she wanted to live in the place where the Jewish state would be established. Her aunt and the family in Canada were infuriated. They interpreted her response as pure ungratefulness, and mental imbalance to boot: they were offering Esther everything, while she wanted to go to somewhere where it wasn't at all clear what would transpire. They cut off correspondence with Esther for many years, until

1966, when the aunt visited Israel in order to meet her. After that, their relationship improved.

Decades later, Yehiel was to hint at Bambi's experiences in the Holocaust. In a letter to the editor, Yehiel wrote:

> It was my good fortune that I did not undergo the horrors of the Holocaust – I spent all my days in Eretz Israel. But for almost fifty years, I have been in the company of a woman who was in Auschwitz and Bergen-Belsen, as well as other camps. I have heard her say: "Even if a person reads everything that has been written in the last fifty years on the Holocaust; sees all the documentaries and photographs that give proof of what happened; and hears from survivors about everything they underwent – one cannot step into the survivors' shoes, or comprehend their emotions."

Following the end of the War of Independence, Yehiel began to search for work. Within a short time he found a job at the Herut Party's Lishkat Ha-Lohem Ve-Ha-Hayal (Office of the Fighter and Soldier), founded and directed by Yitzchak Farger (Yonah) and Reuven Yellin. This office was responsible for providing assistance to the wounded and families of fatalities from the Irgun.

The need for such an office came from what seems, in retrospect, one of the bitterest and most difficult social phenomena of the newly created state: the profound hatred between Mapai and the Revisionists, which not only persisted but intensified and consumed every sector. The formal governmental institutions were headed by David Ben-Gurion, Mapai leader and Israel's first prime minister. The left-wing government refused to recognize the Irgun and Lehi war fatalities and wounded as victims of the battles for independence. Thus, they and their families were not eligible for remuneration. The demands made in the nascent Knesset to prevent differentiation between party affiliations of war victims fell on deaf ears. Knesset member Eliezer Shostak of the Herut Party bitterly described the situation as "the open denial of the state and the present government toward the families of the fallen and wounded of the War of Independence," but his words had no effect. The overwhelming majority of the parties that joined Mapai obeyed the leader's orders. In his book *The Road to the Pantheon: Irgun, Lehi, and the Borders of Israeli Memory* (Hebrew, Jerusalem: Carmel, 2007), historian Dr. Udi Lebel emphasized that from the outset, the government determined that the only individuals eligible for compensation were those wounded between November 29, 1947, the day of the UN declaration of the Partition Plan, and July 20, 1949, the day of signature of the last truce, between Israel and Syria – completely overlooking the war against the British, the main enemy of the Irgun and Lehi. Things reached such a point that the term "military service" was defined by law to mean defense action against the Arab gangs and invading armies. Although technically this definition also overlooked the Haganah soldiers who were killed or wounded before the cut-off date, in reality, many legal and bureaucratic processes protected the Haganah soldiers and enabled them to enjoy government recognition and rights.

The struggle over this issue was bitter and protracted. Fighters in the underground armies, and families of the fallen, viewed it as an attempt to deprive them of their rights, they who had endangered their lives on behalf of the nation – merely because they did not belong to the "correct" political camp. Years passed before a proper and just solution was found for this painful problem.

In early 1949 it became clear that financial difficulties prevented the Herut Party from continuing to give regular aid or assisting the rehabilitation of the underground soldiers, despite its good intentions. The party thus attempted to locate special sources to fulfill this need. The chairman of the Herut Party, Menachem Begin, initiated a special fund for this purpose. He named it Shikum Lohamei Hofesh (Shelah, "Rehabilitation of Freedom Fighters"). Shelah was founded in April 1949, and the Office of the Fighter and Soldier was integrated into it. The project was administered by the Herut Party offices on 17 Tchernichovsky Street in Tel Aviv.

The director of Shelah was Raphael Kotlowitz, and members of the board of directors were Reuven Yellin, Shabbtai Nadiv, Yehudah Bilu, Dov Millman, Yitzchak Avinoam, Eliyahu Lankin, Dr. Litmanowitz, Asher Podhoretzer, Shabbtai Vardi, and Yehiel Kadishai. The welfare department was directed by Reuven Yellin and the department secretary,

Yehiel. Menachem Begin served as committee chairman, Ya'akov Meridor as vice chairman, Aryeh Ben Eliezer as treasurer, and Shmuel Merlin as secretary.

Members of the Herut Party, Yehiel among them, did not wait for the Knesset to include the Irgun and Lehi victims under the law. They began to address the financial problems of the underground fighters who had been drafted into the IDF and faced problems of livelihood; personal problems of all kinds; and of course, the families of the fallen, who were left sometimes without the most basic necessities. Most of the Shelah funds went to medical treatment and rehabilitation of the Irgun wounded and disabled, whom the state refused to recognize. For this purpose, Shelah even established a rehabilitation center in Netanya. Some were sent abroad for complicated treatments. Funding came from supporters of the party in South Africa and the United States.

Many other issues demanded attention as a result of the state's discrimination against Irgun members. Some of these issues included the erection of tombstones and monuments, bringing to Israel the remains of fighters who were killed abroad, and memorial services.

One of the Shelah projects was publication of *Zichram Netzah* (Their memory is eternal) a memorial book for Irgun heroes. The editors were Ya'akov Hetman (Yisrael was his underground alias), Eleazar Pedhatzur (Gad), Avraham Aharoni (Hillel), Shlomo Okon (Nissan), and Yehiel Kadishai (Shimon). "The book was published in 1959," recalled Yehiel, "although it was ready for print seven years earlier. The reason for the long delay was financial, of course."

The book's preface begins with a quotation from Jabotinsky: "There is not one spot of our land that was not redeemed in blood." The preface, written by the Shelah directorate together with the editors, gives full expression to the feelings of Irgun fighters who felt betrayed by their country.

> As few against the many, pursued at home and abroad, the soldiers of the fighting underground rose. In a mighty struggle paved with suffering, torture, imprisonment, exile, and gallows, they threw off the burden of slavery. In the storm of rebellion that preceded the decision of the United Nations

and the war against the invading armies, many fell. Their steadfastness against the enemy was fearless; their heroism stunned an entire world. From their ranks came the martyrs who went joyfully to the gallows so that Israel would rise. But after the birth of the state, which they had attained with their blood, its leaders and ministers did not remember them. On the contrary – the State of Israel did much to obliterate their memory and achievements.

Commemorating the underground, those who carried out operations and the fallen – this was one of the missions that Shelah took upon itself. As part of these memorial activities, and on reaching the tenth anniversary [of independence], we hereby present with the utmost respect the life stories of the fallen of the Irgun Zva'i Leumi to the bereaved families, their fellow fighters, and all citizens of our homeland.

In this book, we have collected the biographies of the heroes of the Irgun who fell in the various fronts of the battle for the freedom of Israel, beginning with the bloody events of 5696 [1936] – when the first buds of self-liberation began to blossom; through the great rebellion against non-Jewish rule, and ending with the war of 5708 [1948] against the Arab invaders. Soldiers of the Irgun stood on all fronts: from defending key positions of the Yishuv against Arab attacks to the British deportation camp in Eritrea; on the Euphrates River in Babylon, and among the ranks of the Eretz Israel units and the Jewish Brigade in the war effort against Nazi Germany; and in direct confrontation with the British enslaver, on the gallows in Acre, and in the death cells in Jerusalem. When the enslaver was banished and the Irgun soldiers, together with the rest of the nation, reported for war against the invaders – they missed not one battle. Their blood soaked the ground of the homeland: "For we planted your fields – in the Diaspora, from the gallows of Acre"[3] – they sang from the dawn of childhood.

---

3 Translator's note: This is a line from the poem "*Kula sheli*" (She is all mine), by Jabotinsky.

The Shelah staff was small, and the problems it encountered endless. There was no money to pay the staff's salaries. Shelah's managers did all they could to find funding for the aid activities, which were irreplaceable. With no other choice, they began to raise funds from foreign countries, and the party leaders went out to all points of the globe. There they met with resistance and lack of cooperation from other fundraisers, who objected to funds that were not authorized by the Jewish Agency or by the directorate of the Joint Distribution Committee. Branches of Herut – Union of Zionists-Revisionists (Ha-Zohar, the international arm of the Herut Party), however, did help them, in those locations to which representatives traveled.

CHAPTER 11

WEDDING IN THE RAIN

In Yehiel's personal life, the bank account was empty, but the heart was full. He had no need to go down on one knee to ask, "Will you marry me?" Yehiel and Esther moved toward a shared future as part of life's natural course.

"We had money only for bread and margarine," Yehiel recalled. "So I went to my wedding not by taxi, as would have been fitting, but on foot." As part of his job, Yehiel spent time in the presence of Herut Party leaders – so it was no surprise that the guest list included Menachem Begin, Ya'akov Meridor, Aryeh Ben Eliezer, and many other high-ups.

Yehiel and Bambi's wedding took place the week before Passover in 1949. Rabbi Aviezer Cycowicz officiated as representative of the Tel Aviv rabbinate. His wife was a friend of Yehiel's mother. A week earlier, the couple had gone to register at the rabbinate office in Tel Aviv. But a problem arose.

"Present a witness," the clerk at the rabbinate instructed Yehiel. Under Jewish law, the wedding had to be witnessed by a Jew who was not a relative of either bride or groom. He scratched his head. Where would he find a witness in the vicinity who knew Esther? Was there anyone appropriate in Israel who knew her?

Yehiel hurried out into the street to try to find a witness. Just then, Yitzchak Avinoam (Yagnes) of Petah Tikva happened to walk by. He had served as Irgun district commander in Jerusalem. Yehiel ran toward him as if he had just found a treasure. "Yagnes," he said, "there's this girl I'm going to marry. Please tell the rabbinate that you know her."

Avinoam agreed, and was full of praise for the virtues of the bride he had never even met. Thus Yehiel and Bambi were able to go ahead with the wedding. It was held, as was the custom in those days – in the rabbi's home at 34 Lilienblum Street. In order to describe the event, we must forget all the trappings of weddings today. There was no hall, no fancy catered dinner, no band, and no endless guest list.

It was a stormy winter day. Outside, it was raining cats and dogs. The room was so small and narrow that some of the handful of guests – including a few who had traveled to Tel Aviv from the Knesset for the occasion – had to go out to the balcony. But who needed hundreds of guests when all that was needed to witness a Jewish wedding was a quorum of ten men? As soon as there was a break in the downpour, blankets were spread on the edge of the low porch railing for the guests to sit on. They shivered slightly, but remained dry. Yehiel's mother baked a *lekach* (honey) cake in honor of the occasion, and the table was graced with a bottle of wine, some small glasses, and candies provided by the rabbi. The guests poured the wine and toasted, "*Le-hayim*! (To life!)" The only one who ate anything was Esther, as she had observed the custom of fasting all day. Yehiel's mother served only her a bowl of chicken soup with noodles, and this was how Esther broke her fast after the wedding ceremony. Yehiel was not strict in his observance on this point.

Before the wedding, Esther wondered whether the Rebbe of Lelov would attend, as Yehiel's father was one of his followers. The answer was negative. His wife would not attend either. This seemed strange, and Esther asked Yehiel's mother why they were absent. Then Yehiel's mother opened the Pandora's box. "Why do you think they're not coming?" she asked. "Because you're already married!"

The story about "Yehiel's wife" had taken root. Yehiel's father had never bothered to ask him whether there was a grain of truth in the story. Perhaps he feared the answer. The Rebbe's followers, at least, believed that the story was proven fact. What would a Rebbe be doing at a wedding of someone who had already married the same bride?

The wedding lasted less than an hour. Afterward, the couple went on a creative honeymoon. Bambi related, "We made a budget, and discovered we had enough money to buy bus tickets to Ramat Gan and back. I had never been to Ramat Gan, so that's where we went. Yehiel showed me the town. To me, it seemed lovelier than Paris, which I had seen before immigrating to Israel. Then we went to Orda Square, where there was a charming park. We sat in the park and talked until our throats were dry, but we didn't have enough money to buy a glass of soda. Yehiel met a friend there and said, 'I'd like to introduce you to my wife.' But the friend didn't believe him. 'When did you get married?' he asked. "Yesterday,' Yehiel answered. 'We got married yesterday.' We were very pleased with our honeymoon. In the afternoon we went back, and Yehiel went to the office."

At that point Yehiel became responsible for supporting not only himself and his family, but also a wife. Where would they live?

Yehiel's older brother Yitzchak saved the day. At that time, the Tel Aviv community, or "the Swamp" as it was called, was in an uproar over the divorce of Cameri theater stars Hannah Meron and Yossi Yadin. Yehiel had advance notice of this from his brother Yitzchak, who was the administrative director of the theater. He also knew that after the divorce, they moved out of their small one-room apartment at 81 Gordon Street. The apartment was under the stairs and had originally served as the building's laundry room. How could the new couple afford to buy an apartment, when their entire life savings was only 150 *lirot*? The information Yitzchak provided proved accurate; and the money he lent them arrived exactly on time.

The room was unfurnished. Even if they had had any furniture, there was nowhere to put it. Bambi brought with her the iron bed from the Jewish Agency, which she had the right to receive by law as a new immigrant. Yehiel's sister gave them an icebox. A nail hammered in the wall was where they hung their clothes. The wedding gifts included a few useful items, such as several electric teapots. Bambi went to a housewares store and exchanged one of these for a broom and floor rag. She exchanged another teapot for plates and silverware for two. They rounded up a broken mug from somewhere and used it to hold their toothbrushes. At least the neighborhood was more pleasant than their little room under the stairs: nearby were Hadassah Park and the zoo, an unparalleled attraction for adults as well as children. Eventually, the zoo lot was repurposed for the Tel Aviv-Jaffa municipal building.

Making a living was their greatest challenge. Yehiel's salary from Shelah was practically symbolic. But they enjoyed life to the fullest. Their many friends constantly crowded into the one-room apartment – it was not hard to fill it – while the spillover stood in the street, laughing and talking, drinking and eating. At first they didn't even have a lightbulb, as electricity was expensive, and so they lit candles at night.

Two years later, they left this address and moved elsewhere. A plumbing business took over the apartment. One day, decades later, Bambi was out for a walk in their old neighborhood. When she saw the place where they had lived at the beginning of their life together, she noticed that the door was halfway open. Curious to see what was there, she moved closer, peeked inside, and saw a young man sitting in the midst of an utter chaos of plumbing supplies. He looked at her, surprised. "Excuse me," she said, "but we lived here many years ago. I saw the open door, and I just wanted to see the place."

"Who lived here?" he asked.

"My husband and myself," Bambi replied.

"Two people?" the man asked, astonished.

"Actually, yes," Bambi repeated, "my husband and myself."

The young man burst out laughing. "I've got to tell that to my father. He says that this room is not fit to live in, not even for one person!"

Bambi peeked inside again and admitted, "You're right, it is really small."

From this small room, they moved to an apartment in Abu Kabir – a larger place, but they were surrounded by sand, and it felt as if they were at the end of the world. After a year, they sold this apartment and paid key money for a place at 184 Ben Yehuda Street. In 1954, they purchased the apartment at 9 Hovevei Zion Street belonging to Yehiel's brother Yitzchak, who sold it as his family expanded. The next apartment in line was on Nahmani Street, and they finally ended their wanderings on 16 Ben Zion Avenue, where they lived for many years, but without the blessing of children.

***

In 1976, the poet Shin Shifra made a speech in honor of Bambi at a celebration in honor of her birthday. Shifra handed out copies to the participants. Part of the speech read:

At first glance, Bambi and "enigma" seem to be opposites. What could be enigmatic about this woman with the open expression, childlike eyes, who says what she thinks, whose deeds and words are pleasant, whose nickname "Bambi" fits her like a glove. And yet – she remains a riddle.

I had never heard the story of Bambi's life in one continuous account. Over the years of our acquaintance, which are not so many in number, I fit piece to piece together like a puzzle, and put them together into a whole. I asked myself repeatedly how Bambi maintained such a strong emotional character in her relationship with the world and with others, despite a life that was not always a bed of roses, to put it mildly. I admit that I did not find any connection between Bambi's biography over there in the land of destruction (which I will avoid mentioning, since Bambi herself rarely mentions it), and the woman I know here and now. I think that even here, once she reached Israel, not everything came easily. From her stories I try to imagine the innocent young girl who came to us without speaking the language, without a family, without a profession, carrying a sack full of terrible memories. Again, it's difficult for me to find a connection between the lost girl of then and the woman I know. In truth, Bambi had the good luck to meet Yehiel (and I imagine that when Yehiel reads this, he'll make a joke), and she was also lucky that Yehiel's family accepted her into their midst, despite her foreignness. Still – how did she manage in this new world in which she found herself? How did she find the emotional strength to accept life, even if not all her heart's desires were fulfilled? Where did she get the innocence that stayed with her all these years – and I use the word "innocence," and not naiveté, because we certainly can't say about Bambi that she doesn't see the complexity of individuals and events.

I've read the text of the riddle to you, and now I'll try to find the solution.

I think that above all, Bambi was graced with love of

life, pure and simple, without asking herself why. From the moment she opens her eyes in the morning, she knows there's a reason for every single moment in her life, simply because there's a reason. She is like an ancient archetype of the mother of all living beings, the source of life, and so she does not pose philosophical or rational questions about the meaning of existence. Through ceremony and ritual tied to the cycle of time, human beings attempt to regain their lost place within nature. Every celebration is a ritual ceremony of this kind. So that these words will not remain abstract, let us observe Bambi with our mental eyes as she receives guests, for example:

You are still in the elevator when the door to the apartment opens in front of you, and Bambi is standing there, smiling. Rarely did Mati and I need to use the doorbell. Then Bambi kisses the guests on both cheeks, sits them down in their places, and offers those with weak backs a pillow for support. When the time comes for refreshment, Bambi lifts her arms and spreads a tablecloth on the table. It's always ironed, and if it's a cotton one, it's also starched. As if performing a ritual, first she serves almonds, chocolate, and snacks. The guests chat around the table, while Bambi goes to the kitchen and sets the teapot on the fire – for serving tea and coffee is a ceremony. She always remembers what each person likes to drink and how – coffee or tea, strong or weak. For herself, she always serves in a mug. This is no small thing. To me, this is a clear sign of attention to others. I've been seriously offended when someone close to me, who has been serving me coffee for many years, asks again and again, "Instant or Turkish?" She slices a cake on a tray, or sometimes two cakes, usually homemade. When they are not homemade, she practically apologizes. She goes to the buffet and takes out a small dish for sweeteners – not a plastic container, heaven forbid – and spoons and forks. Of course we could eat cake with a spoon, but that would spoil the ceremony. She does all of this with a joyous expression adorning her face, as if she just had done all this for the first time. As if these guests were not frequently invited to her home, but rather they were "important" ones. I've never seen an expression of effort or weariness on her face. But we still haven't reached the end of the ceremony. After sitting with us for a short while, she'll bring to the table sliced watermelon or melon, and grapes with a reddish tinge that recalls plums or peaches. This is not just fruit placed on a plate in random shape or form. Once I saw her examining the artistically displayed platter, head inclined, as if she were studying the aesthetic arrangement of a still life. Sometimes she uses a mixed arrangement of tropical fruit, and even then she manages to infuse it with a composition that is also beautiful. Only after this part of the ceremony is over does she allow herself to sit in an armchair at a distance and light a cigarette.

Bambi's ceremonial attitude toward daily activities is a direct result of the positive attitude I described previously. It is as if every day she is reborn anew, like a Jew who gets up in the morning and recites the Modeh Ani prayer: "I gratefully thank You, living and eternal King, for returning my soul within me with compassion – abundant is your faithfulness."

I imagine that this is how Bambi sanctifies herself before each activity she carries out: this is how she puts on her clothes, this is how she irons Yehiel's shirts, prepares a meal, goes to a wedding of friends or any other celebration.

This is perhaps the origin of the love she radiates to all who know her, and the love that her friends and acquaintances radiate back to her. Only a person who accepts himself and his own life as a unit is willing and able to accept others, with all their strengths and weaknesses.

I have attempted to find a solution for the enigma of Bambi. I hope with all my might that I have not succeeded in deciphering this enigma in full, because a living, breathing relationship, and this is the kind of relationship I have with Bambi, always poses new questions.

Now for a few words of a more personal nature. I came to Yehiel and Bambi's home much later than the rest of their friends. Bambi and I are from very different birthplaces and backgrounds, but still we are close. Our lives came together at one point due to our husbands' work – the work of my husband Mati and that of Yehiel, my dear friend. Even when Bambi had criticism, she always chose her words carefully. She never allowed herself to be dragged into gossip or spoke ill of others – her words were measured and never bitter. It was pleasant to laugh with her at bombastic meals that amused us both, and to have heart-to-hearts with her in difficult times.

Finally, I permit myself to assume something that I can't prove: that the secret magic of Bambi and Yehiel's relationship is in the differing natures of its two components. In a poem called "Justice" by Aliza Tur Malka, a man and woman appear before a judge, and present their arguments using colors: "Paint the issue in colors." They both follow the judge's orders. I won't give the details, but the poem ends with an afterword written in the voice of a friend:

Friend: What is the color of the man's soul?

Woman: Blue, red, and gold. These are the colors of fire: "A soul praying for redemption and love."

Friend: What is the color of your soul?

Woman: I cannot know. Not the element of fire, like him. Sunken in twilight. Infused with a strange quality, deep and generous, like a powerful dream that nurses the soul.

"Love your neighbor as yourself. As for the rest – go and learn."[4]

After the honeymoon, which could barely be called as such, Yehiel continued with his job for Shelah. His daily work in this position was never routine. Every day brought with it new stories. Yehiel told of the overwhelming difficulties faced by former Irgun members.

---

4 The sage Hillel's quip, in the Talmud, to a potential convert who requested he teach him the entire Torah at once, while standing on one foot (*Shabbat* 31a).

"The regime abandoned us. Whoever didn't belong to the right party or didn't have the right membership card was like a foreign body. Whoever didn't belong to established society had to take care of himself, because he had no job in any government office or high-up position in the IDF. We did not belong – we were invisible, and there was no attempt to object to this, because this was simply the way things were.

"The scariest thing was the issue of the war wounded and bereaved families. This was not a question of a healthy individual who could take care of himself, who could walk, who could fight the system with his brain and his body, or find work on his own in a private business. We had several hundred cases of people who were unable to help themselves, or bereaved families who needed help to get back on their feet. At the time, people looked askance at the disabled due to their organizational affiliation. He might be lying wounded in the hospital, or maybe he lost a leg in a battle, and they would say, 'He won't get a dime [*perutah*] from the government.' This was a direct order from David Ben-Gurion, the omnipotent prime minister and minister of defense."

Yehiel's activity with Shelah involved lifesaving decisions. He and his comrades attended to the most difficult cases with sensitivity and tireless dedication. The following story illustrates the complications resulting from the discriminatory treatment of the former underground members. Two twin Irgun members were twenty-five years old when they both fell in battle. One was killed on May 19, 1948, in the Irgun battle at Wilhelma. His brother joined the IDF along with his Irgun unit, and was killed two months later, on July 13, 1948, in the battle at Negba. The Ministry of Defense did not officially recognize the first brother as a war victim, because he was an Irgun member, but it did recognize the second, because he was serving in the IDF when he died. These twins, who grew up together, were separated in death by the heads of the new state. Their father wrote a harsh letter to Ben-Gurion: "The prime minister and minister of defense must realize that even if the Irgun fighters were not to his liking, still they gave their hot blood as willingly as the Haganah members."

In another incident, a bereaved mother of an IDF fatality was denied a pension. Her son, Zvi Reifer, was in the Givati brigade. During the battle over the *Altalena*, he had fought for the Irgun, and was killed in the conflict with the IDF. Reifer was killed at Beit Dagan, some eight and a half miles from the Tel Aviv beach, by an IDF unit placed there to block Irgun supporters. After he was killed, the mother received a monthly stipend from the Ministry of Defense. But on the third anniversary of the *Altalena* incident, the *Herut* newspaper published a bereavement notice, on behalf of the Herut movement and Shelah, with the names of those Irgun members who had fallen during that tragic incident. A clerk in the Ministry of Defense pored over the list of names, and found the name of Zvi Reifer. The diligent clerk corrected the record to show that the soldier had lost his life in the *Altalena* battle, and the mother's stipend was stopped. In the end, an appeals committee rescinded the heartless decision of the Ministry of Defense claims officer to stop the payments to the bereaved mother.

Such injustices under cover of the law cried out to heaven in dozens, even hundreds of cases. The fingers of a mere handful of Shelah workers were stuck in a dyke that threatened to collapse under the rising flood of cases. Each case represented a painful personal story.

In his work, Yehiel lived these heart-rending cases day in and day out. He did everything he could so that the discrimination between blood brothers would be erased as if it never existed. On this, he agreed wholeheartedly with Menachem Begin, who stated that, "Injustice is corrected when justice is done."

Doing justice also related to financial assistance. Many of the underground fatalities left behind families in poverty. The death of a father or son brought with it severe financial woes, aside from the endless grief.

Such was the case for Sheila Levi, who was sixteen when her father, a British native who made aliyah during the 1940s, was killed in the Irgun bombing of the King David Hotel in Jerusalem, where he worked as a senior clerk for the British authorities. Sheila and her widowed mother Yael faced extreme difficulties, as there was no one to support their family – until Shelah was established.

Another challenge was the problem of the disabled. Through his work, Yehiel established ties in the Ministry of Defense rehabilitation branch, located in Beit Hadar in Tel Aviv. Through this office, a few Irgun members received treatment – those who were officially eligible under the law for medical treatment by the state. One of these, Jack (Ya'akov) Skovronek, lost his leg in an Irgun operation, and did not even have a prosthesis. Yehiel knew a claims officer named Yo'ash whose heart sometimes broke when faced with the absurd. One day, Yehiel took Ya'akov to see Yo'ash, to try to get the disabled man treatment at the hospital. Yo'ash took stock of Ya'akov's condition and asked, as he asked many others, "Where were you wounded?"

If Ya'akov had cited the name of the site where the Irgun operation was carried out, he would have been sent home at once. Instead, the former soldier played naïve, and instead of giving the place name, he answered, "In the foot." Yo'ash did not ask for further clarification, but signed the appropriate form to send Ya'akov for the needed treatment.

There were other clerks in the rehabilitation branch who gave the right answers to certain requests – mainly for medical treatment for the disabled. Captain Levine, a central figure in that office, was one such individual, as was Olga Stein. Individuals at the administrative level were much more willing to help than those at the political level.

"Sometimes I would come to them with a particular name," Yehiel related. "I would explain that this was a special case, and they would put him on the list of patients. Furthermore, the IDF had a special unit that took care of such cases. Sometimes they enlisted our wounded men, and so they were transferred to the IDF for treatment. For example, thanks to certain clerks with merciful Jewish hearts, one Irgun soldier who was severely wounded in Jaffa and incapacitated for the rest of his life was able to receive treatment at Tel Hashomer. Their true Jewish hearts encouraged them to ignore Ben-Gurion's punitive declaration: 'They [the underground members] won't get a dime from the government.'"

Not all underground members received treatment, because of the criteria of the times. Two Irgun members lost their eyesight, both in their early twenties. David Weiss was blinded in the battle of Jaffa, while Meir Palay was wounded while packing hand grenades to be sent to the Irgun in besieged Jerusalem. In a storage room on Ha-Tabor Street, Palay accidentally pulled the pin of a grenade. Palay was completely blinded, while his fellow Irgun member, Mordechai Aharon Fogeman (Aviram), was killed in the explosion. Under the strict criteria, they did not qualify for any support.

Menachem Begin was involved in the cases of each and every Irgun member. On behalf of Weiss and Palay, after all other avenues were exhausted, a group of former Irgun members went on a fundraising mission to the United States in December 1948. Their party, Herut, was then in the opposition in the Knesset. The travelers included Menachem Begin, Shmuel Tamir, Ephraim Margolin, and Yitzchak Elitzur. They took Weiss and Palay with them. Also traveling with the group were journalist and Irgun member Yitzchak Gurion, and Na'ama Shabto, who had been wounded in an Irgun operation and was left with a paralyzed leg. Weiss and Palay were taken to special medical facilities for the blind, where treatment was extremely expensive. The treatment was paid for by the contributions of supporters who met with Begin and the other members. At first, the wounded men underwent a series of ophthalmological surgeries, but when these did not help, they were taught skills that blind people can perform, such as piano tuning.

Mordechai Fogeman, the Irgun member killed in the same accident that blinded Palay, was also not recognized by the Ministry of Defense as a victim of the War of Independence. Yehiel's main argument in his attempt to convince the Ministry of Defense to recognize Fogeman was that he had died in a war operation, as defined by the law– part of an operation to battle Arab gangs and invading armies. Finally, the Ministry of Defense recognized Fogeman as a fatality of the War of Independence. Then Yehiel was able to argue that Palay also deserved recognition, as he had been wounded in the same operation in which Fogeman was killed, and Fogeman had been declared a "legal" war fatality. His argument was accepted, and eventually, a petition on behalf of David Weiss was also accepted.

Knesset representative Haim Landau – as Yehiel recounted – was deeply offended by the authorities' hostile attitude toward Irgun victims, and he declared vociferously that there was no reason to lobby for aid. They should take nothing from the new government that was so apathetic to their plight, but rather the party should provide for its own. Landau had no idea how many expenses were involved – sums that only a state could bear, not a party. When he realized what was involved, he changed his tune.

"We had no choice but to collect funds from abroad," Yehiel said. "For example, we printed special editions of Menachem Begin's book *The Revolt* and Ya'akov Meridor's book *Long Is the Road to Freedom*, with special leather bindings, decorative metal plates, and the authors' signatures. They were sold in exchange for a donation to Shelah. But no matter how much we collected, it was never enough.

"After many years, the state eventually recognized all Irgun fatalities and wounded, including those involved in the *Altalena* incident, as victims of the War of Independence."

The discrimination affected not only those wounded in battle, but also members of the underground who finished the war unscathed.

"People stopped complaining that they couldn't find jobs," Yehiel acknowledged. "They accepted it as a natural thing that we were not eligible for anything from the state – not the healthy ones, nor the wounded, nor the dead. This is not an exaggeration, it's a fact. With my own eyes, I saw my friends delivering bananas to the market privately. I mean, they worked at Tnuva [a large agricultural cooperative], but as subcontractors, not salaried workers. Why? Because Tnuva wouldn't give a job to someone who belonged to our group of people. Our people didn't complain about this. Actually, maybe they did complain, but they didn't shout it out loud, because what good would it have done?"

In the early fifties, one of the former Irgun commanders, a creative and daring young woman, was given a lowly job addressing and stamping envelopes at the Tel Aviv branch of the nascent National Insurance Institute. She had gotten the job through a private arrangement. After a few weeks, the branch manager called her into his office. His face grim, he informed her, "I'm sorry, but you can't continue working here."

"Why?" she asked. "Have I done something wrong?"

"Don't play dumb," barked the manager. "You don't know why?"

"No, I don't," she replied, mortified.

"You belong to them!" he revealed. That was her last day of work in the office. She found work in a jewelry factory, and earned three times her previous salary. She was eternally grateful that the manager had fired her, but she never forgot the humiliation.

In the meantime, one of the stormiest affairs that rocked the state in its early years was taking place: In 1952, Israelis led by Menachem Begin demonstrated in Jerusalem against accepting war reparations from Germany. The crowd threw stones at the Knesset, which met at that time in Froumine House on King George Street.

Yehiel described his participation: "I was at that demonstration in Zion Square. Begin spoke, and then he called, 'We'll go to the Knesset!' He did not command them to 'advance on the Knesset' or 'attack the Knesset,' but rather to go to the area nearby and continue demonstrating there. We reached the area and gathered in a small hollow that was full of large chunks of gravel. People started to run toward the Knesset, but the police stopped them. There were also barriers in the area. We stood opposite the Knesset, shouting and demanding that the government refuse to accept reparations. We would not agree to accept payment for blood. There was no atonement for what the Germans had done, even for astronomical sums.

"Then one of the demonstrators bent down, picked up a stone and hurled it toward the Knesset. Someone else next to me bent down, and he also threw a stone. Not many stones were thrown, and those that were thrown were insignificant, but the phrase that took hold was, 'They threw stones at the Knesset.' Threw? Yes, but only a few. Begin didn't initiate it; he didn't even support it, because while it was happening he was entering the building, and he could have gotten hurt by one of the stones. Personally, I don't regret for a moment the stones that were thrown, as this only served to emphasize the seriousness, the shame, the humiliation, and the moral dilemma at the heart of this issue, all the more so in light of the fact that the State of Israel could have managed without that money. An approach that supported payments, as in the case of Germany, might encourage antisemitic regimes, governments, groups of skinheads, or anti-Jewish mobs, to carry out pogroms against Jews in far-off communities or even major ones. It encouraged an attitude of, 'It's not so terrible, in the end we can make a deal with them for money, because they'll take payoffs.' Future generations in Israel and throughout the Jewish world could suffer from this."

As for the question of how to build an economic infrastructure in Israel without the reparations from Germany, Yehiel cited an expression he had heard from Begin, who in turn quoted the book of Esther: "Relief and deliverance will arise to the Jews from another place" (4:14).

Years later, that same expression caused a terrible incident with a major Jewish donor in London. This incident was related to the search for the submarine INS *Dakar*, which sunk mysteriously in January 1968 while sailing from England to Israel. The sixty-nine crew members aboard the *Dakar* were all lost at sea, and the submarine was never recovered.

The story began in late 1964 or early 1965, about one year after Yehiel began his position as Begin's secretary. At that time, Begin was still deeply entrenched within the opposition. One day, Shmuel Tamir, a former Irgun commander and a founder of the Herut Party, related that at a certain social event he had met the Soviet ambassador to Israel, Dmitri Chuvakhin. In conversation with Tamir, the ambassador had expressed interest in meeting with Begin. Begin returned the compliment, and after arrangements were made with the embassies, the meeting was set.

That day, Yehiel was at Begin's home on Rosenbaum Street in Tel Aviv. As usual, they went over correspondence, and Begin dictated his replies. At the appointed hour, they heard a knock at the door. The ambassador had arrived. Begin welcomed him. Although Begin knew Russian, they spoke in English. (Begin understood and read Russian, but on principle he did not like to speak languages he did not know fluently.)

Before they began to talk, Begin, who did not even know the difference between cherry liqueur and brandy, asked, "Yehiel, would you be so kind as to pour a shot of vodka for the ambassador?"

The honorable ambassador, who had developed epicurean tastes during his career in the Soviet foreign service, said, "Excuse me, but I would prefer whiskey."

The two began to converse. They began with formalities, then spoke a bit about themselves, and finally moved to local and international politics and global problems. The conversation lasted for about an hour. When it was over, when Chuvakhin already stood beside the door, he asked Begin, "Can I do anything for you?"

Begin realized at once that this was a once-in-a-lifetime opportunity. He said to his secretary, "Yehiel, please bring me Friedrich's list."

Two weeks before this meeting, Begin had received from the Herut

Party representative in Paris, Shlomo Friedrich, a list of some forty individuals who had asked to have immigration requests submitted for them, so that they could obtain exit visas from the USSR. Most were former Prisoners of Zion, originally from Riga and Vilna, which had not belonged to the USSR before the Second World War. These individuals, whose exact addresses appeared on the list, were members of Zionist Jewish communities, and a large number of them were Betar members. The list, written in Cyrillic letters, was two pages long. Begin recognized the majority of the names, although he did not know the people personally, and he was fully aware of their Zionist activity behind the Iron Curtain.

"Yes," Begin revealed to Chuvakhin, "I have friends who are in your country. I would like to see them here."

Chuvakhin laughed. "You know, Mr. Begin, these people will not vote for you in the elections, because they come from a communist country."

Actually, Begin probably assumed that they would vote for him for that very reason, but of course that was not his decision. He replied to Chuvakhin with a smile: "It doesn't matter, they can vote for whomever they want. They're my comrades, and I would like to ask that you release them."

"Okay," Chuvakhin replied, "Send the names to me at the embassy."

After Chuvakhin departed, a glimmer of doubt stole into Begin's mind – should he send the names or not? He revealed to Yehiel: "What? Give him the list? Who will promise me that the authorities there won't take the list and imprison them, one by one?"

Begin also consulted with Knesset members Ben Eliezer and Haim Landau, but he did not reach a decision. Meanwhile, Begin's deliberations reached Shlomo Friedrich in Paris and from him on to the USSR. A few days later, Begin received a letter from Yechezkel Pulerevitz, an old friend from Lithuania. Pulerevitz was a Betar member in Kovno. He was the Betar cultural director in Kovno, and a poet, and some of his songs were sung in Israel by Betar youth. When the Russians invaded Lithuania, he was taken prisoner together with his wife Ela (Elyonka, as Yechezkel called her) and they were deported along with other Jews. He was in exile in Siberia for eighteen years, some of which he served in prison. In 1940, they had a son whom they called Shabi Ya'akov. "Shabi" was spelled *shin bet yod* – an abbreviation for Shlomo ben Yosef, or Shalom Tabachnik, the first Jew executed by the British authorities during the mandate period. He was named Ya'akov for the Irgun hero Ya'akov Raz. Shortly after the birth, mother and baby were separated from the father. She raised him alone, and when they were finally reunited, Shabi Ya'akov was already a young man of seventeen. He registered for university in Russia, completed his studies, and became a physician.

Yechezkel Pulerevitz's letter was first sent to Paris and from there to Israel, because the activists feared that it would be dangerous to send letters directly to Israel.

"I understand," Pulerevitz wrote, "that you have doubts about publicizing these names. Please know, Mr. Begin, that we are asking you to publish the names, and we want you to make a public demand that we be liberated from here, and that we be granted the exit visas."

Pulerevitz's letter put an end to Begin's wavering, and he sent the list to Chuvakhin.

The Russian ambassador was a man of his word, as quickly became clear: just two months later, three of the individuals named on the list arrived in Israel with their families. Shortly afterward, two more arrived, and within a year, the last of the people on the list came with their families. One of them recounted: "The Jews in Riga say that the Betar members have pull with the communists, and so they're letting the Jews out."

One of the new arrivals was Begin's personal friend Yechezkel Pulerevitz, and his family.

After the family came to Israel, Shabi Ya'akov was drafted into the IDF. One day, Yechezkel contacted Begin, and said that his son the physician would like to practice his profession in a submarine. The problem was that because he was an immigrant from the Soviet Union, his security clearance did not permit him to serve on a submarine. Begin wrote a letter to the right person, emphasizing that he recommended Shabi Pulerevitz for service in a submarine with as much confidence as if he were his own son. This recommendation proved sufficient. But unfortunately Shabi was placed on the INS *Dakar* – and was lost at sea along with the rest of its crew.

"Many people contacted Begin over the years asking why we did not conduct a search for the submarine's remains," Yehiel reminisced. "They pressured him to operate at the highest levels he could reach in his role as a Knesset member. Begin also had a personal interest in the *Dakar*, aside from the public tragedy of the loss of its sixty-nine sailors. Begin received requests from citizens, some of them family members of the *Dakar* crew, to do everything in his power to initiate a serious search for the submarine. He did everything possible so that this would come to pass. At this stage, the search had not even begun, because the cost was estimated at half a million dollars. But all of Begin's efforts were in vain.

"One day, after he became prime minister, he had an idea: he would contact wealthy Jews who would band together to donate on behalf of this important ethical project. He thus contacted a Jewish aristocrat in London, a titled lord, and asked him to join the sacred mission of locating the submarine and the remains of the lost crew. He also asked this Jew to encourage some of his wealthy friends to join him in raising the necessary funds. In the past, Begin had made other exceptional requests of wealthy Jews to participate in a unique project and donate for the sake of a worthy cause. Ten days later, the lord replied that there were other projects more important than finding the lost submarine.

"At that point, Begin sat down and wrote his response. He confirmed that he had received the lord's missive, and emphasized that, 'Relief and deliverance would come to the Jews from another source' [Esther 4:14]. Begin wanted to avoid the possibility of offending the lord, so he added in parentheses, 'I refer only to the first half of the verse' [the verse's second half is, '...and you and your father's house will perish'].

"Begin wrote this verse in Hebrew, and added, 'If you do not understand this verse, please have a rabbi translate it for you.' The lord received the letter, but didn't understand the verse, so he followed Begin's recommendation and went to a rabbi. The rabbi explained the entire verse, including the second half, to his astonishment. The lord thought that Begin had intended to communicate a terrible curse. He publicized the letter, and the Jewish community of London broke into a furious storm, all the more so since this insult had been written to one of the greatest contributors to the State of Israel.

"When the reverberations of the British storm reached Begin's ears, he was not particularly upset. He said, 'I don't care. The main thing is he should know that he can't decide whether this ethical issue is less important than another. If the lord had written that he didn't have the money at the time, or that he would check into the matter, or that he couldn't manage it – I would have understood. But to dictate to me, to the prime minister of Israel, which is more important – this matter of finding the submarine or another matter?!'"

This incident went unresolved. Then, on September 30, 1981, Yehiel received a letter from industrialist Ernest Wodak, a friend of the Herut Party and supporter of the settlements. Wrote Wodak: "Last week we returned from Scotland…. In London I read an article that was interesting in and of itself, but also for our concerns. It was about an operation to bring up a warship that had capsized several hundred years ago under rather shameful circumstances. Donors, including foreigners, pitched in to the effort. I used this article successfully in my debate with my friends at Marks and Spencer Company, who were involved in the *Dakar* incident (or 'Book of Esther incident') with Lord S. I believe that the prime minister's request of Jewish donors to assist in raising the INS *Dakar* is by far more justified on all accounts than the British operation for the *Mary Rose*, especially when considering that the families of our lost crew are still alive and raising an outcry. If you wish, please show this article to the prime minister and your media staff, and perhaps also to the Foreign Ministry, so they'll have some support for the argument that is still not over in England."

In the end, appeasement was achieved by Yehuda Avner, the British-born Israeli diplomat and top political advisor, who made a special trip to England in order to end the animosity.

CHAPTER 12

OVERSEAS ONCE MORE

In late 1951 or early 1952, Yehiel accepted the offer of his brother Yitzchak, director of the Cameri Theater, to open an office for presales of theater tickets. Their mother had a room they could easily transform into an office, on 1 Aliya Street at the corner of Ha-Moshavot Square, where she stored the stock of writing implements that remained from the store their father had closed in 1943. This room, whose rent was three *lirot* per month, was on the third floor, with no elevator, of course. One of its great advantages, in addition to its location in what was the commercial section of Tel Aviv at that time, was that it had a telephone line – a valuable commodity back then.

The Cameri, which was then staging its shows in a hall underneath the Moghrabi Cinema, had several productions that were major hits, such as *He Walked through the Fields* and *Of Mice and Men*. Tickets were sold three or four months in advance. Yitzchak gave Yehiel exclusivity for ticket sales. Yehiel added one *grush* as commission, and the tickets sold like hotcakes, enabling him to fill the larder. At any rate, it was a better income than he was making in the Herut Party. The Cameri advertisements included the address of Yehiel's box office, as well as the phone number. At first this was 971, then after the town grew, 3971; as phones were added, 63971; and eventually, 623971. Early on, Yehiel found an appropriate name for his box office: "Sherutron" – a creative amalgamation of *sherut* (service) and *teatron* (theater).

This was an excellent business, and culture aficionados of Tel Aviv were more than willing to climb up three flights of stairs in order to purchase tickets for performances that ran for many months and whose reputation spread by word of mouth. The entire office was just one desk, and the ticket sellers were Yehiel and Bambi. Office hours were from 9 a.m. to

151

5 p.m. When he saw that the business was flourishing, Yehiel began to sell cinema tickets as well. Once a week, a long line snaked outside the little office, and people crowded into the stairwell. This was on Fridays, when people bought tickets to the films shown on Saturday night at the conclusion of Shabbat. Advance sales of tickets ensured they would get in to see the film, because tickets sometimes sold out at the cinema box office, and no one was keen to empty his pockets for tickets sold by scalpers, then a well-known phenomenon on the Tel Aviv entertainment scene. At Yehiel's office, theater goers could also order tickets by phone, which were saved until a pre-determined time. Other box offices were operating in Tel Aviv as well: Ha-Kartiss ("the ticket") box office at 31 Allenby Street and Rococo at Dizengoff Square. The uniqueness of Yehiel's business was that he sold tickets for other events besides the theater – sports events such as soccer games, cultural festivals, and more.

Journalist Shlomo Nakdimon recalled that as a child of eleven in south Tel Aviv, his parents sent him to Yehiel to purchase tickets to entertainment events. "It was a real pleasure to buy tickets from him. He always wore a smile, was already ready with a good joke and a warm remark. I think that the lines that stretched behind the counter were largely due to him."

Yehiel sold tickets for five years, with Bambi's help, until 1958. Then the Jewish Agency offered him the chance to serve as the Betar representative, or *shaliach*, in South Africa for two years. This was his second offer for the same position. The year before he had agreed to serve as the Betar representative in Brazil, but shortly after accepting the offer his father passed away, and Yehiel backed out so that he could help his mother and family adjust to their new reality. Now he was headed to South Africa. Yehiel was a top candidate. He was already fluent in English, and above all, he had a powerful sense that he would do everything possible to serve the movement and its values, to spread its principles in far-off communities, and most importantly: to encourage Jewish youth not only to consider aliyah, but also to make aliyah a reality.

Furthermore, he was armed with firsthand knowledge and the powerful personal experience of meeting Jewish Holocaust survivors. They had considered Poland their home; they had thought that they were Germans of the Jewish religion; they had considered themselves Jewish Hungarians.

Then Poland threw them out of their homes. Germany hunted down anyone who was of the Jewish religion to the third generation and beyond, and sent them to the crematoria. And Hungary put them in their place: there are Jews, and there are Hungarians. The same happened with the Jews in the rest of Europe, the continent that betrayed them. The truth was that South African Jewry was comfortably complacent – those who had just recently arrived in the country as well as long-time residents. They, too, were sure that nothing would happen to them.

Before giving a positive answer to the party members who offered him the position, he asked his younger brother Shmuel, who helped him during peak periods in the box office and was well acquainted with the work there, if he was interested in taking over management of the office for two years while Yehiel was abroad. After all, said Yehiel, it would be a shame to throw away the sterling reputation that Sherutron had built up. Shmuel agreed, and Yehiel handed over the office management to him.

The couple thus traveled to South Africa. Their new home was on Olivia Street in Johannesburg, in the heart of a Jewish neighborhood. The home served as a base for travel to all parts of the country as well as neighboring states with large concentrations of Jews and Betar activity. Betar branches were spread all over southern Africa, including Salisbury (now Harare) and Bulawayo in Rhodesia (Zimbabwe). They also operated in Pretoria, Brakpan, Germiston, Benoni, Cape Town, Port Elizabeth, East London, and Durban. Johannesburg had five branches of its own.

The Betar movement in South Africa was the second largest Jewish youth movement in the country. The largest was Ha-Bonim, a Labor Zionist youth movement; after Betar in size came Bnei Akiva and Ha-Shomer Ha-Tzair (the youth movements of Religious Zionists and Socialist Zionists, respectively). Yehiel and Bambi arrived in the country one year after the first *shaliach* had finished his term. The first representative was Yehudah Bilu, who served in South Africa with his wife, Hannah. Yehudah, a Betar member from Wloclawek, Poland, had made aliyah on an Aliyah Bet boat. He had worked in the accounts department of the Tel Aviv municipality, and then became a *shaliach* for a two-year period from 1955 to 1957.

Yehiel had no need for a special training course for this position, as he was a *shaliach* to the depths of his soul. This had been the case in the DP camps in Europe, and it was again the case in the prosperous communities of South Africa.

A month after their arrival, Yehiel described their experiences in a letter to Petahia Shamir, Betar chief in Israel:

> A month has passed since our arrival, and I can tell you that concerning the movement officers and activists in general, and from what I have seen of activities in the branches in Johannesburg and the suburbs (Pretoria), the situation is exactly as you and Yehudah (Bilu) described in your discussions with me before my trip. The people are friendly and dedicated, and the general cultural level is truly commendable. But as for Betar awareness as we understand it, in the practical sense – aliyah – it is scant. Of course, I have already visited all the branches in Johannesburg and been to Pretoria twice. I participate in the leadership meetings. I spoke to the Shavei Zion class twice on the subject of "Youth in Israel" and "Achievements of the Jabotinsky Movement." The members' interest in issues in Israel is serious, and their intentions are honest.
>
> On Sunday, August 17, we held a festive ceremony at the great synagogue in the city (Yeoville), to grant graduation certificates to district leaders and three counselors who completed the courses. There was a cantor, Captain Yosef Shapira, and the synagogue choir sang. Chief Rabbi Isaac Zwebner, son of Rabbi Avraham Chaim Sha'ag of Jerusalem, spoke to the Betar members and their parents. Members of the Betar leadership, Y. Delsky and Harry Horowitz, gave out the certificates. Rabbi Zwebner, Delsky, Betar head Zvi Brand, and I gave short remarks. The certificate recipients made declarations, and the text of these led to an argument over the extremely compromising nature of the wording: "I declare my willingness to be faithful to our people, to our land, to our language and to our flag, and I will do everything in my ability to be a good Jew in the spirit of the holy members of our people and as a dedicated Betar member."

One evening, I spoke in Krugsdorf, on behalf of the World Association for Hebrew Language and Culture, about the kibbutz and integration of Diaspora communities in Israel. I visited Pretoria for a morning meeting of a women's group (they, by the way, are extremely active) and spoke about the Betar youth village. I also spoke with parents there, and with the Pretoria branch last Saturday night, at a lovely party given in honor of the Hashmonaim class there.

On August 20 I am going to Rhodesia to organize and lead an eight-day seminar camp. On August 29–31, we will hold the three-day camp for Kanaim and Bnei Etzel classes.

There is a good chance of a larger number of participants in the counselors training program next season. At any rate, two definite candidates are Haim Kaplan (son of Yehudit Kaplan) and Zelig Goldschmidt of Johannesburg, who spoke with their parents and received their permission. Other possible candidates are Jenny Chesler (Cape Town) and Yani Kimmel (East London). I will check about them when I visit those locations in late September and October.

Regarding aliyah: there is a chance for a group at the beginning of next year, composed of Ivor Wolf (Aubrey's brother), Yossi Gittelband, Carmela Gal, Zippora Sherman, David Levi, Julian Sachs, Shaul Levitan. But clearly, these candidates still face challenges of a personal and family nature, etc. The only certain ones are Wolf and Levitan.

Every day I give Hebrew classes to some of the Johannesburg candidates for the training program and for aliyah.

Esther (Bambi) caught a serious flu and was in bed for about three weeks. Luckily, the Sieff family came and insisted that we go to live in their house. They took excellent care of her and now she is completely healthy. She sends her greetings to everyone.

> Sending you the Tel Hai salute –
> Yours,
> Yehiel

A significant portion of Yehiel's job was to pass on the movement's ideology to the members. Who better than Yehiel was appropriate for this? He had memorized entire treatises by Jabotinsky and poems by Uri Zvi Greenberg. There wasn't a single Betar song for which he had to fill in the words by humming along. He played a central role in the summer and winter camps, planned training programs for special courses and seasonal seminars, worked together with the local leadership of the movement in the main Betar membership centers of Johannesburg as well as other areas with Betar members. As mentioned, he traveled as far as Rhodesia, which was then under the familiar regime of Britain – but this time he had nothing personal against it. In addition, he participated energetically in Zionist activities in synagogues. Yehiel appeared at meetings of various organizations, such as the local branch of the World Association for Hebrew Language and Culture, at symposia, and at discussions of literary topics.

"Wherever there were Jews, there was a Betar branch," he recalled. "There was no special *shaliach* for aliyah. The *shaliach* for each movement was the main representative." At one conference, in a discussion with parents of young Betar members who were soon to make aliyah, one of the participants criticized him: "Mr. Kadishai, how do you dare to take our children from here?" Yehiel replied with one of Begin's favorite expressions: "This is our raison d'être, our reason for existence." He then added, "This is our ideology. Yes, we are here specifically in order to bring your children to Eretz Israel. And you," he emphasized, "must send them money so that they can establish their own businesses in Israel, to ensure their futures."

One of the listeners asked, "Is this Menachem Begin's opinion, too?"

Yehiel replied, "You must ask him."

The heckler continued to press Yehiel. "Isn't he your boss?"

"No," Yehiel answered. "We don't have a boss. Our only boss is the idea. We serve an idea, and that's what we've come here for."

Harry (Zvi) Brand, Betar head in South Africa, reminisced: "Yehiel and Bambi integrated very quickly into our community, and quickly began to work and to influence. Like his predecessors, Yehudah Bilu and Hertzel Katz, Yehiel led a revolution in the conception of the Betar movement in South Africa. The focal point of the revolution was the fact that previously, Betar was a Zionist movement but did not involve commitment to fulfilling the mitzvah of aliyah. It was a youth movement like the Jewish scouts, without any commitment. Yehiel instilled within us the awareness of and commitment to aliyah. Of my age group, almost all made aliyah and were integrated successfully. They became professors at the Weizmann Institute and Bar-Ilan University, doctors at Hadassah Hospital in Jerusalem, professionals, and kibbutzniks."

"It was a very wealthy Jewish community," Yehiel expanded, "warm-hearted, upholding traditional Zionism. They did not have the problem of anti-Zionist parties – Bund and Agudat Yisrael. This large community of one hundred thousand people in South Africa and Rhodesia was almost completely Zionist. These Jews were dedicated to the Zionist idea and to Eretz Israel, and it was a pleasure to work with them."

Harry Horowitz was a leader of Betar in South Africa and editor of the *Jewish Herald* newspaper. He said, "One day I went to Yehiel, and I told him that a young man named Joe Shapiro had made aliyah with his family. Yehiel was pleased to hear it, and said, 'Thank God. Now I need another one of those.' What did he mean by that? During his term, there were two Joe Shapiros in the Betar leadership. Yehiel had great influence within the community, and while he was there, the entire group of leaders in South Africa made aliyah, except for the two Joe Shapiros. Then the first one made aliyah. The second one emigrated to England and established a few businesses, and this is the one Yehiel was referring to when he said, Now I need another one."

The Kadishai home was a vital anchor for many. Everyone who was on their way to Israel, or who had business in South Africa and had nowhere to stay, found a warm bed and delicious meal in their home. They did not hold regular activities in their home, as it was not a Betar branch in and of itself, but it did serve as a base for Yehiel's work at each location.

The young South Africans wanted to make aliyah, and make aliyah they did. Many of them occupied key positions in various sectors of Israeli society. One member, a former Betar head in South Africa, became a real estate developer; one of his projects was the Tefen Industrial Park in the Galilee. A few years before publication of this book, a reunion of Betar members was held in Shuni Fortress (Jabotinsky Park) near Binyamina, with over six hundred participants, all immigrants from South Africa. During Yehiel's tenure, except for one Betar head, all the members of the directorate made aliyah, and many entered the upper echelons of Israeli society.

Here is an example of the typical schedule of a "Hebrew Camp" held by the Hebrew Federation of South Africa, one of many camps that took place during Yehiel's term. The camp took place on the weekend, from Shabbat through Sunday. The schedule for Friday evening lists the Kabbalat Shabbat service and the evening prayer service. The meal began with Kiddush and was peppered with the traditional Shabbat songs. Then, the program reads: "Mr. Yehiel Kadishai, director of the camp, will give an introduction in easy Hebrew and in English on the importance of the Hebrew camp. After that, at 9:15 p.m., we will divide into three groups for classes, which will conclude with group singing. The next morning, wake up is at 7:30, followed by services, Hebrew class session 1, another class and vocabulary sessions for all groups, lunch, and a break. At 2:30 p.m., Mr. Yehiel Kadishai will lead a study session on Ethics of the Fathers." The study session went on for an hour, followed by bingo games, afternoon prayers, and Hebrew classes between 5:15 and 6:45 p.m. They convened for the evening prayer service and Havdalah, and then ate dinner. Then the participants gathered around the campfire to sing Israeli songs. On Sunday a full day of activities was planned: two Hebrew classes, singing and vocabulary exercises for all classes, reading the students' Hebrew compositions, corrections by the teachers, and two more classes. The students returned home at 4 p.m.

Bambi took an active part in assisting Yehiel. During the camps, she took care of children in the youngest group. She even earned the nickname "Angel in White" thanks to her dedicated care of children who fell sick during the activities. She never forgot a certain child whose friend had a fever and was put to bed in the camp infirmary tent. This child, who was healthy but in need of some pampering, came to the clinic and announced, "I'm sick, too." Bambi asked him, "What's wrong with you?" He pointed to his friend and answered "Same as him."

One of the most well-known Betar activities in South Africa during

Yehiel's time there, which had international reverberations, was the stormy "welcome" Betar organized for the visit of the infamous British fascist leader, Sir Oswald Mosley. Betar members demonstrated near Mosley's hotel in Johannesburg carrying placards that pictured Mosley's hands dripping with Jewish blood. Under the drawings were slogans in English and Afrikaans: "Oswald Mosley and Adolf Hitler are friends in heart and soul"; "You're not wanted here"; "We won't forgive or forget." Another impressive Betar activity was the movement's response to a swastika graffiti campaign in South African cities. Betar organized guard duty for synagogues and Jewish institutions. Some of the graffitists were caught and fined. Betar also sent denunciations of the swastika campaign to the press, making waves in public opinion.

After two years in South Africa, Yehiel and Bambi flew back to Israel, and Yehiel returned to work in the box office. Shlomo Nakdimon wrote in an article published in the *Herut* newspaper on August 1, 1960, under the title, "Completed Illustrious Service and Returned to the Ticket Window":

> Once again, the face with the sparkling spectacles appears behind the ticket window. Once again, the familiar singsong voice answers the incessantly clamoring phone. "Second show?" Yes. "How many tickets?" Four, but what are your prices? Answers are given, and new questions asked. This is how Yehiel spends most of the hours of his day in the Sherutron ticket sales office. He's back to the daily routine after serving as Betar representative in South Africa. For two years, he worked in South Africa, a country constantly in the strident headlines. For many months, he acted and initiated on behalf of Betar – to enlarge it and expand its influence. Yehiel does not toot his own horn. A few days ago, we heard a long report on the success of his term at a party held in his honor by the Betar leadership. The speakers, including former South Africans, spoke nonstop of the "Right Rep."

When Nakdimon asked whether the Jews in South Africa had begun to consider aliyah, considering the tempestuous anti-apartheid demonstrations and the unrest in the country, Yehiel replied: "The whites all share the same concerns. But certain circles within the Jewish community have begun to think about uprooting themselves once again – the eternal wandering Jew. Jewish citizens, and non-Jews as well, have begun to check into the possibility of emigration. In the meantime, the demonstrations have died down, and mostly, the idea has not become a reality. Yet some families have emigrated to Canada, Australia, and Israel."

Yehiel emphasized to the journalist that there was no future for Jews in the South African diaspora, no chance they would remain Jewish, just as there was no such chance for Jews in any other Diaspora country. Assimilation was spreading. The Jews represented only a small percentage of the white population in South Africa (3.5 percent) – on the other hand, they were a significant part of the cultural and economic life of the society. As time went on and the generation that had brought Jewish culture with it from Lithuania and Latvia disappeared, assimilation would escalate. The majority would be lost, while only a small number would be saved.

"In debates and symposia that Betar initiated," recalled Yehiel, "I tried to instill the Betar position, based on the writings of the Betar leader – there is no chance for Jewish continuity in Diaspora countries where Jews are granted full equal rights. Go and learn from meta-historical events: for centuries, our Jews spilled their blood in order to achieve equal rights in their countries of origin. Now that they have achieved it, they have done more harm than good. And why? During the pogroms, the Jews feared for their Judaism and fought for it, but now it's disappearing. No pogroms – no Jews."

As mentioned, when he returned to Israel in late 1960, Yehiel took up his old place behind the ticket window in the box office. In the meantime, things began to change for his brother Yitzchak. His relationship with the Cameri Theater came to a head, mainly because of the hard-and-fast principle he maintained that the theater should be self-supporting and not rely on government or municipal funding. This meant that the productions had to be chosen carefully, as they had to attract spectators. However, the Cameri began to change its approach, and so Yitzchak Kadishson left. He purchased a spacious basement of some five hundred square meters in a new building at 7 Mendele Mocher Sefarim Street at the corner of Ben Yehuda Street in Tel Aviv. There he founded the Theater Club. The concept behind his initiative was to provide a place for actors to meet after their shows, or on their evenings off, to put on performances or improvisations. Theater enthusiasts would come, buy a ticket and a drink, and everyone would profit, including the cash register. Kadishson took the idea from Broadway, where he had seen satirical productions performed before audiences of 150, the number that would fit into the basement he purchased.

The Theater Club began to put on small but regular productions. Yitzchak served as manager, while the director was Yosef (Papo) Milo, who had left the Cameri together with him. The Theater Club was a hit, and became a Tel Aviv mainstay. A long list of well-known Israeli artists began their careers there, including Ha-Duda'im, Beni Berman, Nechama Helena Hendel, and Arik Lavie.

In 1961, Kadishson went to the United States to acquire the rights for several plays, intending to stage them at the theater. In particular, he cast his eye on the American drama *The Fantasticks*, which was an off-Broadway hit for decades, and whose cast was renewed dozens of times. The cast was small – two young actors and two elderly ones – while the plot revolved around love, parents, and children. The scenery was not complicated, and the musical accompaniment was for piano only.

Before going abroad, Kadishson founded the Theater Club in Haifa, at the request of its legendary mayor Abba Hushi, who aimed to place Haifa on the cultural map. Hushi granted Kadishson the use of a large auditorium on Pevzner Street. Four of the actors who performed there became well-known: Shimon Bar, Gideon Singer, Reuven Sheffer, and Yankele Ben Sira. Their sketches had the whole country in stitches, and in the evenings, an endless line snaked in front of the box office. Often, the number of disappointed fans who went home empty-handed was greater than the number of thrilled customers who managed to obtain tickets and get into the show. The disappointed would return the next evening.

Another idea of Kadishson's was to hold a rotation between shows by the foursome and *The Fantasticks* in Tel Aviv and Haifa. Everything was set, but astonishingly, *The Fantasticks* was a flop. The show was performed twice only, and then canceled. The post-mortem revealed that although the reviews were positive, apparently the Tel Aviv audience stayed away because they were used to watching stand-up comedy at the Theater Club, and they preferred that medium to drama, despite the quality of the performance.

Disappointed, Kadishson returned to the US to try to undo the damage, and in the meantime, he asked Yehiel to manage both clubs. One of their sisters helped by managing the Haifa club on a regular basis. Eventually, when Yehiel was working as Begin's personal secretary and right-hand man, when he was asked what it was like to switch from a ticket office and management of a theater club to the Knesset, he replied, "It's not easy. At the theater I had seven actors. Here, I have 120."

He maintained contact with the actors even after the curtain went down. Yankele Ben Sira related: "I attend the same synagogue as Yehiel, the Chassidic synagogue of the Rebbe of Modzitz. We haven't become religiously observant, but sometimes we pray. During the services, I don't always know where they are in the prayer book, so Yehiel shows me – 'Yankele, we're here.' Then I continue with everyone. He knows the entire service by heart, he always knows where we are. I always stand next to him, because if the Holy One, blessed be He, were to suddenly look and see that I'm not even on the right page, heaven forfend, it could be really uncomfortable…"

Yehiel worked at the "real" theater until 1963, when Dov Alpert, secretary of the Herut Party in the Knesset, died. And then, everything changed.

CHAPTER 13

THE NEW JOB

In 1963, Dov Alpert, secretary of the Herut Party's representation in the Knesset, passed away while still a young man in his thirties. In his short life, he managed to make and leave an impression on many party veterans. Many knew him by his nickname, Moishele the Athlete. According to Aryeh Naor, secretary of the cabinet in the Begin administration, the nickname was devised to mislead the British. Alpert had a hunchback, and the nickname directly contrasted his appearance, so that when they came upon him, the British would never dream that he was the "athlete" they were looking for.

His story was unusual. In his childhood and adolescence he grew *peyot*, the sidelocks of the Chassidic Jews, and wore a black kaftan. The son of a doctor, he was born in Germany and immigrated to Jerusalem, where he followed the ultra-Orthodox lifestyle. When he was sixteen, the British caught him pasting Irgun posters on the walls of Jerusalem houses. He sat in prison at Latrun for a period, where he became friendly with other Jews imprisoned there, including Dr. Yohanan Bader. After establishment of the state and the Knesset, the need arose for a secretary of the Herut Party's Knesset faction. Bader, who was a founder of the party, recalled the dedicated young man, and appointed him to the position.

Alpert fulfilled his duties to the satisfaction of all his superiors, but his shaky health was a critical problem. He suffered from heart irregularities. In late 1963 he underwent surgery, but unfortunately he died on the operating table at Tel Hashomer Hospital.

The faction, which numbered only seventeen members at the time, began to search for a replacement. One day, Yoske Giladi, the faction's chauffeur, met Yehiel. The two were the same age, and they knew each other from their Betar days in Tel Aviv. Their shared path had then led them to the British army.

"I have an offer for you," Yoske told Yehiel.

"An offer? What offer?" Yehiel asked.

"The Herut parliamentary faction in the Knesset is looking for a secretary to replace Moishele the Athlete, of blessed memory," Yoske informed Yehiel. "On one of my trips with Menachem Begin, I told him that you would be right for the job. He agreed that I should ask you."

"How do you know if I'm right or not right for the job, when I don't even know what the job is?" asked Yehiel.

"Nonsense," Yoske dismissed Yehiel's question out of hand. "It's not complicated. They're not looking for PhDs. It's mainly secretarial. Anyone who's graduated from high school, or even just started high school, would fit the job. The plus of it is that you're in an interesting crowd and place."

"But I'm already in an interesting crowd and place," Yehiel protested, as he was managing the Theater Clubs in Tel Aviv and Haifa. "But you know what? I'll ask Bambi. Let's see what she says."

"Take it," Bambi said when she heard about the offer from Yehiel. "Grab it with both hands, before someone else does."

"What's the rush?" he asked.

Eventually, Yehiel learned that Bambi did not like his working hours at the Theater Club. Every night he came home at 2 or even 3 a.m., after the shows were over, the scenery was taken down, and the auditorium was cleaned. So he took the job as secretary for the Herut Party.

Yehiel went from being a supporter of political Zionism to conducting political Zionist activism on the ground, and then in the Knesset. He spoke about the beginning of his career in this role: "Yohanan Bader and Haim Landau, who handled my appointment to this position, told me to come to the Knesset and start the job. I came, and I started to find my footing. Two days later, MK Yosef Shofman came to me and asked, 'Here, you've been here for two days already, what do you think about your new job? How does it compare to your previous job in the club and the theater?'

"'It's fairly similar,' I replied, 'because both here and there, everyone wants his name to appear in the paper, and if a photo appears as well, then it's really perfect.'"

Yehiel began his work as secretary of the Herut Party faction in the Knesset in January 1964, at age forty-one. After that, he remained at Begin's side for twenty-eight straight years – at first as secretary of the faction, then as Begin's personal secretary, then as head of the prime minister's office, and finally as private secretary to the former prime minister; and his faithful escort; and always as an apprentice and friend, until Begin's death in 1992.

A retrospective look at the political career of Herut – which merged with the Liberal Party to form Gahal in 1965, and then consolidated with the Liberal Party, Free Center, National List, and Movement for Greater Israel to form the Likud in 1973 – with Begin at its head and Yehiel at his side, may hint at the long path that Begin and Yehiel walked hand in hand. Here is a summary of the representation of the Herut Party, beginning with the first Knesset:

- 1948 – First Knesset: Herut won fourteen mandates, and became the fourth largest party.
- 1951 – Second Knesset: Herut went down to eight mandates. In December, Begin led the struggle against the reparations agreement with Germany.
- 1955 – Third Knesset: Herut won fifteen mandates.
- 1959 – Fourth Knesset: Herut went up to seventeen mandates.
- 1961 – Fifth Knesset: Following the Lavon affair, Herut again won seventeen mandates. Begin was head of the opposition.
- 1965 – Sixth Knesset: Herut and the Liberal Party formed Gahal. In the November 2 elections, Gahal won twenty-six mandates. On May 23, 1967, Gamal Abdel Nasser, president of Egypt, blocked the Suez Canal and began to move toward war. Begin raised the idea of forming a national unity government led by Ben-Gurion, despite the open animosity between himself and the former prime minister. On May 30, Begin was invited to join the national unity government under Levi Eshkol, as a minister without portfolio. On June 1, he participated in a cabinet meeting for the first time as an observer. On June 5, the Knesset confirmed Begin as a

member of the government, representing Gahal along with Yosef Sapir. Together with Yigal Allon, Begin initiated the decision to liberate the Old City of Jerusalem.

- 1969 – Seventh Knesset: Gahal again won twenty-six mandates, and joined Golda Meir's government with six ministers. In 1970, Begin stood against the initiative of US Secretary of State William P. Rogers, who proposed withdrawal from Sinai in exchange for a political arrangement – without direct negotiations. On August 4, the six Gahal ministers quit the national unity government. On September 12, 1973, the Likud was established, as a result of the energetic efforts of Ariel ("Arik") Sharon. On October 6, the Yom Kippur War broke out.

- 1973 – Eighth Knesset: The Likud won thirty-nine mandates. Within a month, Yitzchak Rabin was elected prime minister, following Golda Meir's resignation.

- 1977 – Ninth Knesset: Begin led the "upheaval" in the Knesset elections – the Likud won forty-three mandates. On June 19, the new government was presented to the Knesset; on July 18, Begin held his first meeting with President Carter; on October 24, Dash (the Democratic Movement for Change) joined the government. On November 9, Egyptian president Anwar Sadat declared his willingness to speak in the Knesset, and Begin extended a formal invitation to him. On November 19, Sadat landed in Israel for the historic visit and was received by Prime Minister Menachem Begin. On December 14, Begin met with US president Carter in Washington and presented the plan for autonomy for Judea and Samaria.

- 1978: Begin participated in the Camp David retreat. On September 17, he signed the Framework for Peace in the Middle East in a ceremony at the White House. On September 26, a discussion on the accords was held in the Knesset, with eighty-four MKs voting in support of the agreement. On December 10, Begin was awarded the Nobel Peace Prize, together with Sadat.

- 1979: Begin signed the peace agreement with Egypt.
- 1981: The Iraqi nuclear reactor Osirak was destroyed on June 7. In elections for the Tenth Knesset, the Likud wins forty-eight seats. On December 14, Begin passed the Golan Heights law in the Knesset.
- 1982: On June 6, Operation Peace for Galilee was begun (the First Lebanon War).
- 1983: Begin resigned from his position as prime minister on September 15.
- 1992: Menachem Begin died in Tel Aviv on March 9 (4 Adar II 5752) and was buried on the Mount of Olives in Jerusalem.

***

Beginning at the time when Yehiel was working for Shelah, he did have contact with Begin, although his relationship with him was somewhat superficial. Yehiel consulted with Begin from time to time on Shelah business, mainly aid and rehabilitation. Yehiel came to Begin for advice on the complex problems that arose during his handling of these difficult issues. Begin was always willing to assist with such matters, as the deeds of Irgun soldiers and commemoration of the fallen were close to his heart, and he advised Yehiel to the best of his ability on how to proceed, whom to contact in order to move matters forward, and so forth.

Yehiel's first meeting with Menachem Begin was in early 1942 or late 1943, as described in chapter 7. While on leave from the British army, Yehiel was invited to hear an "interesting speaker" at Metzudat Ze'ev; this man was Begin, but his identity was not disclosed. Only after the man had left, Yehiel, impressed by what he had heard, asked aloud, "Who was that soldier?" Some of those present who had made aliyah from Poland in the late 1930s answered that the speaker had been the Betar head there. At the time, Yehiel and many of his comrades had never heard the name Menachem Begin. They didn't know that he had been head of Betar in Poland, because Betar members in Eretz Israel had no contact with their Polish compatriots.

"I didn't know who the Betar head in Poland was, just as I didn't know who the Betar head in the US was," Yehiel explained. "You have to realize, world Betar was not on our radar at all. We were youths in the Betar unit at Metzudat Ze'ev, living our own lives. Only years later did I find out what Begin had done there. But at that first meeting, at which I was very impressed with his appearance, speech, and his analysis of current events, I didn't know who he was. Even later, when Begin was appointed commander of the Irgun in Eretz Israel, I didn't know anything about it, because I was in Egypt, and then I went to Europe. In June 1948, when I returned to Israel on the *Altalena*, I knew that he was Irgun commander, but of course I couldn't, for example, compare between his style of command and that of David Raziel, because I wasn't acquainted with the style of either Raziel or Begin. I was far from both of them. As an aside, I saw Raziel only once, at the memorial ceremony held in the Metzudat Ze'ev courtyard when we received notice of Jabotinsky's death."

Eventually, Yehiel came to know every detail in Menachem Begin's biography, including the period in Poland. In 1937, Begin was sent by Jabotinsky to establish the movement's branch in Czechoslovakia. In 1939, he took the place of Aharon Zvi Propes as head of Betar in Poland, where he was responsible for the more than seventy thousand Betar members in his country of origin. In May of that year, he married Aliza (Alicia) Arnold, whom he met at the home of her parents. Her father was a contributor to the Revisionist Party in Drohobycz, Galicia, where Begin studied law. Hundreds of Betar members were among the guests at their wedding, and the best man was none other than Ze'ev Jabotinsky.

One of Yehiel's first activities in his role as secretary of the Herut Party in the Knesset was bringing Jabotinsky's remains to burial in Israel. Shlomo Nakdimon, journalist and media consultant to Prime Minister Begin from 1978 to 1980, revealed the full behind-the-scenes story of the government's 1964 decision to bring Jabotinsky's body to Israel for reinterment. In the Spring 5762/March 2002 issue of the journal *Ha-Umah* (no. 147), which was dedicated to Jabotinsky, Nakdimon wrote that it all began with a chance conversation between opposition leader Begin and Prime Minister Levi Eshkol in early March 1964, in the cafeteria of the Knesset, which was still at its original address at Froumine House on King George Street in Jerusalem. Eshkol was more relaxed in his personal contact with Begin and his compatriots than his predecessor, David Ben-Gurion.

Begin approached Eshkol and said, "I would like to bring Ze'ev Jabotinsky's remains to Eretz Israel."

Eshkol was surprised. "So why don't you just bring him over? What's in your way?"

"The deceased instructed in his will that his remains could only be brought over by order of a Jewish government," Begin explained.

"He had a will?" Eshkol asked.

"You didn't know that?" Begin was astonished.

"No," replied Eshkol. Begin was certain that everyone in the world was aware that Jabotinsky's remains were still in a Jewish cemetery in New York because of the last clause in his will, which he had written in Paris on November 3, 1935, and sent in a letter to his wife. Clause number five read: "I wish to be buried, or else cremated (it's all the same to me), in the place where I die, and my remains, if I am buried outside Eretz Israel, should not be transferred to Eretz Israel except by order of the Jewish government of that land, should it be established."

Begin knew that this issue was one of those things whose success lay in keeping it a secret. For Eshkol, this was quite a minefield. First of all, the Labor Party, the successor of the historic Mapai party and the majority in the Knesset, was the major enemy of Jabotinsky's Revisionist Zionist movement, and the two sides had fought intense battles in the past. In addition, Ben-Gurion was even more antagonistic toward Eshkol, with whom he had a long list of political grievances, than he was toward Begin, his open enemy. As is well known, the relationship between Ben-Gurion and Begin was hostile for decades. At its worst, it was reflected in Ben-Gurion's manner of referring to Begin as "The man sitting to the right of MK [Yohanan] Bader," and Begin's advice to Ben-Gurion: "Go out to an intersection, kneel down, and ask for forgiveness and atonement for spilling innocent blood." (A hesitant reconciliation between the two influential leaders took root several years later when Begin, on the eve of the Six-Day War, promoted Ben-Gurion for minister of defense over Prime Minister Levi Eshkol. At one point, Ben-Gurion wrote to Begin, "My Paula has always admired you.")

Two of Ben-Gurion's biographers, Shabbtai Tevet and Michael Bar-Zohar, contacted Yehiel several times and asked to speak with Begin about

Ben-Gurion. Every time Yehiel asked Begin about this, Begin replied, "We have time." Yehiel understood that Begin was looking for a way out, until Begin told him directly: "Get me out of it." Yehiel managed to do so, and one day, Begin explained to him outright, with his characteristic cynicism, the reason for his evasion: "You see, Yehiel, I don't want to say bad things about him, but I don't have anything good to say about him."

As for Jabotinsky's remains, after the conversation with Eshkol, Begin let Yehiel into the secret, saying, "I need a copy of Jabotinsky's will."

Yehiel, who could quote fluently from Jabotinsky's texts and poems, was familiar with the clause in the will about the transfer of remains. At Yehiel's incredulous glance, Begin explained why he needed the document. He also explained the details of the conversation with Eshkol to the secretary of the Herut Party.

Yehiel related: "Begin believed that the moment would soon arrive when the government of the State of Israel would order the reinterment of the remains of the man whose entire life was dedicated to the establishment of the state."

"Yehiel," Begin said excitedly, "we're going to bring over the bones of the leader of Betar!"

Later, in his work at Begin's side, Yehiel would hear many stories about Jabotinsky from his apprentice. During their lengthy trips together in Israel and around the world, Begin told Yehiel that he had often accompanied Jabotinsky on long walks up and down the streets of Warsaw, during which they discussed matters of the utmost importance. Begin also spoke of accompanying Jabotinsky on a carriage ride to one of the Polish towns where the Zionist leader had been invited to speak.

Yehiel also heard from Begin that when two or three of his admirers would travel with him from one town to another, Jabotinsky would say: "Here's some money. You go to the movies. Don't bother coming to hear me. I don't like it when people hear me over and over." The audience paid an entrance fee to hear the speeches, as in the theater. The classic story about Jabotinsky goes that he would repeat his speeches several times, using the exact same hand gestures and intonation. He also had a little trick to check if his audience was awake. He would say a word in Latin, or Hebrew or Yiddish, and ask the audience to translate it into their own spoken language. An audience member would give him the correct word, which Jabotinsky of course knew already. The speaker would thank the participant and continue his lecture. The next day he would speak in a different town and repeat the exercise, using the same word. On one occasion, a Jew in the audience, who apparently had been following Jabotinsky around from one town to another, stood up and said, "I told you yesterday how we say that word in our language, but you've forgotten already?!"

Yehiel also knew about the incident in which Jabotinsky had mocked Begin. This was in 1938, at the Betar world conference in Warsaw. Before that point, Jabotinsky had articulated political Zionism, but Begin wished to push the dialogue in the direction of military Zionism. In addition, Begin proposed an amendment to the fourth clause of the Betar "oath" that Jabotinsky had written in 1935. The oath read:

> I shall devote my life to the revival of the Jewish State with a Jewish majority on both sides of the Jordan;
>
> To this ideal of state building, I shall subordinate my own interests, as well as the calls of my house and class;
>
> The Hebrew language will be my language and the language of my offspring, both in Eretz Israel and in the Diaspora;
>
> I shall prepare and train myself for the defense of my people;
>
> I shall carefully endeavor to fulfill the principles of *hadar* in thought, word, and deed, for I am conscious of the noble heritage of my people;
>
> I shall rise and answer the Betar mobilization – be it for the Legion or for labor, to go up to Zion, or for service in the Diaspora, be it near or far, I shall rise and go;
>
> I shall harken to the laws of Betar and obey the commands of its leaders as a man listens to his conscience; for the law of Betar reflects my own personal wishes and its leaders are my representatives.[5]

---

5 Shindler, Colin, *The Triumph of Military Zionism* (I.B. Tauris, 2006), 129.

After the words "I will prepare and train myself for the defense of my people," an addition was made: the new text that was ultimately accepted by the conference read, "I will prepare and train myself for the defense of my people and to conquer my homeland."

Jabotinsky objected to this step, but at the same time, he admired Begin's determination. In his speech in Warsaw, Jabotinsky referenced the debate over the change to the oath, and remarked, "The young man who is our hope, and when I say our hope, I don't mean only Betar's hope, but the hope of the Jewish people – his speech sounds like a squeaky door." He meant to criticize Begin's ideas as fanciful and unrealistic, for while the Jewish community in Eretz Israel was making practical "squeaks" with tractors and plows – developing the land and laying the foundation for a state – Begin's words were as useless as the creak of a door. The audience called out in both support and disagreement. Dr. Israel Eldad (Scheib) rose from his seat in the audience and said that a squeaky door was also useful, since it could sound a warning against thieves.

In July 1977, after Begin's first meeting with US president Jimmy Carter, the Israeli leader said, "I've met many people in my lifetime, but I haven't been very impressed by them. The reason is that I saw Betar leader Ze'ev Jabotinsky, spoke with him, and spent time in his company. After meeting the Betar leader, no one else compares. But when I met Jimmy Carter, I did feel a certain sense of personality." These words roused a storm among admirers of Jabotinsky, who protested against Begin's whisper of a hint that Carter was the type of personality that perhaps just barely reminded him of Jabotinsky, to whom no other could compare, and for whom there was no equal. Begin rejected these assertions out of hand.

In any case, the Herut Party secretary began to take care of the matter of Jabotinsky's remains at once. Yehiel phoned Dr. Yosef Pa'amoni, director of the Jabotinsky Institute in Israel, where the documents of the late leader were archived. In answer to his question, Pa'amoni replied that he had a copy of the will in his home. Yehiel did not hesitate. He went to Tel Aviv, to Pa'amoni's home at 2 Yavne Street, received the document from him, and rushed back to Jerusalem to give it to Begin.

The issue of Jabotinsky's remains had been raised thirteen years previously, in December 1951, by MK Rabbi Dr. Mordechai Nurock of the Mizrachi faction. He approached Ben-Gurion and said that they should transfer the remains of four leaders: David Wolfson, Nahum Sokolov, Yehiel Chelnov, and Ze'ev Jabotinsky. Ben-Gurion's answer was laconic: "The obligation of the State of Israel is first and foremost to bring live Jews to Israel."

With that, the matter was temporarily closed. In August 1952, a second petition to Ben-Gurion was made by Professor Benjamin Aktzin. The prime minister rejected this petition as well, using the same justification and wording. After that, many of Israel's best and brightest addressed the issue, including President Yitzhak Ben Zvi, Minister of Foreign Affairs Moshe Sharett, Minister of the Interior Israel Rokach, and the B'nai B'rith organization, as well as ordinary civilians. Ben-Gurion replied to Ben Zvi's petition with a letter, to which he attempted to grant a personal touch rather than a formal one: "I see no reason to bring over the bones of the dead who lived always in the Diaspora. I will make an exception for two people: Herzl and Rothschild. It is fitting for these men to be buried in Israel. But what good will the many graves of people abroad do for us? Shall we bring over all the millions of people who died throughout history in the Diaspora – including people no less important than members of our own generation? For what purpose? Do we really need dead Jews? Let them rest where they are – as long as there are millions of live Jews still in the Diaspora."

In 1964 as well, the issue was not a simple one to solve. It became more complicated, and was discussed in various forums. It was raised again on the government agenda, and it provoked stormy arguments among the public and in the media. It remained on the agenda of the Herut Party, and provoked the Jabotinsky family, until finally, in March 1964, the Knesset voted unanimously to reinter Jabotinsky's remains in Israel.

Aryeh (Lova) Eliav, a Labor Party founder who had at one point served as assistant to Prime Minister Levi Eshkol, remarked: "When the decision was made on this issue, I rushed to meet with Yehiel in order to be the first to tell him about it. I knew how much he had admired the man, and I knew how deeply he was involved in the entire incident."

Jabotinsky died on 29 Tammuz 5700 (August 3, 1940), at age sixty. On the twenty-fourth anniversary of his death, 29 Tammuz 5724 (July

9, 1964), his funeral was held on Mount Herzl in Jerusalem. Yehiel was among the attendees. He also served in the honor guard, which changed continually while the casket was displayed at Metzudat Ze'ev in Tel Aviv, before the funeral procession began. When Ze'ev Jabotinsky's casket was buried, Yehiel stood to one side and thought that the small role he had played in this issue was the least he could do on behalf of the personality he admired so deeply.

CHAPTER 14

BOSS AND FRIEND

Yehiel's role as secretary of the Herut faction included several duties. One of these was to find material for members of the faction to use in their speeches, in order to support proposals for the agenda. Not all the members needed his assistance, particularly as some were highly educated. Most knew where to find the materials they needed on their own. Yehiel also served as the whip – he had to know where each party member was located and call them in when it was time to vote. In faction meetings, one of his most important roles was to record the minutes. He also recorded the minutes at meetings of the Herut Party central committee, a job that was hardly impossible, in light of the fact that the number of central committee members was only forty, and not upwards of three thousand as it was in later years. Another one of his duties was to word the parliamentary queries, and he also sent letters on behalf of the faction to various recipients.

Yehiel did not have an office in the Knesset, and neither did the MKs. In those days, the Knesset was located in Froumine House on King George Street in Jerusalem. (The Knesset moved to its present location in 1966.) This location was too small to house all the members, and certainly did not offer a comfortable work space. "When I wanted to talk to someone," related Yehiel, "I would leave the building, cross the street to Ta'amon Café, which was owned by Mordechai Kopp. That's where we would meet. The journalists were there, too, so there was no need for surreptitious leaks."

The only area in which Yehiel required formal training was typing, mainly so that he could type Begin's letters to the countless citizens who contacted him, but also because the faction had no typist. So he went to the Mofet clerical school on Frishman Street in Tel Aviv, near Dizengoff

Street, where he trained his fingers to use a typewriter. Of course, this machine was manual. The course was not so successful as to transform him into a touch typist, but at least he could peck rapidly with two fingers.

His days of work at the Knesset were Mondays, Tuesdays, and Wednesdays until the afternoon. Yehiel always went back and forth using public transportation, mostly the bus. Begin arrived in a taxi. Sometimes Begin went to Jerusalem in the Herut faction car, a Chrysler that looked spacious and impressive but was really no better than a jalopy. But Yehiel did not join him, because Begin always had other riders in the car. Besides, Yehiel always said, what was wrong with the bus? Didn't the driver know the way to Jerusalem and back?

Years later, after Yehiel retired, he made a visit to Los Angeles. After a meeting with a potential donor to Assaf Harofeh Medical Center at Zrifin, he returned to his hotel – by bus, naturally. He went to the station, saw that the cost of a ride was forty cents, and prepared the change. When the bus arrived, he boarded and placed the money in the receptacle. The driver glanced at him and asked if he was a "senior citizen."

"I looked at him like a chicken looking at a human being," Yehiel recalled, "because I had no idea what a 'senior citizen' was. The driver saw who he was dealing with, and asked, 'Where are you from?' I answered Jerusalem. '*Shalom aleichem*!' the driver responded excitedly. 'I'm a Jew, too. I was in Jerusalem just two weeks ago.' He started telling me a long story about his experiences in Israel. The driver also said that he was an engineer, still a bachelor, and was considering making aliyah and trying to find work at Israel Aerospace Industries. I gave him my phone number in case he needed any help."

Often Yehiel had to work long hours. By the time he got around to glancing at the clock, it was already late. On such days, he would spend the night in Jerusalem. At first he slept at Ha-Nasi Hotel on Ehad Ha-Am Street. MK Shabtai Shikhman had a regular room there where he slept two nights a week. One night, Shikhman asked Yehiel to cancel the room because he was going home to sleep. On that night, Yehiel happened to be stuck in Jerusalem. So he didn't cancel the room, but called the hotel late at night to reserve it for himself.

"We have no free rooms," the reception clerk informed him.

"There is a free room," Yehiel corrected him, "Shikhman's room."

"There aren't any free rooms," the clerk repeated laconically.

Apparently, when the hotel staff realized late at night that Shikhman still hadn't shown up, they gave the room to someone else.

Yehiel was furious. "I thought I would find a room somewhere else, because that was no way to give service. I called the Kings Hotel and they offered me a room. Then I discovered that the price of the Kings was a whole lira cheaper than Ha-Nasi – fourteen *lirot* instead of fifteen! After that I stayed at the Kings Hotel regularly when I had to stay over in Jersalem, because it was cheaper, and just as nice as Ha-Nasi. In 1977, when I was appointed director of Prime Minister Begin's office, the Israel Security Agency demanded that I switch to the hotel across the street, the Plaza, which was more expensive than the Kings. Why switch? Because at the Kings there worked an Arab from Beit Safafa who they discovered was a member of the PLO. One of the leaders of the party faction who heard about this supported the ISA decision, saying they had to keep closer watch over me than over all the other MKs put together, because Begin would never allow a situation in which he knew something and I didn't. This statement was of course not true; it was hyperbole that had no basis in fact."

Twice a week, on Mondays before the trip to Jerusalem and Thursdays when he stayed in Tel Aviv, Yehiel would meet with Begin in his home on Rosenbaum Street in Tel Aviv. These meetings were dedicated to two main tasks: answering correspondence, and writing Begin's articles in the *Herut* newspaper, which became *Ha-Yom*, and then in *Maariv*.

Correspondence was done in the living room of the modest home, which also served as a bedroom. To save space, Begin used as a table a panel on two legs that could be folded against the wall when not in use. On this table, Begin would pile a bundle of letters that he pulled out of his bag, which was a schoolboy's satchel. He sat at the table with his back to the wall, while Yehiel sat diagonally across from him.

"Begin used to say," Yehiel recounted, "that if you don't reply to a person's letter, it's as if he held out his hand to you but you don't hold yours out in response – as if you left his hand hanging in the air. He followed a routine method in responding to citizens. He pulled out a letter from the sheaf that he received, read it very quickly, actually photographing it with his eyes, set it aside, and began to compose the reply, dictating to me word for word. His response was finely constructed and organized. It took him five minutes to dictate to me a letter of three to four pages. What was more, he had a phenomenal memory. After 'photographing' the letter, he never had to look back at what was written in it. If the letter had five or six paragraphs, he would reply paragraph by paragraph, in exact order. He remembered each point that the person made. I have never met a person who had such intense powers of concentration. When I answer a letter, I read it twice before I begin to reply. Then I check the letter again to see whether I answered everything. Sometimes, after completing his dictation, he would say, 'Yehiel, in the third paragraph, change this or that word, because I already used it in the first paragraph. Use another word instead.' Of course, he dictated the alternative word to me. Heaven forbid he should use the same word twice.

"To him, answering correspondence was a sacred task. Sometimes, when he came across a specific problem, he would ask me right then and there to call the manager of the welfare office, for example, or any other relevant manager. He would discuss the problem mentioned in the letter with the director and ask him to take care of it. In little more than an hour, he would answer dozens of letters, and the rest he left for the next meeting. 'First thing in the morning,' we would say. Aside from the attempts to solve problems on the spot by dialing to one manager or another, he would say, 'Remember, first thing in the morning we must write to so-and-so,' or call a certain person. This was not always in reply to the letters, but often his own initiative."

One day, Begin received a letter from a student who asked no less than twenty questions. Begin scanned the letter, grinned, set it aside, and said to Yehiel: "This student wants me to write his doctorate for him." Begin didn't write the student's doctorate, but he did answer the questions succinctly. Twenty answers.

"No one answered his letters for him," Yehiel clarified. "No one ever wrote a speech for him. If someone today would say that he once wrote a speech for Begin, I can state with full confidence that this is a complete lie. No one ever changed a word in a letter, no one ever wrote a word in a speech. This was also the case for the weekly articles he sent to the newspaper. Beginning in 1948, he wrote a lengthy weekly article – over two thousand words. These were regularly published for many years. They took up three quarters of a page, the giant pages of newspapers back then. He always wrote each article by hand. Because I was the only one capable of deciphering his handwriting, I read it and then dictated it to the typist at Metzudat Ze'ev. After typing, it was sent back to Begin for proofreading. Then I sent it, including the headline, to the newspaper office. As for reading his handwriting, before I came into the picture, the only one who knew how to decipher it was Moishele the Athlete. I guess deciphering ability was one of the job requirements... Moshe Zak, one of the editors of *Maariv* who received Begin's articles, would sometimes suggest an idea for a different headline. He would call Begin and say, 'I have a great idea for a headline; it's shorter and captures the idea better than yours.' Begin would ask, 'What's your idea?' Zak replied, and then Begin would say, 'Leave it be, Moshe, leave it as is.' Only once in a blue moon, very rarely, was Begin willing to accept a change. Then he would sigh and say, '*Nu*, all right, okay, this time.' But for the lion's share of the suggestions for headline changes, Begin's response was polite but decisive: 'Perhaps your idea is better than mine, but this is what I think.' And with that, the discussion was over."

The bond between Yehiel and Begin became tighter as they spent long hours together in their shared work. They grew to understand each other without words – and above all, they spoke the same exact ideological language. At the same time, Bambi and Aliza (Ala), Begin's wife, became closer. Yehiel and Begin's relationship was almost a personal friendship, except that Yehiel always knew who was boss. They also had a shared hobby – the movies. The two couples visited the cinema together.

Outings to the movies were usually arranged after Aliza Begin phoned Bambi and suggested it to her. At first, Bambi asked what kind of films Menachem Begin liked. Aliza's reply was definite: "Everything. Anything you choose." Indeed, Begin enjoyed every kind of film: drama, history, spy stories, comedy, and romance.

The physical proximity between Yehiel and Begin's homes allowed them to walk to the movie theater together. On the way, passersby would greet Begin, and some would try to give him advice, in passing, on how to extricate himself from the long years of opposition. Yehiel would suggest that they write the leader a letter at his Knesset address, as long and detailed as they liked, and their suggestions would be considered seriously. Eventually, when Begin was elected to the highest position in the state, he was uncomfortable with the fact that his accessibility to the public was greatly restricted, although he understood the security considerations that meant he was constantly surrounded by security guards. He even grumbled that he had to sit in the back of the car, not next to the driver, his seat of choice in the years preceding the premiership. He often shared this uneasiness with Yehiel, who could do nothing but nod his head in understanding.

Aryeh Naor, secretary of the cabinet in the Begin administration, spoke of the unbreakable bond between Begin and Yehiel: "Begin was charmed by Yehiel's loyalty, his honesty, and his knowledge of the movement's ideological sources – Jabotinsky's writings, Uri Zvi Greenberg's poetry. In addition, Yehiel also had a phenomenal memory. You had only to mention one document or another to him, and he immediately knew where to find it – and this was before computers."

"I have a phenomenal memory?" Yehiel laughed. "Begin had a phenomenal memory! He could tell me, for example, 'Yehiel, in 1945, in the *La-Merchav* newspaper of the Labor Federation, on the top left side of the third page, there's an article about Yigal Allon's speech at a certain conference. Find that newspaper.' I would go and find it, but even this I didn't do alone, but with the help of a young man, an employee of the prime minister's office, who sat in a little room and found things for me."

It was no wonder, then, that many years later, after Begin resigned from his position as prime minister, when he paid tribute to Yehiel on an episode of the television program *What a Life* that was dedicated to the man, Begin was quoted as saying:

> Yehiel, my friend and partner, my right-hand man and colleague for decades, is one of the best of Israel's founding generation. He volunteered for the war against Nazi Germany, saved and guided immigrants, taught and trained fighters,

carried out fighting operations in Eretz Israel and abroad in order to free the nation from foreign rule, endangered his own life, aided underground fighters, and carried out pivotal roles of weighty responsibility. This is only a partial list, because this man dedicated his life, in the full sense of the expression, to the rescue of the [Jewish] people and redemption of the homeland. I offer my thanks, esteem, and appreciation for his work over many years. I would also like to thank his dear wife, who was fated as a Jew to undergo indescribable suffering, and who has stood at his side ever since she was saved from the concentration camps. Your friendship, Yehiel, is very dear to me, as I have none deeper. You were my right-hand man at many moments for decades. You assisted me with everything, day and night. You spared no effort to fulfill my requests. With all my heart, out of friendship that could not be deeper, I say to both of you, to Yehiel and his wife; my dear friends, *kol ha-kavod* [well done]!

Hearing this, Yehiel squirmed in his chair, and said only, "Thank you for the honor of serving our nation in your presence."

The friendship that went beyond the job found expression during preparation for one of the ceremonies on Mount Herzl in which Begin participated. Before Begin left for the event, Yehiel passed him a note in his own handwriting: "*Prime Minister. It is very cold on Mount Herzl, and the ceremony will last for over half an hour. I believe your clothes are not warm enough for the cold on the mountain. Perhaps I'll send Damti [Begin's driver] home to bring you a warmer coat (if you have one), or find one with one of the people here. Thank you, Yehiel.*" Begin returned the note to Yehiel, and in the margins, he wrote, "*I don't have a warmer coat at home. I won't wear someone else's coat. 'Those who are going to do a good deed, etcetera.*'[6] *M.B.*"

***

---

6   The *etcetera* at the end of the Sages' dictum that Begin quoted is "…won't come to any harm."

At the beginning, Yehiel's role was more pedestrian. One day, when a law on aid to municipalities came up for discussion in the plenary, Yehiel contacted MK Yosef Shofman to request that he go up to the podium to present the Herut faction's position. Shofman refused, as the issue seemed beneath him. Yohanan Bader saw what happened. He went to Yehiel and said, "If you want Shofman to speak, first ask MK Binyamin Avniel. As soon as you ask Avniel, Shofman will want to do it. Avniel will almost certainly not want to speak. He'll say that Shofman's much better, and then Shofman will want to prove that the compliment is justified. He'll jump at the opportunity and do the job – and your problem will be solved." Yehiel rapidly caught on to the internal system of the job, which involved much jockeying for respect. So much so that once, on a Thursday, as they left the old Knesset building for the weekend break, Bader turned to Yehiel and said, "Before we return to the Knesset next week, arrange it so that on Wednesday Shofman speaks, not Avniel." Yehiel had been the faction secretary for two months.

Begin overheard, and said to Bader, "What do you want from him? First let him learn the ropes a little, and then he can do things connected to the interactions between the members. He's not familiar with that part yet."

Bader retorted, "Not familiar? Who, Yehiel? Yehiel understands it very well. He's already taught me a few decent tricks for managing the faction."

In those times, the faction operated according to an unwritten axiom: when it came to economic issues, one of the three economists would speak: Bader, Shofman, or Avniel. For political matters, usually one of the other three spoke: Begin, Haim Landau, or Aryeh Ben Eliezer.

This was in the early sixties, the height of Begin's "wilderness years" in the opposition, when no one believed there would come a day when he would become head of the government. Begin himself said once, "I've become old in the opposition." Even Yehiel doubted the chances of the party ever joining the coalition.

The media for the most part ignored Begin and the Herut Party MKs, except for the *Herut* newspaper, which was essentially preaching to the choir. The other papers didn't bother to cover Begin's meetings, unless someone threw a stone during one of them. Thus when the name

"Begin" appeared in *Maariv* or *Yedioth Aharonoth*, or when two or three lines appeared mentioning a law proposed by a Herut MK, a feeling of celebration overcame the MKs and party activists. The media – as did Ben-Gurion and all of the Mapai Party – also related to Herut as "Them, you know."

"'Them,'" Yehiel explained, "meant 'the ones who don't belong.' We were never invited to cocktail parties with diplomats, to museum openings or to opening night performances. 'Them' meant in the best case scenario, 'air.' We were two nations. We had already accepted the fact that we were a foreign transplant within the people. We were different – I don't want to use the words 'contaminated' or 'lepers.' But that was the attitude from the political and social point of view. The situation changed for the better with time, but still people would pull out the 'them' on occasion. For example, in 1984 I was featured on the TV show *Such a Life*. One newspaper carried a review that emphasized that 'This time, other people sat in the audience.' Not the usual ones that we see on all the shows, the beautiful people, but 'different,' of another race."

Their dreams – whoever bothered to dream – of taking over the government were modest, secret. Until such time as that would happen, Yehiel learned the duties of his job very quickly. He was aided by his natural talent of interpersonal communication, the sense of humor that always popped up even in situations that seemed insoluble, and above all his prodigious memory. There was not one document, file, or paper that he couldn't find. During those years, Yehiel learned the rules and customs of the Knesset and politics. His relationship with party chairman Menachem Begin was fortified and transformed into firm, close personal friendship, and the trust between them was boundless.

Yiddish American writer Dr. Hillel Seidman wrote about Yehiel in the Yiddish newspaper *Der Morgen Zhurnal*: "Yehiel, like his father who was a Lelov Chassid, is a product of the kind of youth that is passionate about ideology – whether Lelov's or Jabotinsky's – about ideas and philosophies and the willingness for personal sacrifice in order to achieve them. The Chassidic flame is constantly burning within Yehiel, and it will never die. He shines and warms, and thus he softens the rigid diplomatic protocol.

He 'interacts wisely with other human beings,'[7] with an emphasis on 'wisely.' This perceptiveness is part of his Warsaw-style Jewish-Polish sharpness, which comes peppered with a basic understanding acquired early on in life. He is close to the entire world, but he feels most at home with the family-style Jew. He takes no pleasure in cruel, hurtful words, in the poisonous criticism and sharpened pens directed against his boss, who is also his close friend. But he doesn't respond in kind. He never gives his slanderers their fair due. He took a lesson in how not to behave from the Saison and the *Altalena*."

For Yehiel, Begin was first and foremost a leader and boss, and only after that a very close friend. Begin felt similarly toward Yehiel: he was his assistant and his friend.

Yehiel understood Begin's way of thinking. For example, Begin had a library of pamphlets, including material on international laws on borders, peace treaties, and similar topics. "The border with Egypt was not a problem," Yehiel explained, "because the town of Rafiah was on that border, while at the Gulf, Eilat was on the border. In Judea and Samaria, the entire Jordan River was inside the territory of Israel. The fact that the Jordanians had taken control of this territory illegally in 1948, and later annexed it – an act that was recognized only by Britain and Pakistan – did not make the territory Jordanian. In his library, Begin had a book by Professor Julius Stone, an Australian expert on international law whom Begin had met on one of his trips, titled *Israel and Palestine: Assault on the Law of Nations*. In it, Stone proved the legality of Israeli control and our right to be in the Land of Israel.

"Any time Begin had a meeting with an international statesman, I would take along this book. I would pull it out whenever Begin needed to support his arguments not just on the basis of 'our forefathers' heritage' and the Torah of the Jewish people. When Begin was under attack in the Knesset and people demanded, 'Show us someone in the world who agrees with that position,' Begin would respond, 'Has any Israeli politician ever

---

7   Translator's note: this phrase is from the chazzan's prayer recited before Mussaf on Rosh Hashanah and Yom Kippur.

presented our position to representatives of other nations? They don't even know that such a position exists.'

"Most of Begin's trips and speeches were to our people. When he was a minister without portfolio in the national unity government, when the Herut Party's platform was presented by him as a senior official in Israel, or when the Knesset was so kind as to set up a meeting between him and some foreign official who came to visit, things started to be seen in a different light. Eventually, there were several senators who supported Herut. Once I heard Begin say to Abba Eban: 'There's at least one senator who supports us all the way – and there will be more!' His argument was always that creating a new situation was sometimes easier than transforming an existing one."

Yehiel also knew how to turn the tables – at least with issues related to the group of party secretaries in the Knesset. Aryeh Han, secretary of the Mafdal (National Religious Party-NRP) faction for many years, related, "While the politicians quibbled among themselves, the party secretaries found a shared language, and we often plotted together, left and right, from Shalom Friedman who was secretary of the Israeli Communist Party, to Yehiel, secretary of the Herut faction. We assisted each other in parliamentary work. Yehiel was always the central axis of this group, ready with a smile, a good joke, a story from the city. Often, when we wanted to spread a witty joke in the Knesset that hinted at one of the ministers or MKs, we chose Yehiel for the job. He could tell such jokes, while others weren't able to. More importantly: we made frequent use of his phenomenal memory, which was legendary. Instead of running to the library to look up a date of a certain decision or speech, it was easier to just ask Yehiel. Everything was photographed and stored inside his head. We only had to push the button, and the answer popped out. It took him exactly one second to find the answer – faster than a computer."

On one occasion during the Eshkol government, the faction secretaries caused a small but unforgettable tumult. The NRP, as was the usual case, was a member of the coalition. But one time, the members had a falling out with Mapai on some minor issue, and decided to flex their muscles. This was during the golden age of the NRP, when it had thirteen MKs.

At that time, a coalition partner party that voted against the governing party was unheard of (as opposed to common practice in future years). Aryeh Han described the incident: "We decided to annoy Mapai a bit, and I was given freedom to operate. It was Wednesday, and on the agenda was the second and third reading of the proposed bill to raise the price of installing a telephone from three hundred to four hundred *lirot*. This was not a very important proposal, and we thought we could defeat it so that Mapai would see we weren't in their pocket. 'You manage it with Yehiel,' I was told in my faction. I approached Yehiel and told him that this time we were willing to vote with the opposition. Yehiel looked at me in disbelief. He said, 'You? Vote against Mapai? That's impossible.' After I convinced him that I was serious and it could really happen, we began to recruit a majority against the ruling party. Yehiel advised, 'First put them to sleep – act casual, they don't need to know you're not going with them, and in the meantime we'll look for the majority.' Meanwhile, Yehiel orchestrated the whole exercise.

"In the second and third readings, most of the objectors were from the opposition, and Yehiel told me, 'When we bring a majority to the hall, I'll instruct all the opposition members to give up the right to speak. We'll go right to a vote and strike them.' At one point, we realized the opposition was short just two votes to shoot down the proposal. What to do? Less than fifteen minutes passed, and then I spied Menachem Begin's long Dodge stop in the MK's driveway of the old Knesset building. Yoske the chauffeur jumped out from behind the wheel, opened the door, and two people stepped out: MK Rabbi Itche Meir Levin, head of Agudat Yisrael, and MK Esther Vilenska of the Israeli Communist Party. Yehiel received them at the entrance, and pushed them into the hall without making too big of a fuss. He signaled for all his compatriots in the opposition to request that their names be removed from the protocol. Then the vote was held – and the proposal failed. Prime Minister Eshkol burst into the hall, seething with fury. The exercise went perfectly, Mapai understood that Mafdal was angry and reached the right conclusions." The faction secretaries celebrated their small victory, and Yehiel went on with his work as usual.

Sometimes, the work was *unusual*. One day, in early 1966, while Begin was answering citizens' correspondence and taking care of humanity's problems, an old friend of his, Mordechai Neumark, arrrived at Begin's

Tel Aviv apartment. He was bursting with excitement. "I came to bring you a memento from our youth in Brisk," said Neumark, and he presented Begin with a booklet: *Kol-Bo La-Talmid* [literally, Compendium for the Pupil], a 288-page student almanac published in 1927, edited by Shmuel Perlman and Ze'ev Jabotinsky.

"This was the first time I had ever seen this booklet," Yehiel acknowledged. "But it was hardly the first time for Begin. Before [Neumark] left, Begin said, 'You've brought me memories from my old home. I first saw the *Kol-Bo* before I went to Warsaw. I learned a great deal from this little book during my youth. We used to say that this book was an encyclopedia in a nutshell.'

"Dr. Joseph B. Schectman, in his biography *The Life and Times of Vladimir Jabotinsky*, gives a comprehensive history of the Ha-Sefer publishing company [which published the almanac]. This chapter describes Jabotinsky's participation in editing *Kol-Bo* together with Dr. Shmuel Perlman. Characteristically, the booklet did not even mention the names of the two editors – it only had 'Edited by P.J.' on the cover. The editors' names appear only in the advertisements for the first Hebrew atlas, also published by Ha-Sefer in London (1926).

"In Shmuel Katz's biography of Jabotinsky, *Lone Wolf*, he writes that 'in order to encourage the general usage of the Sephardic pronunciation among school pupils, Jabotinsky wrote an article on this topic, which he included in the *Kol-Bo*. His other articles in the book were on Jewish organizations, the Zion Mule Corps, the Jewish Legion, and table manners. He invested much time and effort on other chapters in the same book, such as information on the [Jewish] Scouts movement, and the rules and regulations of various sports.'

A few years later, a copy of this rare book fell into Yehiel's hands. Another copy is preserved in the Jabotinsky Institute in Tel Aviv. "I leafed through the yellowing pages," Yehiel recalled, "and then I had the idea that this wonderful work by Perlman and Jabotinsky could be republished – almost eighty years after its first publication. I thought that had our dear friend [the industrialist] Dr. Reuven Hecht still been with us, I would sell him on the idea. I spoke with my friend Harry Zessler, chairman of Moledet Development Company, who was Dr. Hecht's right-hand man.

He asked me to send him a photocopy of the booklet. A short while later, he replied: Moledet had decided to adopt the idea of republishing the *Kol-Bo*.

"The republication of *Kol-Bo* in its original format is not only a result of the sentiments and caprices of Jabotinsky's old students. I believe that republication and widespread distribution will have educational value today, and will illuminate a lesser-known aspect of the literary and educational activity of the great Zionist leader Ze'ev Jabotinsky. I am certain that anyone who picks up this book will enjoy it immensely, as I do."

CHAPTER 15

A BULLET IN A TREE

It was the eve of the Six-Day War and tensions were high. In the face of mounting aggressive overtures by Egypt in May 1967, Israel called up its reserves in preparation for the war that seemed imminent. What was Yehiel's view of events involving Begin and Ben-Gurion during the waiting period on the eve of the Six-Day War? "Everyone's ears were tuned to the news, and everyone followed each headline and report," he recalled. "They also followed the internal political maneuverings, which mainly focused on Gahal [the union of Herut and the Liberal Party] joining Levi Eshkol's government."

Under pressure to present a strong and united defense, in May 1967 Eshkol invited opposition parties Gahal and Rafi (Reshimat Po'alei Yisrael, Israeli Workers List, Ben-Gurion's breakaway from Mapai) to join his cabinet, creating a national unity government.

"The politicians argued over whether Moshe Dayan [of Rafi] would receive the defense minister portfolio," recounted Yehiel. Until that point in time, Eshkol himself filled that role. "This was a vital issue that the establishment of the national unity government depended upon – Begin insisted that if Dayan did not join as defense minister, then Gahal would not join either. No one understood the reason for Begin's insistence."

Yehiel had been called up to prepare for the war like most other able-bodied men. He was on the Hawk missile base when he heard on the news that Begin was pushing for Rafi to join the emergency national unity government. Yehiel phoned Begin's home to ask him why he was acting so stubbornly. Aliza Begin said that her husband was not at home – he was at the home of Aryeh Ben Eliezer. Yehiel called the number, and Ben Eliezer picked up the receiver.

"Why is Menachem insisting that Rafi join?" Yehiel asked.

"You speak to him," Ben Eliezer replied, handing the phone to Begin.

"Why are you insisting–" Yehiel began to ask Begin. But the statesman did not allow his secretary to finish the sentence, and cut him off: "Because it's good for the Jewish people," he explained.

Yehiel could not argue with this reasoning, coming from Begin. "This response characterized Begin's general approach," Yehiel said.

During the days before the war, the Eshkol government faced troubles. Former prime minister David Ben-Gurion hurled harsh accusations against Levi Eshkol, both justified and unjustified, and tried to prevent going to war. Eshkol had a hard time functioning in this atmosphere. On May 23, 1967, after Gamal Abdel Nasser closed the Straits of Tiran, Begin asked Shimon Peres if Ben-Gurion could return to a leadership position.

The question is why Begin, who supported going to war, bothered to work to change the composition of the government and to convince Eshkol to resign his position in favor of Ben-Gurion. The simple answer is that Begin didn't know that Ben-Gurion objected to war. Yet, it is possible that even if he did know this, he would still have supported Ben-Gurion's appointment. To Begin, Ben-Gurion was a figure who could lead the nation into war and inspire it with self-confidence. Begin sincerely believed that Israel was in serious distress. Many soldiers were serving on the fronts, the economic situation was shaky, and war was on the doorstep. The senior military staff felt that one more day of waiting would escalate the number of losses. Begin thought that shock was the only way to force the agitated political elite to understand that things couldn't go on as usual. He was particularly worried over the nation's low morale. The day after receiving a positive answer from Peres, Begin contacted Eshkol and proposed the switch.

Eshkol rejected the proposal out of hand with his famous Yiddish retort, "*Di tzvei ferd velen nisht shleppen dem vegon tzuzamen*" (These two horses can't pull the cart together). Eshkol was right from his point of view, but Begin's manuever succeeded in producing the desired shock. Begin and Ben-Gurion's history was checkered with bitter disputes, and the panicked nation understood that if Begin was asking Ben-Gurion to return to the helm of the ship, this was a sign that the situation had reached the crisis point.

"Begin's requests of Ben-Gurion and Eshkol also changed Mapai's attitude toward him," Yehiel continued. "The process had begun three years earlier, when Eshkol decided to agree to Begin's request and bring Jabotinsky's remains to Israel, to Ben-Gurion's aggravation. The change continued in May 1967, during negotiations over the establishment of the national unity government. The two principal negotiators with Gahal, Golda Meir and Yisrael Galili, begged Begin not to fight for Rafi, but to be satisfied with Gahal joining the government. In other words, they asked Begin to join the government without Rafi, which was the meat and bones of the historical Mapai [as it comprised most of Ben-Gurion's core supporters]. In internal discussions in Mapai institutions, Herut Party leaders were called 'fascists,' while Rafi leaders were called 'neo-fascists.' [Aryeh] Ben Eliezer tried to convince Begin, arguing that this would be the government that would direct the war – with or without Dayan. But Begin insisted on Dayan's appointment to defense minister. If he hadn't insisted, the government would have been formed without Rafi."

In the end, with Dayan as defense minister and Eshkol as premier, the emergency national unity government was established on the first day of the war, June 5, 1967.

Another key event of the waiting period was Eshkol's famous "stutter" in his radio address to the nation on May 28, which struck fear in the hearts of hundreds of thousands of listeners. The leader came across as hesitant and uncertain of his nation's chances of victory. Yehiel also heard the famous speech. "We sat that night in a tent at the Lod airport, listening," he recalled. "I heard the stutter, and I thought, what's going on here? Maybe there's something unclear written on his papers? I knew that such a thing could happen to anyone, but at the time, the nation's mood was very down, and that stutter aroused fear."

At any rate, Begin focused on one sole purpose: "the good of Israel," as he himself defined it. Interestingly, Begin was the first person to stand up to tell the Israeli nation the truth regarding the treatment of Eshkol in the period leading up to the Six-Day War. He said this some time after he obtained an inside report of the events of the waiting period; he said it in discussions within the institutions of his party; and he said it when he eulogized Eshkol in the Knesset plenary after his death in 1969: "While working with Mr. Levi Eshkol, of blessed memory, I learned how the true image of a person can be distorted by what is known today as 'image.' What was said about Levi Eshkol? Mainly – that he was unable to decide. This is completely untrue." According to Begin, Eshkol's public image as a waverer unable to make decisions was false. Without Eshkol, the Six-Day War would not have been the same – Israel would not have entered East Jerusalem or the Golan Heights. Begin opined that "Israel must realize that Eshkol did a great deal on its behalf."

A seminal event for Begin, and all the more so for his right-hand man Yehiel, took place on the morning when the Six-Day War began. Begin and Yehiel – who was released from military reserve duty at Begin's request – were in the prime minister's offices at the Kirya military headquarters in Tel Aviv. These offices contained a meeting room for the cabinet, and next to it, the prime minister's chambers. It was Monday morning, 11:30 a.m. That evening, the new ministers of the national unity government would be sworn in – Dayan as minister of defense, Begin as minister without portfolio, and Yosef Sapir, also minister without portfolio.

Yehiel was caught in the eye of the storm, witness to the intense atmosphere in the office of Israel Lior, the prime minister's military secretary, who sat in the room beside Levi Eshkol's office. The phones buzzed incessantly, and reports began to stream in from the new fronts as they opened. Lior recorded the reports carefully. In the room next door, Eshkol, Yigal Allon, and Begin stood together. At some distance from them, in a corner, stood Yigael Yadin, who served as the prime minister's advisor on the war. Suddenly Yigal Allon turned to Eshkol and said, "Eshkol, Begin and I want Jerusalem." Eshkol hit his forehead with his palm and said in Yiddish, "*Dos iz a gedank*!" (Now that's an idea!). At the time, reports were coming in that we had completely destroyed the enemies' airports and air forces and that the skies were clear. Begin did not know then that Israel had contacted King Hussein of Jordan, promising that if he sat quietly, he would not be hurt. Yehiel never forgot that shortly before his release from reserve duty, one of the other reservists, a young man from a *moshav* near Ramle, had announced, "Let Hussi come fight, then we'll get to Jordan and we'll have all of the Land of Israel!"

"While I was in that room," Yehiel reminisced, "I remembered that reservist's pronouncement, and I thought how right he was. But on the other hand, we had no reason to attack in the east, because the front there had not yet been opened. An hour later, we left for an emergency session of the Knesset that was called for 4 p.m. Begin's regular driver, Yoske Giladi, had been called up for reserve duty as an ambulance driver in the north. Begin was given another chauffeur, a volunteer named Ephraim. But Begin was used to Giladi's superior driving, and he couldn't stand the substitute's sudden stops and sharp turns. At Sha'ar Hagai we had to turn right toward Kibbutz Netiv Ha-Lamed Heh, because the main road to Jerusalem was clogged with military vehicles. Then Begin caught sight of Golda Meir, at the time an ordinary Knesset member, on her way to Jerusalem. 'There's Golda!' he declared. 'I must speak to her!' I asked the driver to speed up, pass Golda's car, and stop beside her. The driver followed my instructions. Quickly Begin got out of the car and entered Golda's, and I squeezed inside as well. Begin updated her that war had broken out, and told her about the first successful operations. Golda was then [Mapai] party secretary and far from the center of decision-making, so every word of Begin's was news to her. She thanked him profusely. We reached Jerusalem in the afternoon, before Eshkol did. Begin told me to wait outside and report to him the moment I saw Eshkol arrive. I went outside and waited, and suddenly I saw a fleet of cars arrive, including Eshkol's.

"I rushed to Begin and told him, and he ran to Eshkol and asked him to convene a cabinet meeting immediately, before the Knesset session which was planned for swearing in the new minsters. Eshkol agreed, and everyone gathered on the second floor, next to the cabinet meeting room. Earlier, the Jordanians had begun to bomb the area, and two shells fell beside the windows of the room where the ministers had gathered. Two veteran Knesset ushers came running, and they shouted for everyone to go down to a lower floor that was more protected, the basement floor with the committee meeting rooms, and to hold the cabinet meeting there. Accordingly, the ministers went downstairs and crowded into a long corridor, really more of a storage area than a corridor. The space held old sofas brought from the original Knesset building in Froumine House, cleaning supplies, buckets, and brooms. That's where the ministers met. In the meantime, our troops were exchanging heavy fire with the Jordanians, and the issue of Jerusalem rose to the agenda. The ministers accepted the proposal of Defense Minister Moshe Dayan to surround the Old City, but not to enter it yet. In retrospect, this was the first step in the historical decision to liberate Jerusalem. Later, Begin, who had a powerful sense of history, said, 'Yehiel, remind me that I would like to place a special plaque on the storage area wall, stating that on this site, the decision was made that led to the liberation of Jerusalem.'"

In the meantime, the government swore in two of the new ministers, Sapir and Begin (Dayan had to rush to the IDF general staff headquarters at the Kirya in Tel Aviv). Afterward, late at night, the new ministers went to the home of President Zalman Shazar. Shazar asserted that the swearing-in was not valid until the new ministers toasted a *le-hayim* with him. In this, he invoked a tradition that was not recorded in the regulations, the constitution, or any other written document: a minister of the government could not begin to serve in practice until he had gone to drink a toast with the president. As this was already a tradition, and these were two new ministers in the national unity government, there was no other choice – Yosef Sapir and Menachem Begin went to Shazar to toast a *le-hayim* with him.

After this, the swearing-in was completed. Begin and Yehiel went to the King David Hotel to find a place to rest their heads.

"We went there, even though we hadn't reserved rooms," Yehiel related. "When we arrived at the hotel, we realized there was no need to reserve, because the place was empty. Two television crews were the only ones there, running around with their cameras. MK Shlomo Perlstein of the Liberal Party was also there. He said, 'Yehiel, I'm desperate to go to sleep. Where can I go to sleep here?' I went up to one of the rooms with him, opened the door, and said, 'You can sleep here.' The room was empty but Perlstein refused, saying, 'The room is exposed to fire.' Indeed, through the window we could see the glowing crossfire of tracer bullets. We went downstairs, and Perlstein found a place next to a pillar on the ground floor with mattresses spread around it. Local residents were sleeping on them, as they had decided that the hotel was safer than their homes.

"Begin and I couldn't sleep, so we decided to go out for a walk in front of the hotel. It was already 3 a.m. Heavy fog blanketed the street. Suddenly, a very tall figure appeared from in front of the building. I saw it was an elderly Jew. He asked us, in English, 'It's not dangerous to walk around here?' We replied, 'No, the big building is protecting us.' That's what we thought, because although we saw shiny balls, we knew those were flares shot into the sky; yet the next day, we would see a deep scrape from a bullet in the bark of one of the trees at the main entrance to the building.

"By way of conversation, the man related: 'Yesterday I was in Hong Kong, where there were street fights. I was scared, so I got on a plane. I landed in Israel, and I've got war again over here.'

"The next night, Begin heard on the BBC that the UN Security Council had decided on a cease-fire. He phoned Dayan, who said that he would call Eshkol. In the morning, several ministers met at the Kirya and changed our decision: not only would we surround Jerusalem, but we would liberate it. And that's what happened."

***

For the first time in his life, Begin was a member of the government, a minister without portfolio. He held this position from June 5, 1967, until he resigned from the unity government in August 1970. Begin's role as minister in the government broke a certain taboo and paved a new road for the future. Many members of the public, including hundreds of thousands for whom the trauma of the right-wing "rebels" was still fresh, still had qualms about him in the best of cases; in the worst, they hated him outright. But now they saw that even though he did not have a defined role as minister, he certainly could serve as a national representative, and not just an eternal oppositionist. You could say that even though people continued to object to him on the basis of past memories, they now saw that the devil was not so evil and that the Irgun commander had come out from the underground.

Yehiel, because of his intensive work with Begin, his total dedication to the ideology and the man, Begin's deep esteem for him, and the fact that they transmitted on the same wavelength, was the natural choice to become office director for Minister without Portfolio Menachem Begin. Yehiel stayed beside him the entire time. He breathed the air of the top echelons of politics, and he learned. Yehiel's own head was not turned by the height of his new position nor was he moved to put on airs, because to him, it was a position in the service of the man whom he admired and in whose path he believed.

Regarding Begin's term in the national unity government, Yehiel had a small argument with Dr. Israel Eldad, the former Lehi leader and Revisionist philosopher. Yehiel recounted: "Following the Six-Day War, when Begin entered the government, I met Eldad, who said, 'Listen, Yehiel, within three months we won't be in Nablus, Tulkarm, or any other place.' I replied, 'I don't want to paraphrase the Sages' dictum, "Let your tongue cleave to the roof of your mouth? But I'm telling you, your Menachem is a minister in the government!' A few months later, I met him again and said, 'You see, we're still there.' We always had wise-guys in our party, pessimists who predicted failure, great believers on one hand, but suspicious, fearful, afraid that something would happen and we would lose. They lacked confidence."

After war, a period of calm ensued. In his role as office director, Yehiel joined Begin on an Israel Bonds fundraising trip to the US and Canada. This was in 1968 and was the first time that Begin, who was by then a national figure, had ever spoken on issues outside the framework of Revisionism. The exhausting trip began in New York and continued to Chicago, Toronto, Montreal, Edmonton, and Vancouver. They then went south to Seattle, Denver, and other cities. In each place, Begin gave the same speech on the Six-Day War. His speech lasted for about an hour, and when he had finished, the organizers collected donations. In one city, Begin spoke three times in one day – at brunch, lunch, and dinner, each meal before a different audience. To Begin, it didn't make any difference that at a morning meeting, eighteen Jewish lawyers listened to him, while in the evening nine hundred sat in the audience. The same speech, the same intonations, the same admiration from the audience – the only thing that changed in each location was the amount collected. The next speech was planned for Las Vegas.

"We reached Las Vegas in the afternoon," Yehiel recollected. "We were taken to the Caesars Palace Hotel. In the lobby we saw two very impressive rows of what looked like white marble columns, with a sculpted bust of

Caesar on top. But it was all made of plastic. I knocked on them with my fist to be sure, and saw that I was right – plastic. We barely moved a muscle when we saw the gambling machines in every corner, tempting the guests to spend their money while they waited to receive the keys to their room. We weren't tempted. We received our rooms and rested for two hours. The bed was very fancy, with an impressive canopy. Also plastic. In the evening, the chairman of the Las Vegas branch of the bonds came to escort us to dinner. The dining room was also impressive, with enormous chandeliers. They sat me at the table of the bonds directors. I checked to see whether they were made of plastic as well – no, they were real people. Everyone was wearing black tie. The platform was decorated. The head of Israel Bonds, an Israeli who had gone to live in the US during the 1930s, gave the opening speech. Everything was very organized.

"The problem began when Begin began speaking. Then everything went wrong. He spoke with no limit. A cautionary speech, the same exact speech he had given at every location he had visited previously. He had not even a slip of paper in front of him – everything was in his head. He began with a description of the dangerous and impossible situation that had existed before the Six-Day War, how the enemy was equipped with the best weaponry and ammunition, how they had surrounded little Israel from all sides and threatened to throw the Jews into the ocean. He talked about how the IDF implemented Hannibal-inspired military feats, all with drama and his best rhetorical talent. The directors began to wring their hands in frustration. They hadn't expected an hour-long speech, and were afraid that the donors would leave. But no one moved a muscle – they were fascinated by the speech and the speaker. The chairman waved his watch at me in desperation every two or three minutes, but I pretended I hadn't seen him. After an hour, Begin finished speaking, and everyone stood up and applauded at length. More importantly, they gave unprecedented donations. The bonds representative couldn't believe it. Instead of people slipping away one by one, they gave donations that reached the skies. That evening, several million dollars entered the Israel Bonds account, a sum never seen before.

"But these amounts made no great impression on Begin," Yehiel continued. "Of course he knew that fifty thousand was more than twenty thousand, but he wasn't an expert on finances. Dr. Moshe Sneh [a member of the Israeli Communist Party] told me – this was after the move to the new Knesset building and during Begin's tenure as minister – that a Jewish millionaire who admired Begin once came to meet with him and shake his hand. Begin invited him for a cup of tea in the Knesset dining room. The meeting was photographed, and at the end, the excited Jew asked Begin, 'Would it be all right if I give you a donation of five thousand dollars?' What was five thousand dollars, Sneh demanded. That Jew could donate five hundred thousand dollars without even feeling it! But for Begin, it was fine."

On that trip, Begin had just one security guard, named Oved. He was a real character – muscular, dressed to the nines, and with a striking face. "He gave the impression that he was the king of Egypt," Yehiel recalled. "Sometimes people thought he was the minister, and Begin was his assistant."

Oved didn't have to save Begin from any terrorists, thankfully, but he did have to save him from a certain elderly, opinionated, and wealthy Zionist woman. Yehiel related that after one of Begin's speeches in the US they went to the hotel room to drink tea, as they always did. In those days, the government accounting office was not as generous as it became in later years, and Begin, Yehiel, and the security guard occupied the same suite: Begin had the large room, Yehiel the small one, and Oved slept in a small room beside the entrance. This wealthy Jewish woman came up with them to the suite. She had approached Begin after the applause had died down, and asked to accompany him as she had something to say regarding his speech. The Israel Bonds people indicated to Begin that it would be good for the Jewish people and the bonds enterprise if he went along with her request, as she was blessed with an untapped reserve of capital. What he wouldn't do for the country… Begin agreed. Over a cup of tea in the suite, she expressed her opinion at length. At first, Begin listened to her, but then when he realized that she wanted to impose her opinion on the entire world, he just nodded his head. It grew later and later, and Begin's patience grew thin with the situation. He asked Oved in Hebrew if he knew how to escort a woman. Oved laughed, "Do I? I wrote the book on it."

The story of this particular woman could be a small chapter in Oved's book, which was never written.

On their last night in Las Vegas, Yehiel was sunk in thought. Their flight back to Israel was planned for early the next morning. The entire night was before them, and he felt "travel fever" penetrating his bones. He couldn't sleep a wink. What was there to do in the gambling capital of America? He reached the most logical conclusion. He had never set foot in a casino, but this time he decided not to let this opportunity pass him by, especially since he knew – and this was almost the only thing he knew about casinos – that he could enjoy quantities of free, tasty food while gambling. As the hours passed, hunger began to gnaw at him, so this seemed the ultimate solution to while away the time before the flight.

Yehiel knew that he couldn't mention this idea to Begin, so he convinced Oved – he didn't have to work too hard – that they two should go gamble a bit in the casino, which was in one of the glittering halls of the hotel. Oved organized a substitute security guard from the embassy. On the way to the casino he asked Yehiel, "How much money do you want to gamble?"

"Ten bucks at most," Yehiel replied.

"The casino won't collapse if it loses on you," Oved murmured.

"Neither will I," came the answer.

They entered the big hall, which sparkled with lights. Yehiel had thirty dollars in his pocket, but he made the firm decision that he would gamble ten dollars and no more. Yehiel and Oved went to a blackjack table, a game Yehiel had played in the British army. Next to them sat an impressive Saudi sheikh.

"I played for one dollar each hand," Yehiel recounted, "while he put one thousand dollars. The sharp-eyed dealer caught on at once. He shuffled the cards rapidly and let me win each round, while the sheikh lost. Each dollar I earned from the casino encouraged the sheikh to continue, and he would lose a thousand. This happened seven times. When I saw that I had earned seven dollars, I controlled myself from getting dragged into losing, and quit the table. The dealer watched me leave, wearing a disappointed look. Then I continued to the machines, and in between I had a decent meal, on the house. Finally, we had to leave, as the clock showed it was early morning, and we had to rush back to the room to get organized for our flight back to Israel. At the end of the evening, I left the casino with the same sum with which I had entered. Not bad for a beginning gambler."

Begin, as minister, had his own way to propose his ideas so that they would be adopted. Yehiel related, "When Begin had a certain proposal, he knew that if he brought it to the cabinet table, he couldn't be certain they would adopt it because he was the only representative of the Herut Party. (Yosef Sapir represented the Liberal Party, while Moshe Dayan was from Rafi.) Begin knew that the twenty-odd ministers would act as a majority to block any proposal of his. He knew the limits of what he might propose that had a chance of passing, and what probably would not pass. So he took preventive measures and adopted a special system. When he had a creative idea, he would go to Yisrael Galili [of Labor]. They were friends, and Galili usually accepted his ideas enthusiastically. Begin would propose the idea to Galili and ask his opinion, and Galili would say, that's a great idea! Then Begin would say, how about if you propose it? Galili would reply, why not? And the idea would be adopted. Begin didn't look for credit, he just wanted the ideas implemented."

Begin and Gahal reached the end of their role in the national unity government in 1970, after the Knesset gave its basic agreement to the Rogers Plan. This plan was first proposed in December 1969, at the height of the War of Attrition, by US Secretary of State William Rogers, in an attempt to break the freeze in Arab-Israeli relations that had held since the Six-Day War. The plan included several principles: Israel would retreat to the international border with Egypt; the status of the Gaza Strip and Sharm el-Sheikh would be determined through negotiations, so that these would not remain under Israeli control; Jerusalem would remain united and controlled by the three religions; Israeli shipping in the Suez Canal would be secured. Egypt rejected the plan, arguing that it favored Israel. Israel also rejected it, saying it did not ensure its security, did not call for direct talks on a formal peace agreement, and did not state that Jerusalem would remain under Israeli control. Later, the US representative to the UN, Charles Yost, expanded this plan to refer to the Jordanian front as well. The new plan specified that Israel would retreat to the 1949 cease-fire lines, with small border corrections; Arab refugees would have the choice between returning to Israel and accepting reparations; Israel and

Jordan would have equal status in Jerusalem for religion, economics, and civil affairs; and freedom of shipping in the Gulf of Aqaba would be ensured. Jordan agreed to discuss this proposal, while Israel rejected it.

In June 1970, Rogers initiated a second plan, proposing negotiations between Egypt and Israel, to be mediated by the UN envoy from Sweden, Gunnar Jarring, who had already tried to invite Israel and its neighbors to talks on a peace arrangement. The new negotiations were supposed to lead to a peace agreement based on mutual recognition of the sovereignty of all the states, their territorial integrity, and political independence, and on Israel's retreat from territories it had occupied in 1967 – all in accordance with UN Security Council Resolution 242. On June 21, the Knesset rejected the new proposal. Egypt, which apparently feared additional escalation in the War of Attrition, announced that it agreed to discuss these proposals. Following this, American pressure on Israel intensified, and President Richard Nixon sent clarifications of the plan to Prime Minister Golda Meir: Israel would retreat to safe and agreed-upon borders, not the pre-June 1967 borders; the retreat would be implemented only after the signing of a binding peace agreement between the parties; the problem of the refugees would not harm the Jewish character of Israel; the US would guarantee Israel's integrity, sovereignty, and security; and the arms balance would be maintained. On July 31, 1970, the State of Israel agreed in principle to the plan, and in reaction, Gahal resigned from the national unity government. The Gahal resignation was implemented after a vote in the Herut and Liberal Party central committees – two hundred members in total – with a majority of only two votes.

"After the decision to leave the government," Yehiel reported, "Begin said to me: 'You should know, Yehiel, if there had been a majority in favor of remaining within the government, our party would have collapsed.'"

The day after the Gahal ministers resigned from the national unity government, on August 4, 1970, Begin announced on the Knesset platform: "We have completed a chapter in our lives entitled the national unity government. It was a good chapter."

On August 25, 1970, Begin spoke in the Knesset about the Rogers initiative: "The Knesset has to know this; the entire nation must hear it. The result [of this plan] is that when the day comes that Nasser decides to open fire – and being aware of our reality, we must assume that such a day will certainly come – the enemy will have a decisive advantage in artillery and armored divisions. In the past months, our air force carried out the welcome operation of assaulting this advantage and preventing casualties among our sons. But such an operation will be very difficult to carry out without casualties of a sizable number among our pilots and airplanes – that is the reality."

Eventually, the Rogers initiative collapsed. The new cease-fire between Egypt and Israel became valid on August 7, 1970, but because Egypt violated the conditions of the agreement by placing anti-aircraft missiles along the Suez Canal, Israel delayed the Jarring negotiations, renewing them only in February 1971. Another version of the Rogers Plan for an intermediate agreement along the Canal never reached fruition.

CHAPTER 16

WITH A "TERRORIST" IN LONDON

Begin returned to the opposition and to a relatively calm daily agenda: speeches, letters, articles, travel abroad. One of Yehiel's trips with Begin during that period was to Switzerland, on a fundraising trip for the United Jewish Appeal. Billionaire Nessim Gaon sponsored a dinner in Geneva. Many donors came to the dinner, from Switzerland as well as other neighboring European countries. In honor of this occasion, the UJA sent one of its directors especially from the United States. This director conducted the evening as was traditional in his home country – with a celebratory announcement of the names of the benefactors and the amounts they were donating.

"At first, people squirmed with discomfort in their seats," Yehiel recalled. "Then they began to whisper among each other. Finally, the local directors stopped the proceedings, and explained to the announcer that in Europe, it was not acceptable to announce the amounts. 'Why?' asked the UJA representative. 'It's a good way to encourage others to give even more.'

"'Of course,' came the reply, 'but it also encourages the tax authorities to start sniffing around.'"

In total, Yehiel traveled an enormous number of miles around the world with Begin. On occasion, after an intensive speaking tour, friends would say to him, "You're really having a great time with Begin, aren't you? You're seeing the world."

At such times, Yehiel would pull out a story he kept in mind for the appropriate moment. When confronted with such a remark, he would dust off this somewhat immodest story from the shelves of his memory. "You probably know the story about Rivka-leh who never got married," he would reply to acquaintances who were jealous that he was seeing the world. "One year goes by, then the next, but nothing happens. She remains a bachelorette and a virgin. People tell her, 'Why don't you get married? It's so wonderful, you'll enjoy it.' Finally, the happy day arrives, and Rivka gets married. Two weeks after the wedding, she meets up with some friends, and they say, 'So, weren't we right? How are you enjoying it?' Rivka-leh replies, 'Enjoying it? The only thing I've seen since I got married is the ceiling!'

"In other words: we arrive in Vancouver, for example, straight from the airport we rush to the hotel and take a shower. Then we have to go down to the lobby right away, because the UJA people are already waiting for us impatiently. We go to a dinner or meeting, and Begin speaks. From there we go on to another meeting, and he makes the same speech. At night we return to the hotel and stare at the TV for a few minutes. The next morning we rush again to a meeting with the women of one organization or another, brunch with lawyers. We run around like this for a few days, and suddenly we found ourselves at the airport again, on the way to another country, where the UJA people are already waiting for us impatiently. In the end we ask ourselves, wait a minute, was I in Canada? Was I in New York?"

By contrast, London did not await Begin expectantly – he visited that city only twice, on January 9, 1972, as a member of Knesset, and again in 1977 as prime minister. On both occasions, Yehiel was with him.

London was home to one of the most important branches – although not the largest – of the world Herut Party. The directors of Herut-Ha-Zohar, under the leadership of Arik Graus, a reputable antiques dealer, and Marvin Benjamin, a senior attorney, invited Begin to visit England. In January 1972, Begin accepted the invitation, and they planned two events: on the first evening, a public speech before three thousand people, and on the second, a gala dinner for six hundred well-off members and admirers. To seat the event of thousands, the organizers rented a spacious hall from a church. For the gala, they reserved the elegant ballroom of the Royal Garden Hotel at Kensington. Begin and Yehiel also stayed in this hotel. They planned to be in London for three days. Yehiel had a feeling that Begin in London would be a hot story – but he had no idea how hot it would get. As it turned out, the admirers and members were not the only ones who awaited him.

Arik Graus met Begin and Yehiel at Heathrow Airport. The car had barely started, when Graus whispered into Begin's ear that there were "problems."

"What problems?" Begin inquired.

"The church canceled the hall we booked for the speech," Graus informed him.

"Why did they cancel?" asked Begin.

"The church decided to cancel the reservation," Graus said, "because they said that they received threats from various elements – Arabs, antisemites, fascists – that they would prevent you from speaking and cause serious damage to the hall. As soon as they received the threats, they informed the police, but the police said they couldn't take responsibility for what might happen."

There was no need to explain to Begin and Yehiel what and whom the church feared. First of all, at that time, England was home to many former soldiers and policemen who had served in Mandate Palestine, and the name "Begin" and the words "Irgun" and "Lehi" caused them break out into a sweat. Secondly, extreme Islamic and fascist populations had swelled in London. As for the police, it was possible there were factors in the government who did not encourage the police to assist in securing the event, as it represented a thorn in the side for Begin's opponents.

The British media preceded Begin's arrival with potent incitement. The newspapers, the tabloids as well as the serious ones, competed with each other over who could harm him the most. The *Daily Mail* shouted "The Little Murderer Returns"; the *Sun* announced across the entire width of the page, "Go Home, Mr. Begin"; other headlines shouted "Arch-Terrorist Visits"; "The Sergeants' Murderer Arrives"; "King David Hotel Bomber Visits"; "Get Out, Deir Yassin Murderer." Before Begin's arrival, the Parliament held a debate on the whether to permit him entry. Many proposed to deny him a visa – in those days, a visa was required to enter England – and prevent him from landing in the country. Yet these demands were rejected.

"Who needs police protection?" Begin asked. "We'll hold the meeting there without them."

"It won't work," Graus tried to explain the problem to Begin. "The church has already refunded our down payment. We don't have a hall."

Begin thought for a moment, then said, "No matter. Tell the driver to turn around. We'll go back to Heathrow and fly back to Israel." Then, although this was his first visit to England, and all he had seen was part of the way from the airport to the city, he added, "I haven't come to see Buckingham Palace or Westminster. I've seen it in the movies, and it never interested me much anyway."

"But Mr. Begin," said Graus in desperation, "everyone's waiting to meet with you at the dinner."

"So what do you suggest?" Begin asked.

"I just wanted to say that we have some problems," Graus replied, "but we'll solve them. How? At this stage, I don't know yet."

They arrived at the Royal Garden Hotel and got organized. Then a messenger arrived from the hotel owner. He informed them that Begin could stay in the hotel, but due to the severe threats he had received, he could not rent them the hall for the dinner.

"I would like to speak with the hotel owner," Begin requested.

A few minutes later, the hotel owner called the room, and Begin said, "I understand that you are afraid, and I understand your fear. I would like to leave the hotel."

The hotel owner replied, "Mr. Begin, this cannot happen! You are our desired guest, and you must stay. I beg you."

A few minutes later, waiters arrived pushing two carts – one laden with fruit, the other bearing drinks. Begin didn't even glance at the special gift. He said to his escorts, "Look, we have no business being here. If there's no hall for the big meeting and no hall for the dinner, let's go back to Israel on the next flight."

In the meantime, the women's committee of Herut Ha-Zohar, which was responsible for the logistics of the event, was involved in feverish activity. They sat on the phones and searched for another hall.

At one point, Yehiel asked them in astonishment, "Why are you working so hard? Why don't you just take a synagogue hall? You have synagogues with large halls for celebrations, weddings, bar mitzvahs."

"You're right," they replied, "but for this, we need the permission of the chief rabbi, Rabbi Immanuel Jakobovits, and he's on vacation right now."

Begin insisted on returning to Israel the next morning on an El Al flight. In the evening, a young, tall Jew of about twenty appeared outside Begin's room in the hallway, which was packed with policemen. The policemen seemed to tense up, but the youth introduced himself as a Jew from the local community. He asked them to call Yehiel.

When Yehiel came out, the youth asked, "Are you staying in the room closest to Begin?"

"Yes," Yehiel replied. "Why?"

"All right," the youth declared, "I'll stay with you in that room."

"To what do I owe this honor?" Yehiel wondered.

"I'm responsible for security for the Jewish Defense Committee of London," the youth replied. "I don't trust the British police one bit. I'll be with you until Begin leaves England."

Yehiel hosted the young man in his room. He sat beside the door the entire night and did not close his eyes.

"He was one of the dedicated young men of the London Jewish community," Yehiel recalled. "Years later, he made aliyah, and we met in Jerusalem."

Jewish security protected Begin closely until he left the United Kingdom.

The next morning, one of the energetic women succeeded in reserving a hall in which Begin could speak. The pleasantly decorated event hall belonged to Congregation Kedassia, a very Orthodox congregation that had its own kashrut certification. It was located in a London neighborhood that was not particularly exclusive or elegant, but was where ultra-Orthodox, modern Orthodox, and traditional Jews held their celebrations. The Kedassia catering company had an excellent reputation, and was also the supplier of kosher meals for El Al flights out of England.

As soon as the hall was reserved, the enthusiastic women began to phone the dinner guests to inform them of the venue change. The next evening, when Begin and his escorts arrived at the site, they noticed a small group of the London "New Left" (the "Radical Zionist Federation"), headed by local members of Mapam and Ha-Shomer Ha-Tzair. They were holding a huge sign that stretched across the entire width of the street. It read, "Begin, Go Home." Begin did not say a word. His car slid into the parking space reserved for honored guests.

The event organizers – three men and a woman – welcomed their group warmly.

"Before we commence," said Begin, "I would like to see the owners."

An elderly woman appeared. She introduced herself as Mrs. Lesser.

"I salute you, madam," Begin said, "for agreeing at the last minute to hold this event here in your hall. I would like to ask, how is it that of all people in London, you are the only one who is not afraid to host us?"

Without speaking, the woman rolled up her sleeve to reveal the number tattooed on her arm. "After this," she said, "I'm not afraid of anyone!"

The hall glittered with lights and was decorated as if the organizers had prepared a week in advance. The six hundred guests sat in their chairs, excited at Begin's arrival. Begin entered the hall, and it thundered with welcoming applause.

Inspired by the fears of the British, as well as the words of the hall owner, Begin began his speech by saying, "When I arrived here, I was welcomed with a big sign that said, 'Begin, Go Home.' I was happy that, thank God, I have a home to go back to."

Then he began his speech. He outlined the main principles of the Herut Party regarding Judea and Samaria, and also responded to the polemic surrounding his visit. In response to the hostile questions of British reporters, he declared passionately, "Just as we are not afraid of bullets, we are not afraid of questions. What I wanted to say has reached the audience's ears. In the last few days, we've had an Irgun festival on British television..." Begin attacked one of the well-known columnists of the *Jewish Chronicle* for its confrontational opinion against him, and sarcastically noted that "the knock-kneed Jew wants to prove to the *goy* how nice and ingratiating he is. Such Jews will earn only humiliation and disgrace."

The next day, a press conference went ahead as planned at the Royal Garden Hotel. Over one hundred journalists arrived from every type of media, and television crews from all the networks turned out. It was high volume: the journalists attacked Begin without even listening to his answers. They didn't want to hear – they just wanted to be heard. Begin decided to put a stop to the farce. He launched the attack: "You British have forgiven and welcomed Jomo Kenyatta of Kenya, Dr. Hastings Banda of Nyasaland (Malawi), and Makarios III of Cyprus – all the colonial leaders of the British Empire who fought you. The only ones you don't forgive are us Jews. And why? Because we Jews won, and threw you out of our land!"

With that, Begin rose and left the room and the astonished reporters.

"Those were three of the most interesting days of my life," Yehiel later noted. "Those three days when I accompanied Begin on his visit to London. I saw the Lion Cub of Judah fight the Lion of Britain and beat it – this time with words alone, without explosives."

The flight back to Israel resembled the flight to London. They sat in the regular economy section. Begin was then a member of Knesset, and he had no security detail. Yehiel sat in the seat beside him, and each was absorbed in his own book. From time to time, passengers came up to Begin, greeted him, and said a few words, which Begin enjoyed very much. Personal contact was always important to him, whether it was with admirers or opponents.

One of the passengers said, "We heard that the media welcomed you with headlines announcing, 'Terrorist.'" Begin grinned and waved his hand in dismissal. Several times, the question arose of whether Begin saw any comparison between the struggle of the Palestinians and the Jews' war of independence.

On this, Yehiel remarked, "He answered this question at many opportunities. Once, Mike Wallace, the well-known American interviewer, asked him directly, 'Mr. Prime Minister, you were the commander of a terrorist organization. Do you not see any comparison between this and the PLO?'

"Begin replied, 'There's nothing at all to compare. We fought to liberate our land from a foreign regime, from the British. They want to wipe us off the face of the earth and take our land from us, because this land is ours. We threw out the British because this land is ours. What do the Arabs want? To throw us out of our land! There's no comparison between the Irgun and the PLO, or any other group of murderers of theirs. Another issue is the method of battle. They kill every man, woman, and child, whereas we did everything to avoid harming civilians. True, sometimes disasters happened and civilians were hurt, but this was not part of our battle tactics.'"

Yehiel added, "There was no national movement here until the Jewish national movement began. In 1942, when I served in Egypt as part of the British army, Egyptian civilians asked me where I was from. I answered, Palestine. 'Oh,' they replied, 'you mean you're Syrian, from southern Syria.'

"The problem is that over the years, a certain Israeli school of thought has developed the view that there is such a thing as a Palestinian people, and that they deserve rights. This is in opposition to the positions of Ben-Gurion and Golda [Meir]. Golda herself said, 'There is no Palestinian people. I am a Palestinian.' What happened to the Israeli leftist parties is a deviation from the main stream of Zionism."

Begin's second visit to England was in 1977, in his role as prime minister of Israel. This time, it was another story altogether. This was Begin's third trip abroad as prime minister. He visited for three days, and his agenda was crowded. He spoke at several events, was interviewed by various media outlets, met with British Prime Minister James Callaghan, Foreign Secretary David Owen, and senior representatives of government and Parliament.

Begin's British hosts welcomed him at an elegant dinner on the evening of his arrival (and even provided Begin with a kosher meal). Following diplomatic protocol, Begin was allowed to invite his own guests to dinner on the second night. Before they had descended from the aircraft, Begin had said to Yehiel, "Yehiel, at our dinner with the top echelons of the British government, I would like Mrs. Lesser of Congregation Kedassia to join us in the receiving line. Find her."

Accordingly, at Begin's dinner, the top representatives of the British government greeted Begin and his senior advisors and shook their hands, and they also greeted the owner of the Kedassia catering service. The heads of the British government, including the prime minister and his advisors, shook hands with the woman who had shown her proud respect to Begin five years earlier, when he was defamed.

Many years later, when Begin was ill, Mrs. Lesser visited Israel, and asked Yehiel to permit her to visit Begin in his home at 1 Zemach Street in Jerusalem. The visit was arranged quickly, and when she came to wish him a speedy recovery, he reminded her of their first encounter – his question and her reply, the numbers on her arm.

On one of the days of that 1977 visit to England, Begin felt ill and had to cancel his meetings, but he was never one to waste time. "In his hotel suite," related Aryeh Naor, secretary of the Begin cabinet, "he dictated to Yehiel the first version of the Autonomy Plan. When he returned to Israel, he called separate meetings with Foreign Minister Moshe Dayan and Attorney General Aharon Barak. He showed each of them the plan, which was still written in Yehiel's handwriting on yellow lined paper. Begin integrated Dayan's and Barak's comments into the final text of the Autonomy Plan."

Begin's son Ze'ev Binyamin (Benny) related, "I was the second person to hear my father's ideas for an autonomy plan, in a phone call from abroad. The first was Yehiel. 'Yehiel, get a pen' – this expression was quite familiar to me, and my father used to say it even before he was prime minister. My father gave himself time to think. He turned over the idea in his head, and finally he was ready to commit it to writing. Speaking out loud is not the same as writing. 'Yehiel, get a pen' in fact meant, I've now completed the thinking process."

***

The Yom Kippur War, in 1973, caught Begin still in the opposition. "I went to him that night," Yehiel shared. "We were all in shock. As usual, I was optimistic, and said, 'We'll throw them back.' Begin's expression was harsh, and he whispered, 'The situation is not good.'"

Begin received updates throughout the war, which lasted from October 6 – 25. He barely left the Knesset, and he was constantly depressed. After the war, when victory was announced along with the bitter results, he expressed himself at several opportunities, saying, "It was an eclipse…" Yehiel heard him say on more than one occasion: "After we knew what was going to happen, how is it that we didn't strike the first blow before they crossed the canal? Why did we wait until the Egyptians made the first strike, and then attempt to turn the tables? We could have smashed their striking force. If we had done so, we could have had peace with Egypt, if not *de jure* then at least *de facto*, for thirty or forty years."

After that, from the Knesset speaker's platform, Begin repeated the questions that had no answers: why didn't you move the weapons closer? Why didn't you call up the reserves?

The Yom Kippur War was a political watershed, setting off a chain of events that led to the resignations of Golda Meir and Moshe Dayan, the weakening of the Labor Party due to infighting, and general dissatisfaction with left-wing leadership. The reverberations of Yom Kippur were seen clearly and simply in 1977, the year of "the turnaround," when the right, led by the Likud and Menachem Begin, won the elections for the Ninth Knesset for the first time in Israel's history. Yehiel analyzed the results honestly: "What helped to bring about the revolution was the fact that Dash [the Democratic Movement for Change] suddenly popped up and took away votes from Labor. This gave us a shot in the arm, and so we were able to put together a coalition on the night of the elections, just after the results were publicized."

**

In that year, 1977, Prime Minister Menachem Begin made an official visit to Romania, where he met with President Nicolae Ceaușescu, who was eventually executed by the Romanian citizens in a popular revolution. On the flight, Begin received a telegram from the Israeli ambassador to Romania, asking for details of the points Begin would make at the gala dinner with Prime Minister Manea Mănescu. Begin hadn't written his speech yet, and so he said to his secretary, "Yehiel, take down a few words." Yehiel pulled out a piece of yellow-lined paper and wrote out several phrases that Begin dictated. At the Bucharest airport, a number of dignitaries stood in line to greet him, including the Israeli ambassador to Romania, a Mapai member and supporter of Foreign Minister Moshe Sharett. He asked Begin if he could give the hosts the summary of the speech, so Yehiel gave him the page of yellow paper. The page was translated and given to the Romanians, while the original was returned to Yehiel, who gave it to Begin. Unitl this point, everything had gone according to protocol.

The dinner that first night was held in a magnificent palace, in a hall with crystal chandeliers and elegant carpets. Enormous, impressive paintings hung on the walls. Around the table sat about eighty people. The meal, which was strictly kosher, proceeded pleasantly, until the speeches began. When the time came for him to speak, Prime Minister Mănescu rose from his seat and broke into a fiery oration on the legitimate rights of the Palestinian people, the right of return, the evils of occupation, and Palestinian statehood. Yehiel glanced at Begin, who perked up his ears and laid aside the yellow page with his speech summary. When it was Begin's turn to speak, he gave a sharp rebuttal to every issue that Mănescu had raised. His words churned up a storm and later were widely quoted in the media. While Begin spoke, Yehiel peeked at the ambassador's face, and saw him turning paler and paler with every sentence, every word.

After the meal was over, Yehiel addressed the ambassador: "Do you have the text of Mănescu's speech as well?"

"Yes," the ambassador admitted, "It's still in my pocket."

"So why didn't you give it to me?" Yehiel demanded.

"I was afraid that Begin would argue with him..." replied the ambassador.

Begin was very angry at the ambassador's cowardliness, and when he returned to Israel, he told Foreign Minister Dayan about the incident. He didn't ask Dayan to fire the ambassador from the foreign ministry, only to transfer him to a different position. A week later, the ambassador was brought back to Israel, and a new ambassador to Romania was appointed.

During that visit, the Romanian authorities adopted unprecedented security measures. They cleared the streets along which Begin and his entourage planned to walk to synagogue on Friday evening and Saturday morning, and they instructed the residents along the route to stay in their homes and to close the windows and shades. Security was tight around the staff, guarded by uniformed and plainclothes police. The security personnel that surrounded Begin held folding fire-proof mattresses that could be thrown on the VIPs in case of an attack.

As mentioned, at the beginning of his Knesset career, Yehiel served as Herut Party secretary. But as his duties grew and the party could support a small expansion of the clerical staff, Yehiel became Begin's full-time personal secretary. No formal declaration accompanied this move nor was there any change in his status or salary. As part of his position, Yehiel had access to Begin's daily schedule.

"Begin was a very organized person," Yehiel recalled, "as opposed to myself. His daily schedule was sacred. Of course there sometimes were events out of the ordinary, such as a sudden appointment; or an incident that required him to go to a meeting or invite people to a meeting; or a celebration or, God forbid, a funeral that wasn't part of the regular schedule for the day. Usually, though, his schedule was consistent. Some things were set in stone, especially answering correspondence. On Mondays we went to Jerusalem, even before he was prime minister, and on Wednesdays he wrote an article. Following the regular schedule became even more important when he became prime minister. But if suddenly someone came and asked to meet with him, I knew who I could let in, who had to be let in, and who he wouldn't be so happy to receive but would agree to see anyway. Whoever I knew he wouldn't agree to receive but I wouldn't allow inside in the first place. In general, he was very easygoing. I don't think anyone ever heard from him, over his years of work, a word in a sharp tone, unless it was to someone in a high position who didn't do what he had asked – to state an opinion or carry out an organizational task – and Begin knew this person was being evasive not because he wasn't able to do it, but because he wasn't in favor of it; then Begin would say a few sharp words to him."

In the early years of his role as Begin's secretary, Yehiel was an eyewitness to hundreds of the man's town square speeches, which granted Begin a favored reputation despite his many critics. This was a special phenomenon: one man who succeeded in inspiring an audience of thousands, sometimes even tens of thousands, with his carefully constructed speeches. This was before television existed in Israel – when TV finally arrived, it drastically changed the phenomenon of the town square gatherings.

"To tell you the truth," Yehiel admitted, "there were moments when I was truly frightened for his safety. I also felt uncomfortable myself. After he finished his speech, he would walk into the audience, shake hands, get an up-close look at the people he had spoken to from far up on the podium. The audience wanted to shake his hand, look at him, say a few words. Begin would climb down from the stage, and the audience would rush toward him. Behind him there was only a wall – there was nowhere to escape. He had no security guards, of course, just a group of local activists who with their feeble forces tried to prevent the masses from trampling him. I feared for myself as well, because I was always there, and almost no one knew me.

"One day – this was in the historical elections marathon of 1977 – I was approached by Aryeh Goldstein, then in his twenties and assistant to MK Yigal Hurvitz. 'Give me the honor of standing beside Begin during his speech,' he asked. Go ahead, I told him, no problem. That evening, Begin spoke in Petah Tikva. I gave Goldstein my place, while I went down into the audience and listened to the speech from there. At the end of the speech, the audience began to push forward in a wave toward Begin. Goldstein was on stage, and he feared for his life. When he finally caught sight of me, he said, breathless, 'I won't be beside him at rallies anymore. Once was quite enough. They almost killed me.'"

When he was a nonagenarian, MK Dr. Binyamin Avniel said to Yehiel, "I don't understand Menachem. Why does he need to stand up and speak in front of five thousand people? When I want people to know what I have to say, I invite in a journalist, offer him some fine cognac, and I talk. The next day, the entire readership of *Haaretz* reads what I have to say. So why does Begin need to speak at rallies? So that the next day there will be two lines in the paper?"

One day, Yehiel said to Begin, "You know, Menachem, that I like you better when you speak to a group of fifty or a hundred people, at a small meeting in a room, more than on the stage at the Moghrebi."[8]

"I also prefer the living room speech," Begin replied, "but I have to speak to the masses. I have to speak to people in such a way that they'll be fascinated by what they hear. After all, they come to the square an hour before the rally begins, they stand on their feet for an entire hour because there aren't any chairs, and they have to overcome their exhaustion so they won't collapse. When I speak to an audience, I have to take all of that into account." The last elections in which Begin participated were held in 1981. Yehiel again said to him, "It's time to end this business with the town squares." He didn't want Begin to go around from city to city, stage

---

8 "Moghrebi" was their term for the town square. There was a Moghrebi in Ramat Gan, in Haifa, Jerusalem, Netanya, etcetera.

to stage. Furthermore, exhaustion was beginning to take its toll on the aging minister's health. Yehiel added, "People will sit at home and hear you on the radio, they'll watch you on TV, and everything you want to say will be transmitted in an easier way." But Begin did not listen, for a simple reason: on radio and TV, and in newspaper interviews, he could not feel the people in the audience, touch them, or see their eyes. Begin wanted the direct contact. He had to see the people standing before him, listening and reacting with enthusiasm. The feedback between the speaker and his audience was one of the secrets of Begin's speeches, and this was what made each one into a special, even unforgettable event.

Once Begin, in a light-hearted mood, told Yehiel how he and David Yuttan, his childhood friend from Poland, would travel from town to town to speak about making aliyah and freeing the Jewish people from the suffering and difficulties of the Diaspora. Often, the two would arrive in a small town where about fifty Jews were gathered in a small hall or synagogue, waiting to hear them speak. This was after a day of work, after the Jews had closed their shops or finished fixing shoes or sewing garments in their workshops, and they were exhausted. A few minutes would pass after the speaker began, and then the heads of the listeners would flop onto their chests into a heavy sleep. Most often, Begin spoke first, and David Yuttan followed. Yuttan was a well-known Yiddish speaker, and he spoke loudly, not in order to wake them but because this was his habit. He would announce, "*Shteit uf di Yiddishe massen* (Wake up, Jewish masses)," and they would wake up in confusion. Begin loved to describe how Yuttan used to wake up the "Jewish masses" – no more than five modest *minyanim* (prayer quorums)…

Yehiel also related that a similar thing happened to Begin. He loved to appear in front of Christian fundamentalist supporters of Israel, Baptists, and evangelicals. Once in the middle of a speech in front of a large crowd, Begin declared with emotion: "Let us stand together!" To his surprise, the entire congregation stood on its feet.

Upon the "turnaround" of 1977, Yehiel's appointment to the position of chief of staff in the prime minister's office seemed completely natural. For example, on the eve of the 1977 elections, Yohanan Bader, one of the leading members of the Herut Party, approached Yehiel and said, "You could be a Knesset representative – you need only ask. Sign a request, and consider it done."

His loyalty, however, was to the man, not the party. "Yehiel did not give the idea even one minute of thought," his wife Bambi disclosed. "After this happened, he came to the kitchen and asked me, 'What do you think of the offer?' I replied, 'What are you thinking? Leave him?' He replied, 'I wasn't even considering it, I just wanted to know what you thought.'" In 1983, when Begin resigned, Yehiel again did not think of leaving him, and instead became the chief aide to the former prime minister.

Aryeh Naor, who became secretary of the Begin cabinet, affirmed: "I heard it straight from Begin that he was sure that Yehiel would be an excellent Knesset representative, but Yehiel wasn't interested. He was tied to Begin, and that was it."

CHAPTER 17

SURPRISE AT THE VOTING BOOTH

Elections for the Ninth Knesset began on the wrong foot. About three months prior to the elections, before a trip to the United States, Begin came down with gastroenteritis. He recovered, and flew off on his trip. But while in Detroit, the gastroenteritis attacked him again. When he returned to Israel, his physician, Dr. Luria, instructed him to go to Ichilov Hospital to investigate the reason for the repeated illness. In April, on the Monday morning he was supposed to go in for tests, Yehiel went to Begin's home. Begin was meeting with Hanan Porat and Rabbi Moshe Levinger, leaders of the Gush Emunim Jewish settlers movement.

"Begin had great respect for the activity of the Gush Emunim," Yehiel recalled. "But he often suffered in the meetings with them, and there were many. Even as prime minister, his door was always open to them, because as he said to me, 'I want to hear them,' but sometimes it was very hard. I saw the deep suffering they caused him. My impression, a sort of psychological evaluation, was that Begin thought that if he was their age and in their position, he would do as they did. I came to this conclusion based on what I read and heard from people who were present during discussions in the Betar ranks in Poland before the war, people who were what we call activists, but they were more passive types of activists, while Begin was one of the 'hyper-activists.'

"When I observed those meetings, I had a feeling he was thinking to himself – actually, they're right. I mean, at their age and situation, not having national responsibility, they acted as they should have – to demand more, act more, even though there was no consensus on the issue. This sometimes caused him pain. He didn't say anything, but I know it didn't add to his health. More than once, with all due respect, of course, I asked them to free him of their presence. I would walk into the meeting, see what was going on, and say, 'People, the prime minister has another meeting now.' But even if he argued with them sometimes and explained to them why they couldn't do something, afterward he would do everything to pass a decision in that very same spirit. It provoked him to hear them, to feel their pain. He argued with them, but in actuality, he agreed with them, and then he would carry out a decision worrying about the results that might ensue."

At any rate, on that day, before the elections in which he was declared prime minister, Yehiel arrived at Begin's home. Begin told him that he had felt ill in the morning and had phoned Dr. Luria, who told him to go to the internal medicine ward that same day. The phone rang as Begin finished speaking, and Yehiel picked it up – Dr. Luria was on the line, asking why Begin hadn't gone to the hospital. Yehiel replied that he was in a meeting at his home, and that when it was finished, he would go. "Tell him to come at once," Dr. Luria demanded, "because I'm about to leave the hospital."

At that point, Begin finished his conversation with the Gush Emunim representatives. He packed a small bag with his shaving kit, as he realized he might have to remain in the hospital until the tests were completed. Then he went to the hospital along with Yehiel. When they arrived, Dr. Luria announced that he had already prepared a room for Begin with a phone line. He had given instructions as to the necessary tests, and he asserted that "everything would be fine."

After Begin got himself settled, Yehiel said, "I arranged a meeting for you with Moshe Dayan on Wednesday. What should I do?"

"Tell him to come here," Begin requested.

"On Tuesday, I went to him for all kinds of tasks," Yehiel recalled. "Everything really was fine. He spoke with his wife Aliza, listened to the radio, and did the tests. Hospital routine. On Wednesday, I waited at the hospital for Dayan. When Dayan arrived, I left Begin's room. In the meeting, they had planned to talk about the application of the law in Judea and Samaria, and the idea of autonomy. Half an hour later, I went back to see whether they had finished. Just then, Dayan left the room. I escorted him to the elevator and said, 'It will take a few days before he's out of the hospital.'

"Dayan looked at me with his one eye and asked, 'Yehiel, did you ever study medicine?'"

Yehiel didn't reply because in the meantime they had reached the end of the corridor, where they parted. Yehiel returned to Begin's room, and inside he found two doctors and a nurse, wearing severe expressions. Begin's face was sickly gray.

Just a few minutes earlier, Begin had suffered a heart attack.

It took longer than a few days, but he would eventually recover.

"When he was sick, he was always an easy patient," recalled Yehiel. "He never complained or whined. Once he told me that while still in Warsaw, as a youth of twenty, a doctor told him that he was sick. But then Begin went to Siberia, where he went through the harshest trials. Often he felt bad one day, while the next day he was fresh and full of energy. 'You're the proof that the spirit overcomes the body,' I told him more than once. Sometimes he would work from 6 a.m. to 12 a.m. without stopping, with no sign of tiredness. Only on trips abroad would he permit himself a short nap in the afternoon, and only because the schedule demanded it: breakfast, meetings, lunch, a break until 4 p.m., and then more meetings or speeches. We had a regular procedure. At 3:30 p.m., I would go into his room to wake him up. He always napped in an armchair in front of the television. I would turn it off, and he would wake up and ask, 'Why did you turn off the TV?' 'So that you would wake up,' I would reply. 'Is it four o'clock already?' he would ask. Then he would shake himself, and continue with his day."

May 17, 1977: Haim Yavin's pronouncement, "Ladies and gentlemen – turnaround!" on Israel's one and only TV channel caught Yehiel by surprise. Over his thirty years in the opposition, Begin had gained more seats from election to election, but Yehiel did not sense the dramatic shift in public opinion following the Yom Kippur War. "Maybe I was too busy with running around, trips, organizing speeches and appearances," said Yehiel, "so I didn't have time to deal with illusions."

This pessimism came despite the fact that Yehiel supported forming alliances with other parties with opinions similar to the Herut Party. In arguments they had within the Knesset faction, MK Yohanan Bader objected to alliances with all his might. "We're fine on our own," he used to say. "This is our little piece of heaven." More than once, Yehiel would interrupt him: "Dr. Bader, let's say we have twenty mandates, or twenty-four, what will you do with that? We need to put our power together so that instead of just a political alternative, we can become an actual alternative. Otherwise you can make beautiful speeches on the budget and fight in the finance committee against all kinds of biases, but in actuality, you will not be able to implement our policy."

But Yehiel didn't believe they would win, and he thought that after eight failed attempts, Begin was used to it. In one conversation between the two, Yehiel said that he didn't believe they would win this time. Begin listened and replied, "You don't believe it will happen? Okay, so it won't. We'll see." Begin believed.

The Alignment, the existential enemy, also caught a whiff of change. One of the harshest expressions of this was a notice published at the end of the elections, which was a kind of self-eulogy. The word that stood out the most in this notice was "end":

> The screen comes down. The end of the election campaign – May 1977. Will this be an end that is an end? An end of many important and beautiful things that are taken for granted (or seem to be), that were created in this country after much initiative and effort? Or will it be an end that is a beginning – the beginning of a new period that washes away the blemishes of the past and its distortions, but draws from it strength and inspiration? It is in your hands, today, to decide. It is in your hands, today, to enable us – the Labor Party – to conclude and to begin, to renew and to continue.

Those on the left who predicted doom were certain that if Begin won, God forbid, they would have no choice but to pull out their combat boots from the attic, because war with one or another of the Arab countries was only a matter of time. In their wildest dreams, no one ever imagined a peace agreement.

Begin believed he would win, and said to Yehiel on more than one opportunity that he himself didn't feel the need to prepare for the position of prime minister should it fall into his lap. "I've been preparing for it for decades already," he said to Yehiel and others who asked him. "As a youth I began to prepare for the position of prime minister of Israel." Then he added, "Actually, what qualifies one person or another to be prime minister? That his father was prime minister? His grandfather was prime minister? All my life I've dealt with policy, with personal issues, with people's problems. What's a prime minister? He has to deal with issues of the nation, and this is what I've been doing for quite a long time." When asked whether, if and when he was elected, he would make peace with the Arab states, or at least one of them, Begin replied, "I'll manage things differently. In a good way, a Jewish way."

Along with many party leaders, Yehiel was present at Likud party headquarters at Metzudat Ze'ev, now an office building much more elaborate than the small shack he had first encountered on the site, when the votes were counted. Like millions of Israeli citizens, they held their breath. Yehiel pinched himself in disbelief. "We knew we'd have good results," he admitted, "and that Labor would have bad ones, but not to this extent."

The balance swayed farther and farther in favor of Likud. Friends and supporters came to the Metzuda, including fresh devotees who were swept along in the excitement, such as the impatient media – as if at that very moment they were climbing the railing of the *Altalena*. They demanded that Yehiel go to Begin's home, where he had sat the entire evening, and convince him to come to the Metzuda. Yehiel walked over to Begin's home, on the way passing his own home on Ben Zion Avenue. He reached the house on Rosenbaum Street, knocked on the door, and found the leader sitting in his bathrobe in front of the television, sipping a cup of tea. His wife and daughters were in the kitchen. The house definitely did not radiate the overly excited atmosphere of a newly born prime minister.

"They want you to come to the Metzuda," Yehiel announced.

"Let's wait a bit," Begin replied, with utter calm. "Sit, come sit with us. Would you like a cup of tea?"

Yehiel felt that his place at that historical moment was at the Metzuda, so he told Begin he had to return. Begin nodded his head and remained at home. Yehiel went back. Everyone pounced on him – ministers, central party members, journalists, media broadcasters. The media demanded its pound of flesh.

After 2 a.m., following the actual vote count and not just a sampling, it became clear, beyond a shadow of a doubt, that Begin had achieved what he had dreamed of doing for twenty-nine years, most of which he had spent in the "wilderness" of opposition. Only then did Begin leave his home and, together with his wife Aliza and their daughters Leah and Hasia, walked to Metzudat Ze'ev. This time, security guards surrounded him. This was the best evidence that Begin had done it: he was prime minister.

A new page was begun, not only in the history of the State of Israel and the life of Menachem Begin, but in the world of Yehiel Kadishai as well.

"Begin never officially offered me the role of chief of staff for the prime minister's office," Yehiel admitted. "It was simply and naturally understood. I was with him."

On June 20, 1977, the day Begin took office as prime minister, he traveled to Jerusalem in the old Herut Party Peugeot 504. As usual, Begin sat beside the driver. Yehiel sat in back, as this time, for a change, he didn't take the bus. Eliyahu Ben Elissar, who became director-general of the prime minister's office, and Yona Klimovitzky, Begin's secretary, crowded in with Yehiel.

"On the way to the transfer of positions in the prime minister's office, we didn't talk much," Yehiel related. "Begin was sunk in his thoughts, and I in mine. I'm certain that his thoughts were much heavier. We arrived at the conference room next to the prime minister's office. Yitzchak Rabin was waiting for us along with outgoing director-general Amos Eran and several department heads, unit heads, and intelligence service directors. Rabin said a few words and was very statesman-like. Then Begin said a few words, and they drank a *le-hayim*. Rabin was restrained as he introduced us to the employees mentioning their names and positions. He wished Begin success, then walked out. That was it. The new prime minister entered his position: Begin walked into his room, sat down, called me over, and proudly announced, '*Nu*, Yehiel? Shall we begin our work? The nation has been waiting for us for twenty-nine years.' He sat on Rabin's chair as naturally as if he had sat there for a thousand years, or like a Chassid entering his *shtibl* [local synagogue], as if it were the most natural thing in the world."

From that day, and over the coming years, the office employees would hear Prime Minister Begin ask countless times, as he entered his office: "Where's Yehiel?"

Of course, this was nothing new. Benny Begin recalled: "I was witness to this statement many times in our home, directed at me: 'Get me Yehiel,' or 'Call Yehiel,' or 'Bring me Yehiel.' I was the one who phoned Yehiel to tell him to come to my father."

Yehiel continued to describe the first day in the highest office in the State of Israel: "Next they showed me my office. Eli Mizrachi, Rabin's chief of staff, was sitting there. He hadn't yet internalized the fact that there had been a revolution. He didn't want to leave his desk or his position. So what should I do? Throw him out? I couldn't tell him to leave the office. Begin didn't have the heart to fire people either. Most of Rabin's staff remained in their positions. Begin was even surprised one day when he didn't see one of the senior secretaries, whose name was Levana. He asked why she hadn't shown up for work. 'She was Rabin's secretary,' he was told. The only one who started out anew was Yona Klimovitzky, Begin's secretary of many years. All the rest stayed on from Rabin's tenure. The same was true for other members of staff as well. Some even joined us on Begin's visit to the Lubavitcher Rebbe, Rabbi Menachem Mendel Schneerson, shortly after Begin began his term as prime minister."

Begin met with the Lubavitcher Rebbe about two months after he won the election, during his first visit to the US as prime minister. Before meeting with President Jimmy Carter, Begin decided to visit the Rebbe's court to receive his blessing.

"The atmosphere was electric," related Yehiel, who as usual was at Begin's side. "When we reached the street of world Chabad headquarters, we saw hundreds of people on the sides of the road, cheering for Begin. In honor of the new prime minister, the Rebbe came out on the steps of his legendary address at 770 Eastern Parkway, to greet Begin. Begin's limousine stopped in front of the house, and the prime minister got out, waved to the enormous crowd, and went up the steps where the Rebbe awaited him. In an exceptional step, the Rebbe stood in front of the journalists' cameras. He congratulated Begin on his electoral victory, and announced, 'I congratulate him more than one hundred percent, and wish him complete success on behalf of the Jewish people and Eretz Israel. May he merit bringing the full redemption closer through our righteous Messiah, speedily and in our days.'"

Begin went in alone to meet with the Rebbe. "The Rebbe wanted to speak with the prime minister in total privacy," Yehiel explained. "So we sat outside the door and waited for almost an hour until the meeting was over."

Then the members of Begin's entourage were permitted to enter the room and receive the Rebbe's blessing. "We went into the room trembling with anticipation," Yehiel related. "The Rebbe's assistants introduced us, and he blessed each one of us individually. When they introduced me, the secretary told the Rebbe that I was from a family of Lelov Chassidim. At that point the Rebbe raised his head, smiled, and said, "Oh, love of fellow Jews." He was hinting to the motto of the Lelov Chassidic sect, based on love for fellow Jews and spiritual activity with the goal of increasing love among the Jewish people."

Yehiel received a letter from the esteemed rabbi immediately after Rosh Hashanah 1980 (5741):

> During the Days of Repentance, 5741, Sabbatical year, Brooklyn, New York.
> To the honorable, God-fearing, and wise Mr. Yehiel Kadishai, who works tirelessly on the public behalf, may he live a long life.
> Greetings of peace and blessings! In anticipation of the New Year, may it be full of goodness and blessing, I would like to express my good wishes to you and your entire family. May you be written and inscribed for good, and may you have a good and sweet year, both materially and spiritually. I wish you particular success in your position of great responsibility.
> Yours sincerely and respectfully,
> [The Rebbe's signature]
> N.B. We received your prayer note, and we will read it at the gravesite [of the previous Lubavitcher Rebbe, Yosef Yitzchak Schneerson] at an auspicious moment.

Alongside the major events, there were also ordinary days at the office. Yehiel related that although he had found a national position, he couldn't find a chair or table in the office: "I didn't even have a place to sit, so they gave me a chair and I sat beside a small coffee table in the office and worked from there. Eli Mizrachi was a native of Jerusalem, and it was easy for him to get to the office in the morning and sit beside the desk at which he had sat for several years. His job was over, but it was hard for him to internalize that fact. All of a sudden he was 'government' and not someone's political appointment."

"During the winter of 1977, a few months before the elections," recounted Aryeh Naor, "the feeling intensified that golden opportunities were about to arise. For example, Begin had an unexpected meeting in the Knesset cafeteria, as he sat drinking tea. Yehiel and I were sitting beside him when he was approached by Eli Mizrachi. Eli said a polite hello and asked how Begin was feeling. Begin understood that Mizrachi wanted to tell him something, and invited him to sit down.

"Mr. Begin," Mizrachi began, "if you become prime minister, you'll probably bring your own assistants with you, but you've always spoken of a national outlook. Many of the government employees aren't even party members, and some were even in Betar."

"I wouldn't dream of hurting government employees because of their political affiliation," Begin assured him.

After Mizrachi left the table, Begin smiled at Aryeh and Yehiel. "He's speaking in general terms, but of course he means himself. This could be an encouraging sign. No one like him has ever said anything like that to me before."

"I sat at that coffee table for two weeks until I got tired of that game," Yehiel confessed. "One morning I made the trip to Jerusalem early in the morning, or else I slept over in Jerusalem close to the office, and I went to the office very early. I peeked into the room – I jumped for joy! Mizrachi hadn't yet arrived! When he arrived he saw me sitting on his chair. Finally the penny dropped for him – the Rabin period had ended."

Begin appointed Ezer Weizman as defense minister and Simcha Erlich as finance minister. Ariel Sharon was minister of agriculture, which had never been considered an important position. But Sharon was a significant personality, all the more so in light of the fact that he took the issue of the settlements under his wing. But the most important and surprising appointment was foreign minister: Moshe Dayan, the man who had abandoned Labor and switched over to Likud.

Dayan's meeting with Begin in Ichilov was the beginning of his road back to leading the nation. At the time, esteem for Dayan had evaporated not only within his party but also among the public due to the failures of the Yom Kippur War, in which Dayan had served as defense minister, and the world's adoration for him had faded. His party saw him as a burden; Begin saw him as an asset. Begin wanted to bring Dayan into the Likud. Anyone could see that an understanding had developed between the two figures, which matured when Begin picked up the work of assembling the government.

Dayan's appointment provoked an internal storm within the Likud. Yehiel also thought that Dayan did not belong in the foreign minister's office of Begin's government. Before the appointment, in a conversation with Begin, Yehiel expressed doubt about this choice. Things reached a head when the news about Dayan's anticipated appointment reached the public. Families of war victims organized a vehement demonstration opposite Begin's home on Rosenbaum Street in Tel Aviv. Participants even threw stones at the house, damaging a shutter and causing a racket. Yehiel rushed outside and brought representatives of the demonstrators into Begin's home. The prime minister listened seriously to their protests, but he stood firm in his decision, stating, "It's good for the Jewish people."

Begin wasn't particularly interested in admiration or hatred for Dayan, whether public or private. He thought in a different direction altogether: the entire world.

"For the government I head," he said, "I need a foreign minister who may not be loved at home, who may have lost his shine among the Jewish people in the State of Israel, but who is esteemed throughout the world. The world respects him; he is the hero with the patch over his eye. Before they meet with him, every prime minister and foreign minister will make sure the crease in their pants is straight, their clothes are ironed to perfection, and all their buttons are properly closed."

Dayan's image was also the reason why a decade earlier, in 1967,

Begin had insisted that he receive the appointment of defense minister in the national unity government. Begin had essentially paved the way for Dayan's appointment with an eye toward Israel's enemy, who feared the imposing Dayan much more than they feared, for example, Levi Eshkol.

Begin had spent many hours with Dayan. One of their first meetings was during the first period of underground operations in 1944, when Dayan was a senior officer in the Haganah. The relationship between the two was one of mutual admiration. To Begin, Dayan symbolized the daring, courageous Jew, weapon in hand. To Dayan, Begin's worldview reflected his own – that the battle over establishment of the state would be won with firepower as well as political clout. Back then, they met in a secret apartment in Tel Aviv after two operational successes of the Irgun: the takeover of the central radio station in Ramallah in May 1944, and the September 1944 bombing of British CID headquarters in Jerusalem. At the conclusion of their meeting, Dayan said to Begin, "I don't agree with your operations, but you've proved that we can fight the British."

While Begin was engaged in the difficult work of appointing his ministers, "heavy pressure was placed on him by those who considered themselves deserving to be ministers," said Yehiel. "But Begin was well aware of who was capable of being a minister, and who was not. When he decided to appoint Shostak as health minister, people said, 'How can you appoint him to such a vital position? He's not a doctor.' Begin replied, 'He doesn't have to be a doctor, he needs to have a good and honest head on his shoulders.'"

Many also tried to take advantage of their positive ties with Yehiel, pressuring him to give them a recommendation, to propel them toward a soft and smooth landing in a minister's armchair. Yehiel would listen to the request, then discharge the applicant with a short phrase: "We'll see." This was a polite response, because Yehiel never interfered with ministerial appointments. He only served as the messenger.

For chairman of the Knesset, Begin chose Yitzhak Shamir, saying to Yehiel: "*Nu*, look how we've made 'Michael' (Shamir's code name in Lehi) into Knesset chairman." He also told Yehiel that it was important that his former Lehi commander finish his public career in a respectable fashion. Neither Begin nor Yehiel ever imagined that this appointment would serve as the springboard for an even higher position for Shamir, who would take over the premiership after Begin resigned.

As for Begin's own office – Yehiel was appointed chief of staff; party speaker Eliyahu Ben Elissar was director-general; Yona Klimovitzky was chief secretary; and Aryeh Naor became cabinet secretary. In the party, some protested that Begin did not turn over the majority of the main positions to "our people." But Begin paid no attention, emphasizing: "Heads won't roll here." Many of his ardent followers felt that he changed gears, from party to national level. This became crystal clear when he announced to whoever bothered to listen that he had not taken the position of prime minister in order to hand out jobs to his supporters.

Begin's first decision in office was to allow refugees of the Vietnam War to enter Israel. The refugees were fleeing to Japan by boat, but it sprung a leak and the boat started sinking. They were rescued by an Israeli cargo vessel that happened to be passing by. No other state was willing to accept them, so in early 1978, Israel took in one hundred of them, earning an international reputation as a humanitarian nation that took action, while other states took a high and mighty tone but got cold feet when the time came to do something. The operation began, as all of Begin's work did, by calling Yehiel to his office: "Yehiel, please contact Zim Company, and speak to them about bringing the Vietnamese refugees to Israel."

In the closely shared work between Yehiel and Begin, from the long years of opposition and through Begin's premiership, Yehiel always knew exactly where the limits of his responsibility lay, and he refused to deviate from them. For example, he never exploited an opportunity that others in his role might have welcomed: he never participated in a cabinet meeting, not even as a listener. He never stuck his nose into matters that were not in the framework of his position, whether needed or not. "I didn't want to go to cabinet meetings," he said. "I didn't want to know what I didn't have to know. I had a lot of work even without that. I didn't want to know state secrets. I thought it would be better not to know. I could live – and perhaps it was better to live – without knowing the most well-guarded secrets of the State of Israel. Neither did I did not seek out the company of heads of the Mossad and ISA. At that time their identities were considered a state secret of the first order. What did I need them for? To say, 'Yesterday I told the director of the Mossad such-and-such,' or, 'The ISA head told me this and that'?

"In fact, throughout Begin's tenure as prime minister, I participated only once in a cabinet meeting, and this was only after he himself put pressure on me. At our morning meeting in his office, he said, 'Yehiel, this morning you're coming with me to the cabinet meeting. You have to be there.' I asked him what was going to happen at the meeting and why it was important for me to attend. He said, 'You'll see a film made by the Mossad, and you'll see how our soldiers are putting the Ethiopian immigrants onto a boat in the middle of the Indian Ocean. From there they take them to Sharm el-Sheikh, and then they put them on a plane to Israel.' Indeed, at the cabinet meeting a film was shown in which we saw hundreds of Jewish refugees from Ethiopia walking across the desert, on highly dangerous paths. They were placed on a boat in the Indian Ocean, which sailed to Sharm el-Sheikh, and from there they boarded a plane to Israel. It was a top secret operation, and only a handful knew about it. *Nu*, so I saw it and I knew. So what? I could have lived without knowing. I would have lived even had I found out about it together with everyone else, when it was officially publicized. Knowing something before everyone else is not something that makes a big impression on me. The same went for military tours. I left that to the military secretary. That was his job, not mine."

The covert relocation of Ethiopian Jewish refugees to Israel, disclosed at that cabinet meeting, was kept shrouded in secrecy by Israeli intelligence so as not to disrupt the operation. On one of Begin's trips to the US, he spoke at the annual conference of the Zionist Federation of America. Jews in the United States assumed that Israel didn't want to accept the persecuted Ethiopians, thinking that Israelis were prejudiced against the idea of black Jews.

"At the conference, held in the Renaissance Hotel in Detroit," Yehiel recalled, "some radical students began to shout insults at Begin. One of them went wild and began to spit and flail around, and there was one red-haired guy who really went mad. Everyone screamed at Begin, excoriating the State of Israel for not accepting the Ethiopian Jews. But in those very days, each night hundreds and thousands of Ethiopians were arriving. But we couldn't talk about it."

When they saw the students running amok and losing control, Yehiel and Yehuda Avner suggested to Begin that they approach the agitated redhead, and hint that his complaint was unjustified.

"We won't tell him anything secret," Yehiel and Yehuda explained. "We'll simply hint that we invite him to Israel to see that there's no basis for his screams and accusations. We'll even tell him that it would be hard to pull the wool over his eyes and present Russian Jews as if they're from Ethiopia."

Yet Begin stood firm. "Let them stone me and spit on me. I won't allow anyone to give even a hint on this topic."

Eventually, after Begin withdrew from public life and shut himself up at 1 Zemach Street in Jerusalem, the *kesim*, religious leaders of the Ethiopian community, submitted a request to Yehiel. They wanted to present to Begin a parchment certificate, appointing him as honorary president of the Ethiopian community.

"Can I arrange a visit with you?" asked Yehiel.

Again Begin was unyielding: "Yehiel, they shouldn't dare come here. The moment they come, it will be in the papers, and there are still a few more Jews left in Ethiopia. So long as there is one Jew in Ethiopia, I will not permit any leaks that might endanger them."

The person who always had inside knowledge of these secrets and others was Begin's military secretary, Brigadier General Ephraim (Freuka) Poran. He had served in this position under Yitzchak Rabin, and remained in the post under Begin. Regarding top-secret affairs, he commented, "At least in the areas in which I was involved, sometimes I would beg Yehiel: you'll appreciate being inside, in the cabinet meeting. Listen to what they are saying, to what's going on. But he would say: if they call me, I'll go in. If they don't call me, I won't go in. I have enough work on my desk. I do my own work."

Aside from this, "Yehiel brought a wonderful atmosphere into the office," Poran disclosed. "He was a faithful servant in the best sense of the word. In positions of power like his, usually you see a lot of people who try to build themselves up while serving. Yehiel was far away from that approach. You saw that first and foremost, he took care of the person he was supposed to serve in his role as prime minister. Furthermore, the same line that had stretched in front of the ticket office moved over to the prime minister's office – all the needy, anyone who wanted to get to the prime minister. Of course Yehiel couldn't let them all in to Begin, so they all stood in line for Yehiel. He took care of them. In addition, he was always willing to consider any suggestion. He was friends with everyone, from Herut to the Communists. He was willing to help [prominent peace activists] Lova Eliav and Abie Nathan, and anyone else if he thought an issue was worth supporting. In many cases when I wasn't able to convince the prime minister, I would go to Yehiel and say, come, help me. He would come in, and often succeeded in convincing him."

Poran added with a smile: "Begin's handwriting was illegible. In many cases, I was present when he called Yehiel over and asked, 'What did I write here?' Yehiel would decipher it for him."

But Yehiel denied this: "That's an exaggeration. True, he might have said, 'I can't read the word that's here, but in that spot, this certain word should be written.'"

Ilena Binenstock met Yehiel when she began to direct the bureau of public inquiries in the prime minister's office. "Suddenly I realized that he had an independent bureau of public inquiries that he had carried along with him for the past twenty years. There were needy people who came to him, but he also received official public inquiries that fell between the cracks, that weren't answered by government bureaucrats. Yehiel's attention and his vision, the human aspect, charmed me, and gave me the opportunity to work. I knew he worked in the same spirit as the prime minister, but he didn't make a big deal out of it.

"Once, a disabled woman contacted the prime minister's office. She said that two months earlier, she was supposed to receive a wheelchair from the welfare office, but she hadn't received it yet. I checked into it, and the welfare office replied that there were a hundred disabled people who were waiting for wheelchairs, but that the office was also waiting, to get the allocation from the finance ministry. I asked the amount, and I found out that it was a relatively small amount. I went to Yehiel, and he called the finance ministry right away. It turned out that someone had forgotten to send the allocation to the welfare ministry. Yehiel's phone call served to remind them, and the issue was solved. That week, one hundred disabled persons were able to leave their homes."

This young woman's request is typical of those that reached Yehiel's desk: "I am a first-year student in the faculty of architecture and city planning at the Technion. I began my academic studies after finishing two years of full military service in the military government of Shechem. I read in *Haaretz* about the Menachem and Bina Fruchter scholarship fund, of which you are a trustee. I am contacting you to request scholarship funding. There are six people in my family, and my parents are elderly. My father is a clerk in the Petah Tikva municipality, and my mother is a homemaker, so my father's salary is our only income. My parents are making a supreme effort to permit me to study at the Technion, but they are collapsing under the burden and can't continue to support me. I ask that you agree to my request and authorize scholarship funding for me from this fund."

The matter was arranged.

Another request came from an acquaintance of Yehiel's in Haifa, who wanted to help H. R., a friend who had arrived in Israel on the eve of Yom Kippur in 1938 with a group of Betar members from Vilna. "At present, H. is in a terrible state," the Haifa resident wrote. "I have information from a highly qualified source that only you can help to get him into the Sephardic retirement home on Maimon Street in Haifa. Please help us and have mercy on us – all the chances are that he will recover there, according to the advice of a physician who examined him many months ago. He can cover all the expenses, of course – let's not overstate his situation."

The issue was taken care of.

Another request came from Los Angeles in February 1979. The writer, A. K., told Yehiel in her letter: "I am permitting myself to contact you with a personal request, in the hopes that you will be able to help me. I am the secretary of the general consul in Los Angeles, and I have been in this office for over three and a half years. Simultaneously, I am studying at the university for my bachelor's degree, and I'll be finished this September. Recently, a new regulation was instituted in the foreign ministry regarding local employees abroad. This regulation specifies a maximum period of three years of employment for office staff. I understand that under this policy, my position will end on March 31. Because the end of my employment will harm my plans to complete my studies and return to Israel, I request your personal involvement to extend my employment at the consulate until September of this year, when I will finish my studies. Again, please excuse me for contacting you personally, but I do so in the absence of another solution for my dilemma."

The matter was resolved.

On another topic, H. K. from Kibbutz Sa'ar in the Western Galilee wrote to Yehiel in September 1983: "Several months after the signing of the peace agreement with Egypt, I thought to create a sculpture symbolizing this event. The sculpture is of two hands placed together in the shape of a dove. The thumbs point upward, symbolizing success; the palms placed together symbolize peace. Within the hands I sculpted the busts of Menachem Begin and Anwar Sadat. I planned to send you the sculpture some time ago, but this plan was delayed. I'm sending you two photos of both sides of the sculpture, made in clay. The existing sculpture is cast in plaster and looks more exact than in the photos. If you are interested in the sculpture, I would be glad to send it to you." Yehiel replied: "I am very grateful to you for your wish to grant the prime minister a precious gift of your own creation, a sculpture symbolizing the peace agreement between Israel and Egypt. Perhaps we should discuss this by phone in order to arrange sending it to the prime minister. Thank you for your kind attention and the lovely compliment."

Ilena Binenstock spoke of Yehiel's "open door" policy. "He didn't have a regular office with reception hours from 2 to 4 p.m. People arrived at his office exasperated with the bureaucracy, and they were astonished to find that his door was open wide and he was more than accessible. They told him that sometimes they would knock for two months on the door of a junior clerk, asking him for an explanation of why they weren't eligible for a loan or other type of assistance, but the clerk never had time for them. After exhausting all other avenues, they would arrive at the prime minister's office, and the door was open. There was not one civilian whose requests were not answered, who wanted to see Yehiel and was not admitted. There was not one case when a civilian received the answer, you can't meet with him. Often, when I was asked to find out why the clerk in the relevant office had deferred or ignored the civilian, I was given the answer, 'He's an annoyance.' In retrospect we found out that the number of actual annoyances was small, while the number of civilians who just wanted to hear an explanation of what and how was large. Sometimes, people got a full answer from Yehiel or the office, and sometimes they didn't get an answer, but they went away satisfied, because they knew that they had been taken care of appropriately."

"One day," related Yehuda Avner, Begin's advisor for Diaspora Affairs, "I saw a strange figure leaving Yehiel's office. The man was wearing shabby clothes, and a tattered coat was slung around his shoulders. I recognized his face. Then I remembered – this was the beggar I often saw in central Jerusalem."

"What's that beggar doing in your office?" Avner asked Yehiel. "Do you know him?"

"He needs help," Yehiel replied. "Yes, I know him. His name is Kreisky."

"What?" Avner was astonished.

"Shaul Kreisky," Yehiel replied. "He's the brother of the chancellor of Austria, Bruno Kreisky."

Yehiel's voice was calm, but Yehuda Avner gaped in amazement. Kreisky was the Jewish Austrian statesman who opposed Zionism, and one of the severest critics of Israel's position on the Arab-Israeli conflict. He was one of the first in the world to recognize the PLO, and permitted the murderers' organization to operate in his country as the legitimate representative of the Palestinian people. He turned a cold shoulder to Prime Minister Golda Meir when she met him in Vienna, announcing that he was the only leader in Europe who hadn't been blackmailed by her. Avner peeked again at the beggar, and saw that he had already made his way to the end of the corridor toward the steps outside.

"You're joking," Avner said to Yehiel.

"No joke," replied Yehiel. "Kreisky's been living here for years. He's a big fan of Begin. Run after him and ask him yourself."

"I did so," Avner related, "and everything was perfectly true."

The son of Betty Cohen of Degania was a navigator whose plane went down in the Yom Kippur War on Egyptian soil. His was one of nineteen missing bodies. Betty's desperate efforts to locate her son's body took her to Yehiel's office. "I found a man whom words cannot describe. I found a father. A father for these boys, the MIAs. A worried father. To every letter I sent, all around the world, Yehiel added a few words, and I knew those words added value to the letter. It wasn't what I wrote that was important, but what he added. With all of his energetic political activity, Yehiel's basic principle was human contact, interpersonal relations. I would get to his office at a quarter to seven in the morning. I had many hesitations about whether I could add to the burden of a man who was already so busy. When he saw me, he would say, 'Good morning, Betty, come in,' and together we opened the office. He opened the windows, showed me a chair, and never forgot to tell me that if I ever needed him, I shouldn't hesitate. Once, when I was in Jerusalem, he called and said, 'Betty, come to the office right now. I have hot pizza, we can eat it together.' I grew up without a father, but in him I found a father in every sense of the word."

Mati Shmuelevitz, director-general of the prime minister's office, related that he often went by Yehiel's home to take him to the office in Jerusalem, to save him the trip by taxi – about which Yehiel himself never once complained. Sometimes he caught a glimpse of the "office" that Yehiel had at home. "There was always someone waiting for him in the street," Shmuelevitz divulged. "There was always someone who needed something. Once I saw Yehiel sitting on a bench on Ben Zion Avenue with someone, listening to his complaints. On the way to the car, Yehiel would pass by his mailbox and pull out the bundle of letters people had left him overnight. He would finish his conversation with the man in the street, jump into the car, and read the letters on the way. From time to time, he would hand me a letter and say, 'Here, you read this,' or 'Take a look at this' – they were all requests, some of them truly strange. Sometimes, in his room in the prime minister's office, at 11 a.m., you could see him sitting there, listening and taking care of the complaints of a Jew he had met on the taxi trip to Jerusalem, on the days when he didn't ride with me. His output in this area was massive. No lists, no index cards, no diary – Yehiel beside the phone would solve between thirty and forty issues in a day. Everything was recorded in his memory, and when he finished one subject, he would sigh deeply and say, '*Nu*, this matter is closed.' Also, we must recall that this heavy burden was in addition to his role as chief of staff."

Shmuelevitz added, "Throughout the history of the prime minister's office, we can always find examples of friction between the director-general and the chief of staff. Yehiel's tenure was an idyllic period." Indeed, Yehiel's acquaintances say that in the office, as he was throughout his work with Begin, Yehiel was never a man of conflict, but a man of service. Above all, the people he knew over his career, in all his dealings, say that he was a good person. It sounds better in Yiddish, the language he loved best: he was a *mensch*.

"Begin became very dependent on him," said Shmuelevitz. "I remember dozens of cases when Begin would finish a conversation with the words, 'Let's ask Yehiel what he thinks.'"

Yehiel denied this, saying "He didn't have to hear from me whether I agreed on certain things. He could tell by the look on my face. We spoke with our eyes. I don't recall if I ever criticized him. On rare occasions I might say something, but it was much easier for me to say it in another's name.

"The work between us was never limited to certain hours," Yehiel continued. "For example, when we lived on Nahmani Street, one day I went by Begin's home to check whether there was any change in the next day's agenda. As I approached his home, I saw him standing outside with Yosef Sapir. I found out later that a second before I arrived, Begin said to Sapir after they concluded an issue, 'I'll check into it with Yehiel.' Then I suddenly appeared from around the corner. Sapir asked, 'How did Yehiel know to come to you right now, the exact second that you needed him?' Begin replied, 'Yehiel just knows…'"

The day began in the prime minister's office when Yehiel entered Begin's suite. Together they worked on short- and long-term projects, went over the schedule, decided what they wanted to postpone, pushed up what they wanted to get done early, and canceled what they wanted to cancel.

The only pause Yehiel had in his daily schedule was when Begin took an afternoon nap. When this happened, Yehiel would take off his shoes, put his feet up on the desk, and converse with the people around him in "the language of the people," as Aryeh Naor described it. At those times, he was completely relaxed.

***

Yehiel's political nemesis, who was of course also Menachem Begin's, as well as his ideological opponent, was leftist MK Yossi Sarid. Yet Sarid asserted, "Yehiel was a man after my own heart. He was always pleasant and in good humor. With Yehiel, you could sit at a table without opening an account, without closing an account – no accounts. It wasn't easy for me to maintain a friendship with someone who was on the other side of the fence – a friendship beyond the tensions, beyond the battles. Through Yehiel, we proved to ourselves that we weren't only opponents, but also human beings."

Aryeh (Lova) Eliav, also from the enemy political camp, asserted: "Yehiel was a man with a soul. He was able to rise above political calculations. His open door was open to people from all ends of the political spectrum. I worked closely with Yehiel on the issue of the prisoners and MIAs, in the days when we took care of the widow of Eli Cohen, who was hanged in Damascus. He took care of matters of the soul. Begin was able to grant him the freedom and the initiative to attend to these matters, and Yehiel did above and beyond. I could contact him in the middle of the night, just as during the day, on a painful matter, and he would come to my assistance. Yehiel's worldview was based on his being the address for every needy individual. In short – he was a man who loved his fellow Jew."

An apt description of this quality was presented by Baruch Duvdevani, director of the Jewish Agency's aliyah department, in an award ceremony for "Honorees of Yeshivat Nir Kiryat Arba," which was held in the Chagall Auditorium in the Knesset in April 1983:

> I would like to introduce you to a modest Jew with a generous soul, a humble Jew who is a symbol of unity, one who does for all with persistence and loyalty, and does not ask for anything for himself. He does everything to glorify the Name of Heaven and for the sake of the issue itself. He is against titles, but there's no way out – he'll have to live with it, just as he lives with many other things.
>
> This man is not just chief of staff of the prime minister's office, and [proverbial] chief armor-bearer to our prime

minister. He has his own long past. He grew up in a Chassidic family, and his soul has Chassidic roots. During the war, he served in the British army and in the Jewish Brigade, and then he was active in the refugee camps in Germany and Italy. I recall that in Italy, we met once by chance on a train that was taking us to camps in the south, in the most difficult days after the Holocaust. He was going there to check the Irgun weaponry in southern Italy. (Then as well he was an armor bearer, but for a different kind of armor…) After that, he returned to Israel. For years he helped families who had lost their loved ones in the War of Independence, with modesty and humility, with his characteristic love for the Jewish people. Like everything he does, he did this job diligently, patiently, and graciously. In 1964, he became aide to Menachem Begin before he became prime minister, and then chief of staff of the prime minister's office.

Many know, but others are unaware, of how he transformed his office – the hallway that led into the prime minister's drawing room – into an institution. He transformed it into the office of the entire nation. Everyone came to him: ministers attending to their business, directors, civilians of all strata, people who struggled, who needed all kinds of social assistance, who had serious personal problems. He welcomed all with a friendly expression. Aside from welfare issues, some requested his assistance on matters of education – and he guided them kindly, with his unique sense of humor, with the optimism that characterized him so deeply. He was always optimistic, happy, always polite and full of love for fellow Jews. He was always running to help others, calling offices, calling ministers – and so he became an institution in and of himself, an institution for research, for love of other Jews, and the love of friendship.

He really doesn't want what we're giving him today. He always says to me, "I'm only a *shammash* [a sexton]." Once I replied, "You're that *shammash* candle [the "helper candle" used to light the Hannukah candles] that Herzl mentions in one of his texts about Hanukkah candles. Night after night he lights another one of the candles, and he explains to the children the meaning of each candle. Then he comes to the last candle, the *shammash*, and says, 'This candle is the most important one of all.' Why? Because it lights all the other candles, but for itself, it asks nothing." The reward for doing a mitzvah is another mitzvah. May you continue serving as armor-bearer for Mr. Menachem Begin, our prime minister, for many long and prosperous years.

This is indeed what came to pass. Yossi Sarid added: "In Yehiel, I found something unusual, unique. He was a man who knew his place. He knew that his place was beside Begin – at Begin's side, but not in Begin's place. I knew so many aides and public relations directors and advisors. They would get confused at times. Yehiel, however, stood in the shadows for so many years, but he never turned pale. He always maintained his own color."

Yehiel himself used the title of *shammash*, but with a small correction: he was in service not to a human being, but to an issue. He defined it as such: "I don't find any inferiority in serving as a *shammash*. In the synagogue, the *shammash* has a very important job. Without him, there would be no light, no Chumashim, and no *siddurim*. He attends to public matters faithfully, and does a valuable service."

One of the former office staff members emphasized: "Yehiel was far from being a fanatical follower of Begin. He did not shrink from disagreeing with him, but always gently, avoiding conflict. Often this came in the form of a mere aside, formulated with the utmost tact. But it was obvious that the prime minister absorbed it."

All of Yehiel's acquaintances noted his modesty. But only a few noticed that in addition to modesty forming an inseparable part of his personality, this characteristic also served Begin – and that was the most important thing to Yehiel. He wasn't waiting for compliments on the fact that he rode the bus to the office, but realized that by doing so, he sent a message to the public that this was a modest office, not wasteful, and this was helpful to Begin. He transferred the compliments to Begin, and did not keep them for himself.

"Yehiel was not simple," said Aryeh Naor. "But on his list of priorities, service to Begin always stood in first place, with no demand for any recompense. This also explains the fact that when Begin wrote his will after the Six-Day War, he chose to give it to Yehiel for safeguarding, above of all his children."

"The fact that my father gave his will to Yehiel to keep," said Benny Begin, "is a microcosm of their friendship, of the trust and personal relationship between them. To me, it's like an embrace. The document is short and to the point, with nothing in it except where to bury him when the time came. It begins with, 'Dear Yehiel,' and ends, 'With love.'"

CHAPTER 18

SHARPENING SWORDS

The first year of the Begin government, 1977, was bursting with activity, as if someone thought they had to cram in as much as possible, because they didn't know how much longer Begin's strength would hold out to complete the tasks that had awaited him for so many years. He was already not in the best of health.

A prime minister's office, by nature, is like the heart within the body that absorbs everything, and also the head that leads. Yehiel sat in the midst of it all. All these activities – of which a selection is enumerated below – were within Yehiel's field of operation as part of his position. In addition, he made the effort to reply to the flood of personal letters that reached the office.

- July: The government recognized settlements beyond the so-called Green Line.
- August: The government decided to establish three new settlements in Judea and Samaria.
- September: After a long period of calm, Katyusha rockets were fired from Lebanon into Safed and Kiryat Shemona. Gush Emunim requested to establish twelve settlements. The US government condemned settlement activity in Judea and Samaria. At the end of the month, the Housing Ministry issued its plan to expand Yamit, then a settlement in the northern Sinai peninsula, to a city of 100,000 inhabitants.
- October: The Americans and the Soviets publicized a joint declaration under which any Israeli-Arab peace agreement would have to ensure "the legitimate rights of the Arab people," an announcement which caused anger in Israel. An economic

transformation began when the government rescinded control over foreign currency and the value added tax was raised to 12 percent.

- November: Three residents of Nahariya were killed by Katyusha rockets. The IDF retaliated with artillery and air power. President Sadat of Egypt announced to the Egyptian parliament his willingness to visit Israel in order to conclude a peace agreement. When this became known in the prime minister's office, Yehiel warned Begin, "Watch out for him – he looks like a big bastard." Begin replied, "Yehiel, the good Lord has given us a measure of brains as well as him." Begin extended a formal invitation to the Egyptian president, Sadat accepted, and landed in Israel in what was understood as a history-making event. He came for a three-day visit, and when he returned to Cairo from Jerusalem, his people gave him an enthusiastic reception.

- December: The first El Al plane landed in Cairo, bringing with it the Israeli delegation to the Cairo conference between Israel, Egypt, the US, and the UN. Defense Minister Ezer Weizman flew to meetings in Cairo with his Egyptian counterpart. Begin raised the issue of the Autonomy Plan for Judea and Samaria. Gush Emunim demonstrated throughout Israel against the government's peace plan. While deep fear reigned in Judea and Samaria, the Gaza Strip and the Rafiah salient, Begin went to a summit meeting with Sadat in Ismailia, and the Knesset approved the government's proposed peace plan. Inflation rose to 34.6 percent.

Undoubtedly, a pivotal moment in history for many Israelis was the moment when Sadat appeared in the doorway of his presidential airplane at Ben-Gurion Airport. Yehiel was present, and he was in the Knesset when Sadat spoke. What were his feelings in those monumental days? Yehiel shared: "I'm not the type to get particularly emotional about things, but definitely his arrival was a historical moment, and his visit to the Knesset was a historical event. It was interesting, no doubt about it."

During the long process of peace negotiations between the two countries, Begin visited Egypt several times. The euphoria that surrounded him led him to ignore basic security regulations, to the horror of his Israeli and Egyptian security guards. Yehiel revealed: "Several times, when we went to Cairo or Ismailia, and he saw a big crowd cheering for him, he would ask us to stop the car. He would go out into the crowd, mix among the people and shake hands. He was received with great enthusiasm. His guards almost fainted, and rushed to tighten protection against any unexpected attack. Begin's last visit to Egypt was to Alexandria. He and his entourage stayed in a glittering palace, while the journalists who accompanied him stayed in an average hotel some three hundred meters away."

After the visit, Begin and his staff were supposed to return to Israel on a morning flight. First they went down to the dining room for breakfast, where Begin noticed that the staff physician, Professor Mervyn Gottesman, was missing.

"Where is Professor Gottesman?" Begin asked Yehiel.

"He went to visit Noah Moses, the publisher of *Yedioth Aharonoth*," came the reply.

"What happened to Moses?" Begin pressed.

"He felt ill in the night," Yehiel informed him. "Apparently something in the stomach. Professor Gottesman went to examine him."

"So we have to go visit Noah Moses," Begin decided. All their equipment was already packed for the trip to the airport and onward to Israel. The security guards had already completed their briefings and final checks of the travel route, and suddenly Begin made a change of the planned route – something that security personnel do not particularly appreciate. The Egyptian chief of protocol, who was in charge of the Egyptian security personnel, realized that something was going on. He asked Yehiel if something unexpected had happened.

"Yes," Yehiel replied. "Apparently Mr. Begin is going to visit Noah Moses, the publisher of one of the major Israeli newspapers. He's in the hotel under our physician's care."

The moment the chief of protocol heard this, he jumped to make the unplanned arrangements. First, he instructed the Egyptian security personnel – in Alexandria these were navy soldiers – attached to the entourage. The strict ceremonial protocol called for trumpet fanfares as the entourage exited the hotel. In addition, on both sides of the road, along the entire route from the hotel to the destination, whether to a restaurant or theater, navy soldiers had to stand guard. After Begin's announcement, the chief of protocol had to make these arrangements not just from the palace to the airport, but also from the palace to the journalists' hotel.

"A few minutes later," Yehiel recalled, "we left the palace. The trumpets sounded their fanfare according to protocol, and security personnel were on guard on the road to the hotel. Begin's convoy made its way to the hotel within two or three minutes, and Begin went up to Noah Moses's room. Dr. Gottesman explained that Moses's status had stabilized, but he still could not fly, and needed at least another day to recover. Begin wished him a full recovery, returned to his car, drove to the airport, and flew back to Israel with his entourage."

The next day, Moses flew back to Israel. Paula Moses, his wife, called Begin and thanked him warmly for his special attention to her husband, which her entire family appreciated.

***

The year 1978 was also packed with activity for Israel with Begin at its helm:

- January: Begin warned that if Egypt did not agree to retain the Israeli settlements in Sinai, Israel might be forced to retract its offer to return the Sinai Peninsula. Eventually, things did not turn out that way, but in the meantime the government decided to expand these settlements. The town of Katzrin was established in the Golan Heights.
- February: The "Orange Attack" – consumers in the Netherlands discovered imported Jaffa oranges that had been injected with mercury, an act of sabotage by Palestinian terrorists.
- March: A terror attack on the coastal road near Glilot junction outside Tel Aviv took the lives of thirty-five Israelis. In retaliation, the IDF began Operation Litani to wipe out terrorist cells in southern Lebanon.
- April: Lieutenant General Raphael (Raful) Eitan was appointed as IDF chief of staff, and Yitzhak Navon as president.

- May: Israel celebrated thirty years since its founding.
- June: An explosive device blew up a bus in Jerusalem, killing six.
- July: Defense Minister Ezer Weizman met with Sadat in Austria in order to set the wheels of peace in motion again. The foreign ministers of Israel, Egypt, and the United States met in London.
- August: Terrorists attacked shoppers in the Carmel market in Tel Aviv as well as El Al staff in London, killing two.

In September, Begin and Sadat and their diplomatic teams arrived at Camp David, the US presidential retreat, for nearly two weeks of peace negotiations mediated by President Jimmy Carter. The treaty that emerged from these talks, "A Framework for the Conclusion of a Peace Treaty between Egypt and Israel," is considered the highlight of Menachem Begin's political career, the act for which he and Sadat shared the Nobel Peace Prize.

Yehiel, naturally, accompanied the prime minister to the historic meeting. "The Camp David summit was the most exciting experience of my life," Yehiel acknowledged.

Brigadier General Ephraim (Freuka) Poran, Begin's military secretary, who was also a member of the Israeli delegation to the Camp David talks, reported that "There were many instances throughout that dramatic conference, not just at the end, in which Yehiel served Begin as a barometer of public opinion. Begin would prepare a proposal, for example, on the issue of autonomy. He would sit for hours and edit the proposal, which was entirely his own idea. After he finished writing, the first thing he would do was to read the text to Yehiel and ask for his opinion, which he definitely respected, and he would often even make changes according to Yehiel's advice. Then he would show it to other people and listen to their comments. But Yehiel was always the first one to see things and express his opinion."

Yehiel revealed what he heard from Begin regarding the framework autonomy agreement ("Framework for Peace in the Middle East"), which was to establish an autonomous self-governing authority in the

West Bank and the Gaza strip. The entire purpose of this agreement, Begin asserted, was to define the issues exactly, leaving no possibility of misunderstanding or deviation. The moment one of the negotiators on the Israeli side questioned the intent of the terminology, the entire course of the negotiations could be changed. Begin therefore gave exact definitions for many points that seemed strange to other members of the Israeli delegations. For example, the expression "legitimate rights." Begin said, in the presence of the Egyptians, that to him, legitimate rights were defined as rights to autonomy, for the Palestinians to manage their own affairs, all under the framework of self-rule. Each time the word "council" was mentioned, Begin said the intention was "administrative council" – not referring to a law-making body, an actual Palestinian entity, or what they called "self-determination." The moment the Palestinians had the right to self-determination, they could establish a Palestinian state, and so everything he wrote was designed to prevent this, even after the five-year initial period defined in the agreement. Begin never intended to give the Palestinians the right to establish a Palestinian state in the territories of Judea and Samaria. God forbid, he would say – God forbid.

"A look at the composition of the delegation reveals Begin's intentions," said Aryeh Naor, who was then cabinet secretary. The Camp David delegation included Attorney General Aharon Barak; Israeli Ambassador to the US Simcha Dinitz; Major General Avraham (Abrasha) Tamir; Foreign Ministry Attorney General Meir Rosenne; Ephraim Poran, Begin's military secretary; Major General (Res.) Ilan Tehila; Dan Pattir, Begin's media consultant; Naphtali Lau-Lavie, Dayan's spokesman; Elyakim Rubinstein, Dayan's assistant; and Yehiel. "There were two [ministers]: Dayan and Weizman. Their positions were more moderate than Begin's. He didn't include any of the Herut Party members as advisor – not from his office nor from among the MKs – except for Yehiel. He did not invite ministers who might have taken a more hawkish position, such as [Haim] Landau, who had already participated in a discussion with Carter on the Autonomy Plan the previous December. Begin was well aware of the positions of Barak, Dinitz, and Tamir, the most senior of the advisors: throughout the internal discussions, and in meetings with the Americans and Egyptians, their positions were more compromising than his. Undoubtedly, he chose this composition purposely, in order to reach an agreement, in order to make peace.

"He knew that during the summit, he might be forced to make difficult decisions. He could avoid this by leaving the decisive authority in the hands of the government, but he did not want to do so. He proposed granting the ministerial team the authority to decide, depending on the circumstances that would develop, because he wanted to conclude the summit with an agreement, not with a postponement and certainly not with a breakdown."

"Several times," Yehiel recalled, "Begin asked me how far off he could go, how the party would react to these things. I told him that the majority would accept it. Was this a consideration he was willing to take into account? I think that if he wasn't willing to take it into account, he wouldn't have asked. Dayan had a big influence on the negotiations, but my personal role was not significant. After all, I wasn't on the negotiating team. I could only talk about what happened in the meetings, in Begin's room, or when he would come into my room, or when we sat and drank tea together. When he would ask [my opinion], I would answer.

"All in all, to characterize the negotiations, Dayan, Weizman, and Attorney General Aharon Barak were more flexible; attorney Meir Rosenne was on the side of the right-wing extremists; Dinitz was on Begin's side, but then he changed his position. There were a few others like me who didn't participate, because we weren't on the negotiating staff, but we listened. Our contribution was not political or contemplative. In personal conversations after the sessions, I would tell Begin what I thought.

"In the discussions themselves, they discussed every comma and period. Weizman didn't like to hear all the arguments over fine points, and he would always say, 'Leave it, move on, keep going!' or something like that. He didn't propose any formulations, certainly not legal ones, but not practical ones either. He was a catalyzer – he would jump up and down, leave the room and come back. There was no organized discussion with him on any topic. He would make a comment on one issue or another, whatever he heard the others talking about. In our private conversations, Begin called him 'mischievous' and a 'nice guy,' meaning he was not serious. Begin, by the way, was not particularly influenced by Weizman's position. Dayan was dominant. But as American writer William Quandt, who was also a member of the US National Security Council, wrote in *Camp David: Peacemaking and Politics*, the only one who knew what he wanted, and achieved what he wanted, was Begin."

Yehiel emphasized: "All of the staff – including Begin, Dayan, and Weizman – were new to international politics, even if they had previously held government positions. At the stage of discussions held before the actual negotiations, at Begin's request I brought him a pile of books from the Knesset library with peace agreements from the eighteenth and nineteenth centuries. Begin studied this material for many long hours, so he could bring proofs from various peace treaties. He delved into each word and comma, but unfortunately, he didn't have a supportive precedent from the previous governments of the State of Israel.

"He also had to battle within his delegation," Yehiel continued. "In fact, Begin met with a three-pronged front. First of all, disagreement within his delegation, as Dayan and Weizman said specifically that they did not appreciate his exacting approach to every jot and tittle. The legal argument didn't interest them at all. Begin also battled the American and Egyptian delegations, who said these things were 'unimportant.' It was good he insisted, because there were Egyptian position papers that he rejected immediately. Clearly, if things had reached the point where Begin couldn't implement the minimum conditions necessary for autonomy, and I'm not talking about Sinai, then peace with the Egyptians would never have come about.

"After he was no longer prime minister, he said about the framework agreement for autonomy: 'It depends who handles the negotiations. If they are directed by people who are in agreement with us, then autonomy will continue as long as the Arabs want it. If the Arabs want something more than autonomy – it won't happen. Negotiations will be held, and we'll come and say: This is Eretz Israel, we have to apply the law. In any case, the situation will return to the previous state of affairs, with no peace agreement, and the forces will continue to stand in the places they reached on June 11, 1967. If the people handling the negotiations are willing to establish a Palestinian state, no matter which party they represent, this will be a disaster for the Jewish people. Even a Palestinian state in Jericho alone will carry the flag of November 29, 1947, and demand that the borders be changed in accordance with the UN [Partition Plan], which includes Ramle, Lod, Jaffa, and the Galilee.'"

One afternoon, Yehiel went out for a walk with Begin on the charming paths of the Camp David grounds. On the left they passed Sadat's cabin, while behind them was Ezer Weizman's, with Carter's in front. As they strolled leisurely, the door of Carter's cabin suddenly opened and the US president came down the path. He walked up to Begin, and as they stood beside a majestic tree they struck up a short conversation. In the meantime, Moshe Dayan joined them.

"We have to conclude the issue of the settlements in Sinai," Carter said to Begin.

"We can't conclude," Begin replied. "We're authorized to make an agreement, but whatever we agree on has to be approved by the Knesset."

"I hope you won't participate in the discussion," Carter said, as he knew that Begin would object and influence the others.

"How can the prime minister not participate?" Dayan asked.

"I'll think about it," Begin promised.

"That was the end of the conversation," Yehiel reported. "We returned to Israel, and the Knesset passed it with a majority." Yehiel himself objected with all his might to dismantling the settlements in Sinai. But he kept his mouth shut. Actually, he didn't have to say a word, because Begin knew how to read him, just like Yehiel knew how to read Begin, and Yehiel had no doubt that Begin was well aware of his opinion.

Begin's relationship with Carter was cool. There was no chemistry between them, but on some level, they had shared interests. Around that period, Begin visited Jewish communities in the US. He had no intention of meeting with Carter, because the order of diplomatic events did not call for such a meeting. The problem was that at that time – unlike during the term of Ben-Gurion, who visited the US often without meeting the president – it was accepted protocol that whenever the prime minister of Israel came to the US he would meet with the president as a matter of course, as obliged by the reality of the situation, and as a demonstration of close friendship. During Begin's trip to visit the Jewish community, no meeting was planned with Carter, and the media exulted: "Carter Belittles Begin," shouted the headlines.

At one point, while Begin was conversing with Secretary of State Cyrus Vance in his hotel room, the White House called and asked to speak with Vance. The American took the phone, and he was told that President Carter was just three blocks from the hotel, and he requested to meet with Begin at 1:30 p.m. Vance returned to the room and told Begin. Begin said to Yehiel, "This whole meeting is just to discharge his obligation. It has no meaning. Maybe he needs the meeting for some internal matter of his own." Begin's analysis turned out to be correct, but he couldn't refuse the request of the president, who was in the home of a Jewish millionaire just three blocks from Begin's hotel.

In preparation for the meeting, Yehiel rushed to pull out a book from his suitcase – *The Trial and Death of Jesus* by Supreme Court Justice Haim Cohn. What was the story behind this book? Carter had expressed interest in the book during his visit to Israel in March 1979. Begin had told him about it in recognition of the fact that Carter was a believing Christian. Carter's messengers had run to the bookstores, but they couldn't find the book in English translation. Yehiel even called the home of Justice Cohn to check if he had an English copy, but Cohn could not help. Yehiel then turned to Abe Foxman, of the Anti-Defamation League, who searched the organization's library and found a copy in good condition. The book was sent to Yehiel, but by the time it arrived, Carter had left Israel.

When preparing for their next trip to the US, at the possibility that Begin might have an unexpected meeting with Carter, Yehiel packed the book.

Begin quickly penned a dedication on the flyleaf, and they went to the meeting. The trip from the hotel to the home of the wealthy Jew, whose name was Kraine, was extremely short.

"We approached the house," Yehiel recalled, "and we saw a large number of people out front, in the street. They had heard that the president was coming, and they had come to cheer for him. We learned afterward that Kraine was a supporter of the Democratic Party. He was hosting a fundraising event for the Democratic candidate for governor of New York. Carter attended in order to help the candidate with his presence. When Begin's car stopped, Carter came out of the house, walked up to Begin, who was still in the street, and hugged him in front of the cameras. Yehiel handed Begin the book by Justice Cohn, and he gave it to the president, right there on the sidewalk."

"I promised to get you this book," Begin said to Carter, "and here it is. This is the book by our supreme court justice, Haim Cohn."

Carter thanked Begin and escorted him into the house, where the guests greeted them with applause. They held an informal conversation while leaning on the brass rail in the reception room. Carter put his arm around Begin's shoulders, and the journalists photographed them as they faced the door.

"I watched this scene," Yehiel related, "and I couldn't believe my eyes: to show his support for his candidate for governor, the president of the great United States of America invited Begin to be photographed with him. The photos appeared the next day in all the papers, and all the Jews of New York, voting citizens, saw that the president wasn't exactly belittling Begin – and perhaps, so Carter hoped, they would vote for the Democratic candidate for their state's governor."

Yehiel affirmed that Begin respected Carter in his role as president, but no further. "There was no hostility between them, but there was certainly a lack of mutual sentiment," he admitted. "For example, Carter came to Israel twice after Begin was no longer prime minister, but he did not request to meet with Begin. Protocol, at least, required that two statesmen should meet after working together in a political process, surviving disagreements and reaching achievements. Once when Carter was in Israel, there was a meeting of all the 'Camp David survivors' at President Chaim Herzog's office in the Israeli presidential residence. Carter and Herzog received the guests when they arrived, and when I approached, Carter said, 'Hi, Yehiel, there you are. I'd like to speak to Menachem Begin.' Someone who's really interested arranges the meeting in advance, and doesn't start planning it when he's standing in a reception line. 'I'll call him,' I told Carter. I went into a side room, phoned Begin, and said that President Carter wanted to speak to him. 'I'd be happy to speak to him,' replied Begin. 'Have him come and we'll talk.' I knew that Carter had no intention of going to Begin's home, and so I responded, 'Please wait on the line.' I went back into the reception hall and told Carter that Begin was on the phone. 'Please, Mr. President, you can speak with him now.' Carter cut away from the reception, went into the side room, and they spoke for exactly one minute. Begin asked, 'How's Rosalynn?' Carter answered, 'She's just fine.' Begin said, 'Thanks,' and hung up the phone. By contrast, when Begin came to the US to meet with newly elected President Ronald Reagan, we flew to visit Carter at his home in Georgia. We even ate lunch with his whole family. True, it was all a show, and not from the heart. A show of respect for a former president. But that's the custom."

One individual whom Yehiel described as a "true friend" was former US ambassador to Israel Sam Lewis. "One day in the Knesset cafeteria," Yehiel related, "I saw Erwin Frenkel and Ari Rath, the editors of the *Jerusalem Post*, and beside them David Landau, the paper's diplomatic correspondent. Landau was virulently anti-Begin, and once he even wrote that the US State Department had to replace Sam Lewis because he supported the Israeli government. It was that bad. I approached Landau, who was an observant Jew, and said: You pray every morning, and of course you know the phrase, 'May there be no hope for those who slander, and may all the wicked perish at once,' which is part of the Shemoneh Esreh prayer. So why do you write that the Americans should replace Ambassador Lewis because he approves of the Israeli government? Landau turned pale and was shocked into silence. Sam Lewis was indeed a friend. That's the truth. Sometimes he got a scolding from Begin because of the policy he represented, but he was and remains a true friend."

Looking inward, inside Israeli society, Yehiel commented, "Begin did not object to criticism. He just didn't like (to put it mildly) when personal issues hid behind the criticism. When political rivals criticized him, then of course he responded with full force and repelled the attack. If it was internal criticism within the party regarding organization, or the composition of certain groups, then of course there were arguments. In politics, as in life, there are always arguments. After a prolonged correspondence on some point of disagreement, in which letters flew back and forth and he wanted to end the cycle, he would end his letters with the statement, 'Let's agree to disagree.' In public he would quote the saying of the Sages, 'There are as many opinions as faces' (*Berachot* 58). For example, regarding different views such as that of [the activist group] Peace Now, or demonstrations on various issues, he never negated anyone's right to have a different opinion, and he certainly considered it legitimate for others to express their opinions and demonstrate."

In March 1978, Begin received a letter which later became known as "the Officers' Letter" in which 348 soldiers and officers in the reserves called for him to work toward peace with Egypt, and to prefer a peace agreement over the concept of maintaining Jewish control over the whole of the biblical Land of Israel. Yehiel related that this letter had no effect on him. After that, the uproar caused by Peace Now later that year made no impression on him either. In general, the positions of the groups who opposed to his policy on Eretz Israel did not affect him. This was similar to his underground days: when the Brit Shalom groups attacked him, he was unmoved, because his worldview was different from theirs: if the Jews wanted our own state, they would have to fight for it. He was not swayed, then or in later years, from his position.

According to Yehiel, "another example of disagreement was related to Begin's party opponents in 1949. The issue surrounded Eri Jabotinsky, Hillel Kook, and Shmuel Merlin, Herut Party members of the First Knesset whose vision was 'Canaanite.' They wanted to include their principles in the party's platform. They distinguished between 'Hebrews' and Jews. By their definition, those who lived in Eretz Israel were Hebrew, while those [ethnic Jews] who lived in the Diaspora were 'Jews'. The establishment of the State of Israel meant the foundation of the Hebrew nation. They thought there should be a Hebrew republic in Eretz Israel, which distinguished between religion and nationality. They spoke of cooperation with the local population, meaning the Arabs, whom they defined as 'Muslim Hebrews,' or 'Hebrews of Arabic origin.' They called for the dissolution of the Jewish Agency and for Arab participation in the government. Debates with them were conducted in writing. After they entered the First Knesset, these arguments became philosophical and ideological. Begin once told me that Eri Jabotinsky, who was anti-religious and a proud atheist, wanted the Knesset snack bar to sell sandwiches with cheese and meat together. Eri said, 'I would understand if Begin was religious for coalitional purposes, because he needed the votes and the support of the religious. But the problem is that he's really religious!'"

Yehiel added that Begin did not fear public opinion, which he said was like wind across the ocean, like breaking waves. Begin read hundreds, even thousands of articles that opposed him, and he did not budge a hair's breadth from his opinion. Headlines such as "Begin Incites War" and "Sadat the Peacemaker" did not even move him to raise an eyebrow. He was insulated from all that. Similarly, he was not particularly impressed by the Peace Now representatives who came to demonstrate in his support when he returned from Camp David after signing the peace agreement. The only thing that caused him pain were the harsh words he received after Camp David from those with whom he identified, whom he would have joined had he been their age or in their position, whether in the opposition or majority – and those were the Gush Emunim. They were his people, and they were angry at him and opposed him and hurt him by throwing eggs, cursing him, and writing articles. He valued their opinions, but not those of others. Of course, if someone wrote positive things about him, he was pleased, but those occasions were very rare.

Yehiel never hid his opinion about journalists and their responsibilities. He often said to *Haaretz* journalists Yoel Marcus, Uzi Benziman, Avraham Schweitzer, and others: "You have a big plus. If you write an article today, it's printed and appears in the paper. But no matter – it doesn't change anything. Two weeks later you can write the opposite, and even then, nothing will happen. But when the prime minister or a statesman has to make a decision, this decision is carried out. As the Sages say, it moves into the realm of action, and once it's done, it's done. It's no newspaper article that people won't even use the next day for wrapping up their fish."

So, Yehiel emphasized, articles made no impression on Begin. He continued marching to his own beat, and was very careful not to cause long-term damage as a result of a careless decision.

Begin's first political step as prime minister of Israel was toward peace. And yet, for thirty years, when Begin represented the major opposition to the Mapai and Labor governments, he was presented as a warmonger, as a man whose very essence was opposed to peace.

"There is no bigger error," Yehiel asserted. "In order to understand the magnitude of this error, we must go back and read things Begin wrote long before the State of Israel was established. One of the principles of his worldview was what he called in English the 'overriding consideration,' and that was the Jewish people. The overriding consideration was the assurance of the Jewish people's survival through the establishment of the state. It all came from Jabotinsky's philosophy, and of course from the vision of the prophets: 'And they shall beat their swords into plowshares, and their spears into pruning hooks [Isaiah 2:4].'

"Begin would also ask, why are our prophets called 'true' prophets – Isaiah, Jeremiah, and the others, including the minor prophets? They never fixed a date [for their prophecies], so their prophecy is 'true prophecy.' We must not fix dates, but rather do all we can so that [the establishment of a Jewish state as a fulfilment of biblical prophecy] will happen earlier, in order to prevent disasters and pogroms, and to raise the banner of Israel among the nations – and afterward to ensure that 'from Zion will go forth Torah' [Isaiah 2:3]. We must understand why Begin was considered a warmonger, although he always called for the Arabs to live together with us in peace.

"In order to understand Begin, we must quote Jabotinsky. In 1977, each time a journalist asked me about Begin's motivations for his steps toward peace, I would say: Do you want to understand Begin? Go study Jabotinsky. What did Jabotinsky say at every opportunity? He also had the image of a warmonger. Everything started with an article he wrote in 1923 entitled 'The Iron Wall,' and another article he wrote on the topic called 'The Ethics of the Iron Wall.' The second article was a reaction to critiques of the first, in which he wrote that in order for us to obtain a Jewish state, or to achieve what we needed to achieve, we had to be strong in all aspects, and to create an iron wall that would protect us from the Arabs. In his article he wrote that the Arabs would never agree for us to take Eretz Israel for ourselves by law, unless they saw they had no chance of preventing it. For this, his opponents called him a warmonger. Today there is a consensus on this approach, except perhaps for a few remaining followers of Martin Buber, Yehudah Leib Magnes, and Yeshayahu Leibowitz, who think that this isn't true and that we must be weak, or better, appear weak, or perhaps be strong but not reveal it publicly. Jabotinsky argues the exact opposite: those who think that if they supply electricity and water to Arab homes, the Arabs will be grateful to us and allow us to establish a Jewish state – they are living in total illusion. Because no group of people will

RIGHT-HAND MAN | 257

agree to permit others – with quotation marks or without – to come and settle among them or beside them, all the more so when they think the new group will take over their land. This was how it was in America, in Africa, and every other place in the world. There are those close to Jabotinsky's ideology who, today, would perhaps say, here, this is the situation; the moderate majority will agree to enter negotiations over a modus vivendi, in order to live. This is exactly what happened with Sadat and Egypt.

"As for the Palestinians, today there are those who assert that the PLO is 'moderate' and the problem is only Hamas. Indeed, above all, we must have peace. Jabotinsky was a big liberal and a big supporter of peace. His MA dissertation in 1912 was on 'Rights of National Minorities.' All this was integral to Begin's thought. People close to him knew that he was a man of peace, but they didn't fight the image he had acquired. Even if they had fought, nothing would have helped, because the concept that dominated Zionism was that we didn't really need force. Here and there, some people made sure that we would have a few guns to protect ourselves, but we didn't really need force. In eastern Europe, Jabotinsky and Begin were both mocked for playing with wooden guns, or as they said it in Yiddish, *holtzene bikslech*. Begin was already involved in all those activities, and as he was a leader of Betar, the largest youth movement in Eastern Europe, he learned all those things and wanted to bring the Jewish people to live peacefully in a Jewish state. This was the 'overriding consideration.' If force has to be used along the way in order to achieve the goal, then we had to use force – until it was achieved. Of course, people who had a different concept, another outlook on life, advocated restraint and appeasement. Begin did not support the view that we had to lay low and keep quiet in front of the non-Jews. If we had an issue with non-Jews, if they raised a hand against us – we should strike them back.

"Uri Zvi Greenberg expressed this concept in his famous poem, 'One Truth, Not Two':

> Your Rabbis taught: A land is bought with money
> You buy the land and work it with a hoe.
> And I say: A land is not bought with money
> And with a hoe you also dig and bury the dead.

And I say: A land is conquered with blood.
And only when conquered with blood is it sacred to the people,
With the holiness of blood.
And only one who walks behind the cannon in the field,
Wins the right to walk behind his good plow
On this, the field that was conquered....

*

And I say: If your generation holds back
And does not hasten the end
And does not test the shield of David by fire
And in blood the knees of his horses do not wallow –
The Messiah will not come, even in a distant generation
And Judea shall not arise.[9]

"These writings were part of Begin's life. On the one hand, his character was that of a man of peace, easygoing and quiet, but when he battled for the 'overriding consideration,' he made no compromises. He said: 'In order to achieve this goal, I am willing to fight, I am willing to die.' Moshe Sneh, who studied with Begin at the University of Warsaw, once told me that he served with him in a group that defended young Jewish women and men from attacks by the youth of the antisemitic National Democratic Party of Poland, and that Begin was the archetype of a real fighter. Shortly before his death, Sneh told me: 'Yehiel, you don't know anything about Begin. I know him better than you.' As for his image, you have to see the statements made by the Histadrut working committee in the pre-state period about the [Irgun] 'terrorists' and 'fascists': 'Don't give them money. Don't help them. They're bringing disaster upon the Yishuv.' All these expressions, which were repeated over the years, were the rubber stamp that marked Begin and his followers. But he was the symbol, and he had to absorb it – especially when it became known that he was the leader of the Irgun, because until 1948 only a select few knew this.

"But no one could argue about his desire for peace. From the Six-Day War until his dying day, Begin was unwilling to say that the land

---

9   Quoted in part in Anita Shapira, *Land and Power: The Zionist Resort to Force, 1881–1948* (Stanford University Press, 1999), 243.

on the other side of the Jordan was Palestine – things that Arik Sharon and even Yitzhak Shamir were already saying. After the peace agreement with Egypt, at a memorial ceremony at Jabotinsky's grave on 29 Tammuz 5741 (1981), the anniversary of his death, Begin declared: 'Your students fulfilled your will, your lifetime desire for Eretz Israel. The entire western side of Eretz Israel is in our hands, and we hope that the day will come when through an alliance of friendship, peace, and understanding, a confederation will arise, and your vision will be fulfilled:

> From the wealth of our land there shall prosper
> The Arab, the Christian, and the Jew,
> For our flag is a pure and just one
> It will illuminate both sides of my Jordan.'[10]

"A confederation with the east side of the Jordan, one state including land on both sides – this is a dream that has yet to be realized, and we hope it will be one day," said Yehiel. "This is also proof of Begin's desire for peace. Begin aspired to see the fulfillment of this dream of Greater Israel united in a federation; the Jewish state on the western side of the Jordan united under an administrative federation with an Arab state on the east side of the Jordan. Of course, some might say that this dream belonged to the nineteenth century, that this was no longer possible. Rhodesia was established and dismantled, Yugoslavia fell apart, and so did the Soviet Union, because nationalism and ethnicity are stronger than any other body. Or else, perhaps this is a vision for the end of days.

"In general, Begin did not budge from the line he repeated endless times, until it became a refrain: 'Without a peace agreement, Israeli forces will remain in the places they reached on June 11, 1967.' The Camp David Accords were also based on this statement. He said this when he was part of the national unity government; he said it after he resigned from that government. He did not put forward his own peace initiative at that time, because the Arabs were touting the three 'no's' of the Khartoum

---

10 From Jabotinsky's poem "The East Bank of the Jordan" written on November 18, 1929, popularly known as "Two Banks to the Jordan."

summit (held in Sudan's capital in August–September 1967): no peace with Israel, no recognition of Israel, and no negotiations with Israel. Only many years later did Jabotinsky's 'Iron Wall' begin to reach fulfillment, when we began to see indications in certain sectors of the Arab public, that they recognized they would have to reach some kind of agreement. Only then could we try to start this process, which ended in March 1979 with the signature of the peace agreement with Egypt – only after at least one Arab state agreed."

Yehiel continued: "Begin's image as a warmonger had no weight in any decision. He really did not care. On the contrary, he even mocked it. When he was prime minister, suddenly in one day he became a celebrity, and everyone wanted to meet with him. All the Jewish federations in the world invited him, along with Jewish organizations and communities. He received a constant stream of invitations. For thirty years he had been ostracized from general society. He wasn't even a foreign implant, because he wasn't even implanted. Then one fine day he became a VIP. He asked me, 'Take a look at me, Yehiel. Tell me – have I changed at all? Am I a different person? Do I talk differently? Do I look different? Do I think different? Look how everyone is running circles around me.' Every single town in Israel wanted to make him an honorary citizen. But he was only willing to accept Jerusalem, and he barely agreed even to that. On this issue, he had a teacher whose example he wanted to follow, but he feared that if he did so, he would be accused of arrogance and conceit for imitating his teacher."

The teacher was Rabbi Aryeh Levin, the zaddik of Jerusalem, who had ministered to prisoners of the Jewish underground. One day, Teddy Kollek, Jerusalem's mayor from 1965 to 1993, contacted Begin and asked him to try to convince Rabbi Levin to accept honorary citizenship in his city. He had already contacted the rabbi on the matter, said Teddy, but the rabbi had rejected the offer outright.

"I was told," Teddy added, "that if you talk to him, he'll agree."

"I'll try," Begin responded.

Begin and Yehiel went to Rabbi Levin's home, and Begin tried to convince him to accept. He said, "If you agree to accept the honorary citizenship, you'll be honoring the fighters as well, the underground fighters whom you served as rabbi. We know you don't want the honor, but perhaps you'll do it for us."

Rabbi Levin looked into Begin's eyes, grasped his hand, and replied: "I can't. After I finish my 120 allotted years, when I go 'upstairs,' they'll ask me, 'Aryeh, how could you accept the award?' I won't even be able to say I didn't know what it was for, because it says clearly, 'Honorary Citizenship.' The word 'honor' is written there on paper, so how could I…?"

He refused.

***

In October 1978, talks were held at Blair House between Israeli and Egyptian representatives on the wording of the peace agreement. That same month, Begin and Sadat were declared winners of the Nobel Peace Prize. They received it in December, although Sadat did not attend the ceremony.

The October summit was the second time Begin had ever met with Carter. The first time, just after the "revolution," Begin flew to the US to meet with the president in the White House and many journalists were forced to swallow their pens: Before Begin's election, humiliating and degrading comments were written about him by so-called objective journalists: "The guy with the Polish manners? Who's going to speak with him, if he gets elected, God forbid? Who will bother to go visit Israel if he becomes prime minister?" Begin read all these remarks, and he didn't even bite his lip, because he knew he was doing exactly what he was supposed to be doing. He had the Jewish people before his eyes, not the journalist community.

This is what happened in 1979 before the Nobel Prize award ceremony, to the horror of reporters who never learned and never forgot. At that time, the peace process was in a lull, even a freeze. The peace treaty that had been discussed at Camp David, the peace treaty that was at the door, had suddenly encountered barriers, and progress was slow. The media launched a frontal attack against Begin, calling for him to stay home, not to go to Oslo to receive the prize. Why? Because a real peace had not yet been achieved, and this was Begin's fault.

"One morning I entered his office," Yehiel related. "Begin said, 'Look, Yehiel, maybe I really shouldn't go to Oslo?' I looked at him and said, Don't you understand that they don't want you to have the honor of accepting the prize in person? Then I added in Yiddish: *Oif tzu pikanish* – literally, 'Let them burst' (or in English you would say, 'Let them rot') – but go! We went. The office prepared a list of guests, and each one paid for the hotel expenses and the flight. The event was very impressive."

There was even an unforgettable moment between a real-life flesh and blood king and an Israeli brigadier general. "An hour before the opening of the prize ceremony," Yehiel explained, "Begin's military secretary, Brigadier General Ephraim (Freuka) Poran, arrived at the palace. I saw him walking down the corridor just as the king emerged from a side corridor. In a gesture of respect, the king motioned broadly with his arm for Freuka to proceed before him."

***

In 1979, the most important events for Begin, and Yehiel as his right-hand man, were the meeting and talks with President Carter, the Knesset authorization of the peace agreement with Egypt, and signature of that agreement in Washington. Yehiel recalled meetings with the US president in Washington. "The meetings were arranged by the Foreign Ministry through the usual diplomatic channels. Begin preferred talks in person with Carter to telephone conversations. This was because he could see the man, read his body language, look him in the eyes, and study his facial expressions. I accompanied Begin on his trips abroad. When his wife Aliza was with him, Bambi also came as her personal advisor but mainly as a close friend. I was very busy arranging meetings with all sorts of dedicated Jews who wanted to meet with the prime minister while he was there, either as individuals or as representatives of organized bodies."

In March, just to remind Israelis of where they lived, a horrific terror attack in Nahariya killed three members of the Haran family – a father and his two daughters – as well as a policeman who arrived on the scene. These events took place in the same month as the signing of the Camp David Accords. Each tragic incident in which Jewish blood was spilled gnawed at Begin's heart.

- May: IDF soldiers clashed with residents of Moshav Ne'ot Sinai, who protested against the retreat from Sinai. Three women were killed in a terrorist bombing of a bus shelter in Petah Tikva. Israel and Egypt began discussing the Autonomy Plan, and President Sadat visited Be'er Sheva.
- June: IDF aircraft shot down five Syrian planes in the skies of southern Lebanon.
- July: Begin and Sadat met at Ismailia.
- August: The first Israeli tourists traveled to Egypt.
- October: Foreign Minister Moshe Dayan resigned following a dispute with Begin over the autonomy talks, and the prime minister took over his portfolio.
- November: The IDF continued its retreat from Sinai. Inflation reached record levels of 78.3 percent.

In those days, Yehiel found himself in presence of world leaders – presidents, kings, and prime ministers; princes and barons. While Prime Minister Begin had prepared himself for this position for the past twenty-nine years at least, as Begin himself declared, Yehiel was suddenly launched into the world's spotlight. His school days in *cheder* and the Tachkemoni school and even his period of service in South Africa were certainly not enough to prepare him for this.

"Those are externals that don't matter much," Yehiel protested. "I had a custom – for every Israeli ambassador or consul I met before he went abroad for his position, I printed the famous Betar oath that Jabotinsky wrote, and suggested he place it under the glass desktop in his new office abroad. I pointed out one verse whose meaning I had implemented for myself, and I suggested that he internalize it. The verse reads:

I shall approach the company of nations gallantly

Like a lion approaching lions, my brethren, not my conquerors

I am a Betar soldier, a soldier trained with a bow, on the threshold of Tel Hai.

"The idea is that first I have to have a weapon, so that I'll be strong," Yehiel explained. "Then I can approach the alliance of nations, as one lion approaches another, as one among equals. I'm neither superior nor inferior to them – I'm equal to them. I relate to every individual, Jew and non-Jew, as an equal. I was educated according to these words, and I try to live by them. Another verse of the Betar oath reads, 'Prevail – in order to forgive.' If others would try to follow this ideal, in the Knesset and the government, in political parties as well as society, in city centers and in neighborhoods – if everyone would prevail with the intention of forgiving, everything would look different. Some might say: Why should I bother to prevail, to convince others that my opinion is correct, if only to forgive afterward? If I prevail, there is no reason for me to forgive. But this attitude is wrong, because if more people behaved this way, there would be much more peace in the world. I tried to follow this code, perhaps because I'm from a Chassidic family, and also because I was brought up in Betar, so maybe I understood and could adopt certain values."

During one of the prime minister's trips to the US that year, he flew without Aliza. Though they would usually fly first class, just before Yehiel reserved the flight tickets, Begin suggested that perhaps this time they should fly in economy class, because the cost of first-class tickets was so high. Yehiel reserved economy class tickets for the entire entourage.

"When the day arrived," Yehiel related, "we boarded the plane and took our seats among the other passengers – the prime minister along with the ordinary Joes. The funny thing was that dozens of journalists and photographers, including *Newsweek*, *Time*, and others, had bought first-class tickets in advance. They paid at least three times as much so that they could say, 'Our reporter accompanied the prime minister on his trip.' They had counted on catching a shot when he was scratching his ear or sleeping. But in fact, when the journalists saw that the prime minister wasn't next to them, they all came down to economy class and stood the whole flight so that they could catch the shot they would have missed upstairs."

***

The year 1980 was also chock-full of events:

- January: Begin and Sadat met at Aswan, Egypt, for discussions.

- February: An Israeli embassy was opened in Cairo, and Israel's first ambassador to Egypt came from the prime minister's office: Director-General Eliyahu Ben Elissar.
- March: El Al inaugurated regular flight service to Cairo. Yitzhak Shamir was appointed foreign minister.
- April: Terrorists attacked Kibbutz Misgav Am and murdered three residents.
- May: Terrorists attacked Jews in Hebron as they returned from Friday evening prayers, murdering six. Defense Minister Ezer Weizman resigned in protest over the government's stance on the issue of the autonomy talks. Begin took on the additional role of defense minister until the elections of 1981.
- June: The mayors of Nablus and Ramallah were severely injured when members of the Jewish underground placed explosive devices in their cars. A kidnapping and murder shocked the nation – Zvi Gur kidnapped Oron Yarden, age eight, of Savyon, a wealthy community near Petah Tikva. Gur demanded and received ransom, but then the child's corpse was found.
- July: The Israeli Air Force received its first F-16 warplanes. Six people were killed in an explosion at an Israel Military Industries factory in central Israel. The Knesset passed the "Jerusalem Law": "Jerusalem, complete and united, is the capital of Israel."
- August: Major IDF forces attacked terrorist bases in Lebanon. In retaliation, Katyusha rockets were fired at northern settlements. Justice Minister Shmuel Tamir resigned from the government.
- October: First visit of an Israeli president, Yitzhak Navon, to Egypt.
- November: The price of gasoline rose by 25 percent. The Herut Party secretary canceled Ezer Weizman's membership after he supported a vote of no confidence in the government.
- In 1980, inflation reached 131 percent.

Alongside the accomplishments, the behavior of those whom Begin called "spoilers" trailed the government like a shadow. These were some government ministers whose behavior – leaking information and behaving in an unfriendly manner – was considered by many to be reckless.

"When I observed this," Yehiel related, "I told them a Chassidic story about the good hell and the bad hell. A man who dies is summoned to hell. At the heavenly acceptance committee hearing, it turns out that the number of sins he committed is only a little bit bigger than the number of mitzvot, and this difference earns him the right to choose to which type of hell he'll be sent. Before the final placement, he's given a tour of the easier hell, Level 1, and the harsher hell, Level 2. In Hell Level 1, the more comfortable one, the man sees a large hall, and in middle sits a giant pot full of fragrant Hungarian goulash, hot and tasty. Sitting around the pot are corpulent people, and each one has a big spoon growing out of his elbow. They can't reach their own mouths with the spoons, so each one takes a spoonful of food out of the pot and feeds his neighbor. Then the man is taken to Hell Level 2, the worse one. There as well, in the middle of the room is a huge pot, and it's also giving off the wonderful scent of Hungarian goulash. But to his horror, around the pot are sitting people who have big spoons growing out of their elbows – and all of them are skeletons with massive ugly burns on their bodies. The man asks his escort angel what's going on, why in Level 1 the people are fat and happy, but in Level 2 they're thin and miserable? The angel replied: In Hell Level 1, each person feeds his neighbor. But in Hell Level 2, each one tries to eat by himself.

"The moral of the story, as I said to the ministers, is that twenty people sit in the cabinet, but no one tries to help each other in cabinet meetings or media interviews. One minister should get up and say to the transportation minister, I saw a new road being paved, a train station built; someone should step up and say to the welfare minister, I read about a new soup kitchen that was established in a poor neighborhood. For once, David Levy could say something positive about Gideon Patt, and Gideon Patt could say something good about Yitzhak Moda'i, and Moda'i about Simcha Erlich. The names don't matter. The main thing is that they should say positive things about each other – they can also say good things directly to each other – and then they'll feel comfortable, like in the good hell."

One of Begin's big "spoilers" was Ezer Weizman, who leaked information, humiliated Begin behind his back, and even called him "the deceased" – which Begin knew about but never acknowledged to Weizman. In the end, Weizman sawed off the branch on which he was sitting. Weizman's political career in the Herut Party began with a powerful takeoff, but ended with a total crash. It began with his surprising 1969 entrance into the national unity government, under Golda Meir. "The appointment was made in collusion," Yehiel revealed. "He retired from the IDF on December 15, 1969, and that evening he was appointed transportation minister, representing Gahal. The government had contact with him while he was still in uniform as deputy chief of staff. Then Joseph (Yoske) Kremerman came in as the straw man who paved the way for Weizman into the government. What's more, Begin himself said that as long as Weizman was a soldier, his name couldn't even be mentioned as a political candidate, and anyway, he personally preferred Dr. Yohanan Bader in the government, not Weizman. But things were managed differently."

Weizman served as transportation minister for eight months, until Gahal resigned from the government in the wake of the Rogers plan. After that, Weizman was appointed chairman of the Herut Party. His relationship with Begin deteriorated, and he resigned from politics and began a new career in private business. In his opinions, which he expressed from every available pulpit, he was a hawk, the very bone and sinew of the Herut Party. In 1976 he returned to Herut, played a dominant role in the elections, and was appointed defense minister in Begin's government. After jump-starting the peace process with Egypt, he developed a close relationship with President Sadat and led the Israeli delegation to the peace talks in Cairo in January 1978. Apparently, it was during this period that his political views began to shift. He began to speak out against the settlements and the Begin government's actions, and in May 1980 he resigned from the position of defense minister.

"A person has the right to do what he wishes with himself," Yehiel confirmed. "He can change his opinion – just as Moshe Dayan once said,

'Only a donkey never changes his mind.' It's perfectly legitimate for a person to change his opinions, because sometimes circumstances change, your age changes. But it's different when you belong to a certain group that has an opinion, and when you represent people who uphold that view.

"In one of our discussions during that period, after Camp David, I told him, Ezer, we don't have electoral regions. We have only one electoral region, and that's the Herut Party. You don't represent the liberals. You represent the Herut electoral region. Let's say that in a certain electoral region in the US, the residents earn their living from tobacco farming. As a representative of that region in the Senate, you can work either for or against religion, for or against abortion. You can choose what to say about those topics, because there are residents in your electoral region who think one way and residents who think differently. That's completely legitimate. But if all the residents grow tobacco, you can't work against the interests of the tobacco growers. The tobacco growers in our party are the creators of the State of Israel. You can't get up in the Knesset and speak out against the interests of the citizens who voted for you."

Yehiel said that Begin felt the same way. "Once while at the airport in New York waiting to return to Israel, Begin learned that Weizman had declared that the government he was part of did not want peace. He tripped Begin up, stuck a knife in his back."

Many wondered why Begin didn't fire the rebellious Weizman. Yehiel explained, "Begin never fired anyone. Not one clerk, not one secretary in the office, which had many staff left over from the Rabin era. He expressed his disillusionment with Weizman's statements, he said he disagreed with Weizman, he realized there was no way for them to sit together in the same government – and he let Weizman decide what steps to take."

In the national unity government led by Shimon Peres and Yitzhak Shamir in rotation between 1984 and 1988 Weizman served as minister without portfolio (representing his party, Yachad). He epitomized the left wing, as he openly supported returning territories and negotiations with the PLO. The next chapter in the story was no less turbulent. In 1988, he was appointed minister of science and technology in the unity government under Shamir. In late 1989, Shamir demanded his removal following Weizman's contact with representatives of the PLO, which was forbidden by law and considered taboo. After the national unity government was dissolved, Weizman resigned from the Knesset.

Moshe Dayan resigned from the government in 1979. Before the chain of events involving Weizman, after the peace agreement with Egypt was signed, Foreign Minister Dayan developed significant differences of opinion with Begin regarding the implementation of the agreement and negotiations over autonomy. Dayan thought that Israel should grant the Palestinians broad autonomy, and not impose Israeli control, in opposition to Begin's view that the autonomy would be established under Israeli sovereignty. Dayan wanted to push forward in the negotiations and score achievements. Begin, as Dayan saw it, wanted to dissolve the negotiations, thinking they didn't have to be concluded so long as the Egyptian interest demanded cooperation, in the period when Israel had to fulfill its obligation to retreat from Sinai. These differences of opinion led to the appointment of Yosef Burg, who was minister of the interior, as head of the Israeli staff of the autonomy negotiation, although Dayan had considered himself the natural candidate for the position. This prompted Dayan's resignation.

The government was also clouded by a chain of corruption incidents in its coalition parties. For example, in 1979, the mayor of Rehovot, MK Shmuel Rechtman of the Likud Party was convicted of taking bribes and was sentenced to prison. He earned the dubious honor of being the first member of Knesset to be given a jail sentence while still in office. Minister of Religions Aharon Abuhatzira, a Mafdal Party representative, was involved in a series of criminal affairs, and his ministerial immunity was removed. He battled the party head, Interior Minister Yosef Burg, who was responsible for the Israel Police, and asserted that Burg tried to "liquidate" him. Then Abuhatzira declared he would run for Knesset on a separate list – which he indeed did, establishing his own party, Tami. Burg then clashed with the director-general of the police, Herzl Shafir, whom he fired, claiming Shafir had lied to him about Abuhatzira's interrogation. Shafir did not sit idle. He revealed the existence of an intelligence report, called the "Peach File," which included suspicions of criminal conduct by Burg. Shafir then claimed that his order to check the information in this file was what induced Burg to fire him.

***

270 | Sharpening Swords

- January 1981: Finance Minister Yigal Hurvitz resigned from his position following a disagreement over teacher salaries. Begin proposed advancing the elections to June, and in the meantime appointed Yoram Aridor in his place. The one-shekel coin entered circulation.

- February: The Finance Ministry announced reductions in the price of cars and electric appliances, while the opposition dubbed this "election finances." The Tel Aviv stock market crashed and stocks fell 15 percent. Strikes of teachers and lecturers caused severe disruptions in schools and universities.

- March: Physicians, engineers, and other professionals went on strike. Thousands of ultra-Orthodox demonstrated on the Ramot Road to protest traffic there on Shabbat.

- April: There was tension on the northern border with terrorist penetrations, and Katyusha rockets in the Galilee. The Israeli Air Force attacked in retaliation.

- May: American envoy Philip Habib arrived to present a program for the Lebanon problem and a solution for the crisis of Syrian anti-air missiles placed in the Lebanese region. Two families became the first to renew Jewish settlement in the Old City of Hebron.

- June: Begin and Sadat met at Ophira, Egypt. The IAF destroyed the Iraqi nuclear reactor at Osirak. President Ronald Reagan expressed his objection to the operation by delaying delivery of F-16s to Israel. The UN Security Council condemned Israel for the operation.

Despite being the person closest to Begin, Yehiel did not hear one word from him about the plan to bomb the Iraqi reactor. Of course, this was not because Begin suspected that Yehiel might leak the news. Rather, Begin respected the fact that Yehiel chose to remove himself from government discussions. Yehiel never asked to know what he didn't need to know in his role as chief of staff. But to say he knew nothing at all about the plan would be an exaggeration. He did know a little something; he had heard a casual comment dropped by someone who was certain Yehiel was party to privileged information. That person mentioned the second postponement of the operation within earshot of Yehiel, complaining that "'It' fell through once again because of a leak."

"A lightbulb went on in my head, and I sensed that something was about to happen," Yehiel said, but that hint was all the information he had about the classified topic. At one point, Begin thought Yehiel knew about the operation, and he asked him what he knew about it. Yehiel replied, "I don't know the details, but I know the principle."

A few days before the operation, Yehiel accompanied Begin's entourage to a meeting with Sadat at Sharm el-Sheikh. Yehiel and Bambi had decided to take a few days' vacation in Eilat after the meeting, and they reserved rooms in advance. So Yehiel did not return by plane with Begin to Jerusalem, but traveled in the prime minister's car from Sharm el-Sheikh to Eilat. When he reached his hotel, he found an urgent message awaiting him, instructing him to return to Jerusalem immediately.

When he arrived in Jerusalem, Yehiel was asked to come to Begin's home. He arrived at 3 Balfour Street in the Rehavia neighborhood of Jerusalem, and watched as all the government ministers began to arrive as well. When he entered, Begin asked him to come into the library, which was separate from the living room. He closed the door and instructed, "Sit here and wait for a phone call from the chief of general staff. As soon as the phone rings, call me at once!"

The phone was a hotline from IDF command headquarters to the prime minister's home. Yehiel sat and waited for it to ring. In his mind he tried to imagine the content of the message. Half an hour went by, and then the phone rang. Raful, the chief of general staff, was on the line. Yehiel called Begin over.

"The boys [bachurim] are on the way home," Raful announced succinctly.

"The voters [bocharim] are on the way home," said Begin's political enemies, pouncing on a play on the Hebrew words. They asserted that the operation was designed to help the prime minister in the elections, which were due to be held on June 30. Begin vehemently denied these claims. "If the operation had failed, God forbid, would that have helped him as well?" asked Begin's supporters in response.

Yehiel returned home. Only then, on the road to Tel Aviv, did he think of the unusual phone call he had received at home on the eve of his trip to Sharm el-Sheikh. On the line had not been the prime minister or the chief of general staff, but Reb Yosef Frankel, a businessman and follower of the Rebbe of Lelov. Yehiel had been surprised. What did the Rebbe's court need of him at such an hour? When Reb Frankel had given him the Rebbe's message, Yehiel had not been particularly moved. "The Rebbe says to inform the prime minister," Reb Frankel had said, "that with God's help, everything will be fine. It will be a success." Yehiel had replied quickly, "Okay, okay," thinking this was a kind of blessing for the upcoming holiday of Shavuot.

"I had no idea what he was talking about," Yehiel admitted, "so I didn't rush to tell Begin about it, but waited a few days, or even weeks."

This story later became a legend that was passed down among the followers of the Rebbe of Lelov. One Chassid reported: "At the time, the Rebbe was immersed in holy meditation. On Motzei Shabbat, the Saturday night before the holiday of Shavuot, Reb Yosef Frankel and Reb Benderley came to him for a *melaveh malkah* meal following the end of Shabbat. After the meal, before they left, the Rebbe called Reb Yosef over and said, 'Call Kadishai and tell him to tell Begin that I said everything will be fine, and it will be a success.' The guests went outside, but the Rebbe sent a messenger to call Reb Yosef back. So Reb Yosef went back in, and the Rebbe repeated, 'Don't forget to call Kadishai and tell him what I told you.' Reb Yosef had no idea what his Rebbe was talking about, but as a dedicated Chassid, he did not delay, and phoned Kadishai to give him the message."

The Rebbe often used to say to his followers: "In war, even when you win, you lose." Now he said something unusual, to his closest followers. He said that he "would take upon himself any damage or mishap that might happen to any of the Jews, God forbid." They had no idea what he was talking about, and when a Rebbe doesn't expand, one doesn't push the matter. Soon after Begin's chief of staff received the Rebbe's message, the IAF bombed the reactor, and all the pilots returned safely to their bases. But the Rebbe did not come out of it safely. The night after Shavuot, he suffered a stroke and died. His followers said that he had taken upon himself, on his physical body, every possible danger to the pilots. In other words, he willingly paid with his life for danger from which the daring pilots were saved. How did the Rebbe know? How did he become aware of the most well-guarded secret in the state? He took this mystery with him to the grave.

***

The election campaign was about to end, and the Likud was in hot water. Would it lose its hold on the government to the Labor Alignment? Surveys showed near parity between the camps. The Likud needed an advantage, an edge. Help came from the most unexpected quarters: comedian Dudu Topaz.

Herut media consultant Uri Porat related that as election day approached, the media became increasingly hostile toward the Likud. In May 1981, a month before the elections, it seemed as if all the media outlets – both print and electronic – had banded together to oust the Begin government and destroy it forever. The picture formed by radio and television was painted in ominous shades of black. Begin was described as old, sick, and helpless, with moods that fluctuated according to the quantity of pills his doctors ordered him to swallow. *Haaretz* began an unprecedented drive to defame him, the *Jerusalem Post* competed with *Haaretz* in printing false reports and intentional distortions of reality, which were picked up in the main by foreign reporters.

The Labor Alignment had already sewed itself a new governmental suit. As part of the campaign, Labor recruited actors, artists, journalists, and entertainers to its ranks. One author spoke at Mapam's Tzavta cultural hall about the "central bus station hoi polloi," advising Labor to leave these voters to the Likud and not to bother pursuing them. Another writer spoke haughtily on TV about "two cultures." Comedian Dudu Topaz, not known for his sophistication, simply called a spade a spade: we are the beautiful fighters, while they (the Likud) are *chach-chachim* – "riffraff."

Topaz stood on stage in Malchei Yisrael Square, facing a crowd of thousands who had come to express their support for Labor, and to the sound of their cheers, he announced: "It's nice to see this crowd, and it's nice to see that there are no *chach-chachim* here to ruin election rallies.

The *chach-chachim* are all over at Metzudat Ze'ev. They barely serve in the guard booths in the army, and that's if they serve at all. The fighters and the elite unit commanders are here. The beautiful Israel is here." Topaz was trying to separate the destruction of the reactor from the Likud's achievements and destroy the Likud with one blow, but his words instead proved fatal for Labor in the elections.

Begin didn't hear this misguided speech in real time. The next morning, Porat entered Begin's office. He was holding a copy of *Haaretz*, which contained Topaz's remarks in the square word for word. The sentences were highlighted, and Porat showed them to Begin. The prime minister scanned the report and said, "*Nu*, what do you want? Why are you surprised? Villains. Are these slanders new to you? What are you so excited about?"

Porat replied, "Mr. Prime Minister, if we take advantage of this properly, it can cause a complete transformation in the public opinion."

"What are you talking about?" asked Begin.

"He said that Likud voters are <u>*chach*</u>-*chachim*," Porat said.

"They're what?" Begin asked, unfamiliar with the word.

"*Chach-chachim*," Porat repeated.

"*Chach-chach<u>im</u>*?" Begin said again, giving the word an academic pronunciation, with the accent on the last syllable. "What are *chach-chachim*?"

"<u>*Chach*</u>-*chachim*," Porat corrected him, with the accent on the first syllable as the word was said on the street.

"What's so awful about that word?" Begin asked.

"Mr. Prime Minister," Porat said, "if you want to understand what's so awful about that word, I suggest we bring in your driver, Menachem Damti, and he'll tell you what it means. He's a Yemenite, and he knows exactly what it refers to."

"Okay," Begin agreed, "bring in Menachem."

Damti was hardly surprised at the summons, as he thought they merely wanted to arrange a trip somewhere, as usual. He came into Begin's office.

"Damti, if someone calls you a *chach-chach*, what would you do to him?" asked Porat.

Damti gave him a furious look, and said, "If someone calls me a *chach-*

chach, I'll destroy his face. Because it's a swearword, it's rude. It's a racist expression that the Ashkenazis use for the Sephardi Jews."

Begin raised his eyebrows.

"Tonight we're in Malchei Yisrael Square," Begin said to Porat. The Labor Party had held its rally there the previous night, that night it was the Likud's turn, and the elections were the following day. The timing couldn't be better. "Remind me about this *chach-chachim* business before I get up to speak."

"Okay, sir," Porat agreed. "I just want to remind you, sir, again, that it's pronounced with the emphasis on the first syllable, not the last."

Then Porat went over to Yehiel's room and said, "Tell me, Yehiel, what's going on? Does he always switch the accents from first to last syllable?"

Yehiel laughed.

"He learned that from Jabotinsky," Yehiel explained. "When something or someone annoys him, he intentionally mispronounces terms and names to show how unimportant these things are to him, that he doesn't even know how to pronounce the words properly…"

That evening Begin went to the square, with Yehiel and Porat escorting him in the car. Predictably, Begin fully exploited the golden opportunity that had come his way. He played with Topaz's name (pronounced *To-paz*), intentionally accenting the first syllable instead of the last – *To-paz*. Then he played on the word *chach-chachim* by accenting the last syllable, giving rise to cheers from the thousands in the square, turning the slur into a joke and a badge of pride. After his speech, he asked the audience: "Go to the voting booth and put in the right slip, slip after slip, slip after slip, a flood of the right slips: Likud, Likud, Likud, get those slips…"

The audience broke into cheers: "Begin! Begin!"

CHAPTER 19

GRAVE NEWS FROM AFAR

Two days after Begin's speech in the square, on June 30, 1981, the Likud won the election. Begin won forty-eight mandates while Labor won forty-seven, but this was enough to enable Likud – led by the man who had been called "outdated" – to put together a coalition. Accordingly, on August 5, 1981, Begin established his new government, supported by sixty-three Knesset members. He chose David Levy for the position of deputy prime minister and Ariel Sharon as defense minister.

- July: Katyusha rockets again targeted northern Israel, killing five Israelis. The US mediated between Israel and the PLO and obtained a cease-fire.
- August: Archeological excavations in the City of David provoked stormy battles with ultra-Orthodox Jews. Begin established the new government, comprised of Likud, Mafdal (NRP), and Tami, with sixty-one MKs, and the external support of Agudat Yisrael. Begin and Sadat met in Alexandria and decided to renew the autonomy talks.
- September: Autonomy talks between Israel and Egypt began again.
- October: President Sadat of Egypt was assassinated during a military demonstration commemorating the eighth anniversary of the "October War" (the Yom Kippur War). A high-ranking delegation from Israel led by Menachem Begin participated in the funeral. Moshe Dayan died. An Israeli-Egyptian document was signed regarding completion of the withdrawal from Sinai.
- November: Religions Minister Aharon Abuhatzira was accused

of theft, fraud, and breach of trust, and took leave from his ministerial position as he went on trial for the second time.

- December: In protest against the anticipated evacuation of their settlement, residents of Yamit barricaded themselves inside the town. The Knesset passed the Golan Law, applying Israeli sovereignty to the Golan Heights, fueling protests around the world. In reaction to the law, the US suspended the Memorandum of Understanding they had signed with Israel the previous month. Reduction of subsidies for basic food items caused price hikes of 25 percent.
- In 1981, inflation reached 116 percent.

"On one of the trips to the United States," related Azriel Nevo, Begin's military secretary, who replaced Ephraim Poran in 1981, "we arrived in Washington. We were sitting in the lobby, and suddenly Yehiel says to me, 'You know what, Azriel?' I've been here so many times, but I've never walked around the streets, just casually. I always go from the hotel to the car, from the car to the White House and back. Let's go for a walk in the street for once. Do you know Washington?' I replied, 'No, I'm not familiar with it, but you know what? Let's go out and walk around a bit.' 'But how will we get back to the hotel?' he asked. I reassured him: 'Don't worry, I'll make sure you get back.'"

The two went out and wandered around. They saw display windows, buildings, offices. Then Yehiel noticed an elderly lady walking slowly along the street, holding a shopping bag. Yehiel stopped her and asked, "Excuse me, where is such-and-such street?"

Azriel noticed that the name of the street he was asking about was written on a sign across the road. Meanwhile, the elderly woman replied politely, "You have to cross the street and look opposite. It's right there, not far."

Yehiel thanked her, and she continued on her way. Then Azriel asked him, "What are you up to, playing a joke on that old woman? That street is right across the way!"

Yehiel replied, "Did you see her? Poor thing, she's probably a widow. No one has spoken to her all day. After I asked her, she definitely felt that she did a good deed by showing me the street. Why not give her that satisfaction?"

"Another good deed Yehiel did during our visits to the US," Azriel related, "was to visit a certain store at the Waldorf Astoria to purchase gifts for all the secretaries in the office. This was a task he never overlooked."

Yehiel recalled that relationships in the office were sometimes very informal. For example, one Friday, pay slips were handed out to the employees. Everyone was ready to leave for the weekend, and Begin was standing at the door to the office, when his secretary Yona Klimovitzky pulled out her pay slip. She protested, "Mr. Begin, look what kind of salary I get." Begin glanced at the slip and responded, "It's really not worth it for you to come to work for that."

Yehiel met Yona in 1973 when she was completing her military service in the intelligence branch. Eliyahu Ben Elissar knew her, and he offered her a job in the public relations department of Gahal. She accepted the position, even though she had grown up in a communist family – her father was active in the Communist Party. Her office was on the twelfth floor of party headquarters in Metzudat Ze'ev, the same floor where Begin sat.

On her first day at work, Yehiel went into the office, saw a new face, and as was his habit, he began in Yiddish and ended with humor: "Oh, *maidele*, what is a lovely girl like you doing here?"

"I'm new, I work with Eli."

"No matter," Yehiel joked. "You'll get used to him."

After a short silence, Yehiel offered, "Would you like to meet Begin?"

"No," Yona replied, "No, thanks."

Yehiel raised an eyebrow and left the room. The next day, Yona was waiting for the elevator on the first floor, when Begin and Yehiel showed up. Yehiel informed Begin, "You know, she doesn't want to meet you."

Begin glanced at her, and she murmured, "Why would you want to see me anyway? You have no reason to know me, and you're a busy man…" Somehow she squirmed out of the embarrassing situation.

Later, on one of Yehiel's tours of the office, he went into her room and asked her about her background. She shared. Eventually she had a conversation with Begin. He asked about her, she replied, and then he responded, "I admire ideological people." Shortly afterward, Yona became his secretary. Yehiel brought her letters, and she typed them on an old typewriter. Begin's office was a chaos of files and papers from his many years of activity, and she began to organize them. As she worked, she read, and a new ideological world opened up before her.

"Yehiel very much appreciated the fact that I studied the material," she explained.

Later on, she typed Begin's articles, which he wrote at home and sent to the office. "Yehiel was the only one able to read his handwriting," she confided. "Besides his handwriting, he could also read his thought process. Eventually, I also learned to read his handwriting fairly well. While typing, sometimes I had questions on what Begin wrote, which I referred to Yehiel. Sometimes he would call Begin to clarify the issue, saying, 'Yona has a question.' Begin would explain patiently. Other times, I would ask questions, but Yehiel would say, 'What do you care? Just type and don't worry about it.' In the meantime, I became friendly with Yehiel and Bambi, and they became like a second set of parents to me. Once I even stayed with them in their hotel room when they were on vacation at Ma'ale Ha-Hamisha.

"Of course, there were fanatics in the party who didn't exactly appreciate my presence. They even said that Begin gave back Sinai because of me. Yehiel retorted, 'Maybe Yona's not one of us, but she's very loyal. There's no one else like her.' Over the years, I discovered what a soft heart Yehiel had. He answered every citizen who contacted him. He pushed to arrange meetings with Begin, even if sometimes I thought they were unnecessary.

"A clear-cut division of roles developed in the office: Yehiel was good the cop, I was the bad cop. Sometimes people came to the office bordering on violence. If I didn't let them in to see Begin, they would threaten me. I refused, and Yehiel would always defend me. This was even before Begin became prime minister. I didn't believe that he would get there. I wasn't alone in this, Yehiel didn't believe it would happen either."

When Begin was elected, the titles changed – Yona became assistant to the prime minister, and Yehiel chief of staff – but the jobs were the same: bad cop, good cop, and leader.

Dan Meridor, who served as cabinet secretary from 1982 to 1984, agreed that "People talk a lot about Yehiel as a joker. And it was true.

I don't think anyone remembers Yehiel ever getting angry or shouting. But in order to properly understand the importance of this, you have to understand his situation. Working closely with the prime minister for six years is a very difficult job of enormous responsibility. There were periods that were not easy at all. His jokes created a radiating atmosphere of calm. This was the special atmosphere of every conversation with him, as soon as he walked into a room. I never saw anyone leave his office without a smile – it could be a minister who went in to see him before a meeting with the prime minister in order to know what to say and how to say it, or after a meeting in order to consult with him. It could be someone from the long lines of people who wanted his advice. But first and foremost, you have to remember that he managed the prime minister's office, and this is a huge, complex job. He did everything with a smile. His manner was vastly different from the administrators who followed him, when the corridors of the Knesset were filled with people who considered themselves very important and who pushed to advance themselves to positions of power. This notion was as distant from Yehiel as east from west."

"Yehiel's loyalty to Begin was unconditional," Yona Klimovitzky added. "But he wasn't a fanatic follower. He was very opinionated. He swallowed books and newspapers, and had vast knowledge in a sea of topics. His ideology was well established, strong, and stood on firm foundations, and sometimes he was even more extreme than Begin. In this respect, he was closer to Benny Begin, Menachem's son.

"They were taken care of in the ideological arena, but when it came to basic technology – good heavens! Begin and Yehiel had two left hands. Yehiel would not give Begin advice. I didn't have that kind of awe of him, because I came from outside. One day I got annoyed with Yehiel, and I shouted at him, 'Because of the loyalty of people like you, he sat in the opposition for twenty-nine years!' One time Yehiel admitted to me openly, 'I can't do what you do, because I have the soul of a servant.' When Yehiel was in the same room with Begin and they would try to make or receive a phone call, they would get completely confused with the buttons. They would cut off calls in the middle, and sometimes they should shout, 'Yona, the call got cut off!' Of course it got cut off, because they were the ones who cut it off."

"When Begin left the political arena," Yona concluded, "Yehiel went with him. He wasn't willing to listen to any suggestion of continuing on the political path. He didn't want to be by himself, he didn't want to leave Begin by himself. Because he and Begin, and I have no doubt about this, were twin souls."

***

In that year, 1981, journalist Uri Porat was appointed as media advisor to Prime Minister Begin. Beyond transmitting press releases to the journalists, he also rebuked them when they published misinformation, unintentionally or otherwise.

"One day," Porat related, "Yehiel entered my office. I was on the phone, and I was dressing down a well-known journalist over a false item that he had published. Yehiel came over and said, 'Uri, give me the phone and I'll explain something to him.' I gave him the receiver and he said, 'What are you, a *freier* [a sucker, a patsy]? You could make a lot of money in one blow without even working.' The journalist said something in reply, and Yehiel attacked: 'What you have to do is go to the principal's office in your school, and ask him to refund you all the money your parents paid for tuition, because you didn't learn anything there!'"

Benny Begin gave a similar report. "Yehiel was a good person with an agreeable character. I never heard him get angry. It's even funny to think of him as angry, as it made such a weak impression on the object of his anger. He knew how to behave pleasantly with others, even in a minefield. When he criticized a journalist who was usually serious but occasionally failed and published foolish and adverse reports, Yehiel would say, 'Go eat a lot of fish, because you're missing a lot of stuff in your brain.' The journalist wouldn't even get mad at him."

Ha-Olam Ha-Zeh, Uri Avneri's newspaper, regularly published reports and articles that bore only a coincidental resemblance to the truth. When Avneri was an MK, he published a gossipy report about Begin's chauffeur, Yoske Giladi, and a cafeteria cashier. The report was completely fabricated, and Yehiel said to Avneri, "Why couldn't you ask me, or Yoske himself, is this story is true? We wander around here all day, what's the problem?" Avneri's reply: "Too many stories have fallen apart due to too many investigations."

Another article published in *Ha-Olam Ha-Zeh* gave a detailed three-page report of an expensive fur coat that Aliza Begin was said to have purchased in a chic store on Ben Yehuda Street in Tel Aviv. In this case as well, a short inquiry would have pulled the rug out from under the story. The real story was that one day, in preparation for a short trip abroad, Aliza Begin needed to prepare a particularly elegant wardrobe. Aliza Begin had a friend named Aliza Odem, who had a friend who owned a fur shop. The friend went to the shop and borrowed the coat for Aliza Begin for a few days as a one-time favor. The day after Aliza Begin returned to Israel, the driver returned the coat to the store, and this gave rise to the scandalous story that was designed to shake the newspapers' readers in their armchairs.

In general, Yehiel took a highly critical view of journalists. "Some of the fabrications and tall tales in the media resulted from spite, others from naiveté or stupidity. I think spite was in first place. I never understood why the media printed malicious distortions of things that were so simple to check. I think journalists are simply lazy, or else they don't know how to work."

For example, on July 10, 1992, Uri Dan wrote in his *Maariv* column, "The Week in Politics": "Yehiel Kadishai doesn't give a lot of interviews, so it was informative to hear him on the [radio] program *Ha-Kol Dibburim* ["All Talk"] with Razi Barkai. Why did Yehiel agree to be interviewed? To repudiate a terrible sentence that *Hadashot* newspaper ascribed to him. In its front-page headline, *Hadashot* announced that Yehiel had said the following about Likud leaders, in an interview with Amnon Barzilai: 'They're fighting each other, as saliva drips from their stinking mouths…' But the actual interview with Yehiel printed in *Hadashot* made no mention of this disgusting, crude sentence. As Yehiel announced on *Kol Yisrael* radio: 'Those words never came out of my mouth. That's the reason why even though I don't usually give interviews, today I am giving this interview – to correct the injustice done in attributing those words to me.'"

One of the incidents recorded in the annals of the office staff was set against the backdrop of the feverish political activity during that period. Senior clerks, military officers, assistants, and consultants came and went.

A certain photographer also happened to be hanging around, and when he saw something going on, he would try to get a good shot.

"I'm begging you," he pleaded with Yehiel, "Give me a scoop!"

"You want a scoop?" asked Yehiel. "Here's one."

To the photographer's astonishment, Yehiel climbed on the table and broke into a spirited jig. Unfortunately for the photographer, though, by the time he focused his camera, Yehiel had already got down from the table.

"You missed," Yehiel mocked the disappointed photographer. "Better luck next time."

***

The year 1982 was marked by the evacuation of Yamit and Operation Peace for Galilee (the First Lebanon War).

- January: An agreement between Israel and Egypt was signed, formalizing completion of the retreat from Sinai and normalization of relations.
- February: The UN General Assembly called for an international boycott of Israel.
- March: French president François Mitterrand visited Israel. Dismantling of settlements in the Rafiah salient began.
- April: The Yamit area was declared "closed military territory." On the Temple Mount, an IDF soldier, an immigrant from the US, opened fire indiscriminately, killing two and injuring twelve. This incited riots and demonstrations throughout the Arab world. The IDF clashed with residents of Yamit who refused to evacuate. Israel completed the return of the Sinai Peninsula to Egypt. The last residents of Yamit were evacuated by force, and the town was razed.
- May: Katyusha rockets were fired into the Galilee. MKs Amnon Lin and Yitzhak Peretz left Likud and joined Labor. IAF airplanes downed two Syrian airplanes in Lebanese airspace.
- June: A Palestinian terrorist shot and severely wounded

> Shlomo Argov, Israeli ambassador to the United Kingdom. Israel attacked a terrorist base in Lebanon in retaliation. The terrorists fired Katyushas from Lebanon into the Galilee. In early June, Operation Peace for Galilee began.

Yehiel said of Begin that he was an admirer of John F. Kennedy's statement during the Cuban missile crisis of 1962, that the moment when war begins is not the first shot, but the first threat. When the enemy informs you that he wants to destroy you, you don't have to wait until he fires the first shot. When a power comes from Lebanese territory and fires Katyusha rockets at Israel, Yehiel emphasized, they have the full right to self-defense, according to UN principles.

Yehiel related: "On one of his visits to Israel, American mediator Philip Habib said that an agreement regarding non-retaliation only applied to Israel, but not to Jews abroad. Begin retorted, 'No, we're responsible for Jews abroad as well.' This was perhaps a reply to those who wondered why Israel responded as we did after the attempt on Ambassador Argov's life. Begin believed in the principle of mutual responsibility."

At one stage of the war, in the afternoon hours, Begin gave Yehiel a piece of paper with several lines written on it.

"Send that immediately for publication in the media," Begin instructed Yehiel, bypassing his media consultant, Uri Porat.

Yehiel peeked at the paper and read the press release that Begin had written by hand. It said that Israel had to uproot the enemy and its leaders from their underground bunker.

"The metaphor was blatant," Yehiel explained. "This was an almost exact comparison between Yasser Arafat and Adolf Hitler – Arafat hiding in his bunker in London, and Hitler in his bunker in Berlin. I did not like the connotation of this announcement one bit, so I delayed sending it to the media. I thought that I would let an hour pass, and maybe I would manage to convince Begin to soften it or change the wording. But Begin pressed me. An hour passed, and he asked, 'Yehiel, why isn't the radio broadcasting my announcement?' Two hours later, he asked again, 'Did they broadcast the announcement yet?' I replied, 'They haven't broadcast it yet because I haven't given it to them yet. I'll give it to them soon.' I hoped he would change his mind. He became very dissatisfied, and said, 'Yehiel I'm asking you to send that announcement to the media.' Then I said, maybe we should change the wording. Begin replied categorically: 'Don't change anything.' I had no choice but to send the announcement, and it was broadcast and quoted. The next day, all the media outlets attacked Begin for making a comparison between Arafat and Hitler."

On June 15, at the height of the war, Begin went to the United States for talks with President Reagan. The IDF had penetrated deep into Lebanese territory, beyond the forty-kilometer (twenty-five mile) invasion Defense Minister Sharon had stated in the framework of a limited operation. The question began to arise whether the events were a natural development under the circumstances, or whether Sharon had dragged Begin and the entire government behind him. Following this, Israel found itself in Lebanon for three years. From the beginning of the fighting until late 1982, 454 Israeli soldiers fell there; 2,435 were wounded; eleven were taken prisoner; and five were declared missing in action.

In Lebanon in September 1982, Christian Phalangists massacred Palestinians in the refugee camps Sabra and Shatila. Yehiel was in Nahariya when he received the news. Nations around the world held Israel responsible for the butchery, dragging after them the Israeli far left, which harshly condemned Begin and his government, mainly Sharon.

Eventually, the Cohen Committee was established to investigate what happened in the Lebanese refugee camps. "This was the worst, most traumatic event for Begin personally," Yehiel recalled. "He decided to establish the committee, and as prime minister, he testified before it. We sat there, in a lecture hall at Hebrew University, with Cabinet Secretary Dan Meridor on his left and me on his right. The committee was composed of Justice Yitzhak Cohen, Major General Yona Efrat, and Aharon Barak. They sat on a raised platform, while we sat below them, like accused criminals before the judge. That committee would never have taken place in any other country in the world. Look at what happened in Vietnam, at My Lai, American soldiers carried out horrific acts. Afterward there was a trial. But in Vietnam or Cambodia, when the Khmer Rouge carried out massacres, for example, when they murdered a whole village of farmers with the American army nearby, did they establish an investigative committee against the commander of the American battalion? Or against the commander of the US forces? Or against the US secretary of defense? Has such a thing ever been heard of? Or in the war between the Serbs and the Croats, let's say they invaded a refugee camp and carried out a massacre. The UN was there, the British were there, but were they guilty? I'm just saying, let's say there's a difference – they are peacemakers, and we were a foreign force. But is that a reason to establish an investigative committee and blame the prime minister? Begin himself called the event, 'Non-Jews murdering non-Jews and blaming the Jews,' and he was fully justified, because that's exactly what it was.

"What broke Begin was that the ones who created all these complications and directed the finger of blame at us were themselves Jews, Israelis. So the IDF was nearby, that was true. But we didn't spill one drop of blood – and suddenly we are to blame. The Christians who carried out the massacre, they weren't responsible one bit. Only we were. In truth, we weren't responsible at all, and Jews were the only ones who blamed us. The demonstration of four hundred thousand people in the square, and the committee that wanted to accuse Sharon and Raful and Begin of participating in murder – these were unacceptable. The committee never should have been established, and when they did form it, they should have reached clear conclusions that our army was not guilty for anything that happened there. The fact that they are murderers by nature, that they behave like wild animals – how can our army be guilty for that? Begin answered the accusations honestly and clearly. He gave exact answers, the pure truth. He did not take a lawyer for himself, and did not prepare any answers. He replied to the questions that were asked. He did not hesitate in his replies, he did not stutter, but spoke fluently and candidly. He described what happened according to his understanding. If they had passed any sanctions against him, he would have got up and left. But the honorable committee did not do so. Begin took a long-term view. He saw that this was a war of deliverance, which others saw only a decade later. If they had not done everything, including Beirut, including forty kilometers and beyond – if they had not banished all those terrorists, down to the very last one, our entire position in the Gulf War would have been different. If we had not banished them, then in 1991, the number of terrorists would have reached two hundred thousand, maybe a quarter of a million, with much greater quantities of weapons and ammunition. Undoubtedly they would have dragged Jordan with them, because it was on the side of Saddam Hussein anyway, and Syria as well. If we hadn't banished them then, in 1991 they could have reached Tiberias and Safed."

Another derivative of this war was the libel suit filed by Arik Sharon against *Haaretz* newspaper in June 1996. Yehiel gave a deposition in which he testified that Sharon did not deceive or lie to Begin and that the prime minister was aware of all the proceedings. Yehiel also stated: "Menachem Begin saw the main purpose of Operation Peace for Galilee as banishing the terrorists from Lebanon and removing the threat to the entire State of Israel, and specifically to the northern settlements. Military experts explained to Begin that the minimum distance that the IDF had to reach in order to remove this threat was forty kilometers and that it was advisable to do so. Therefore, the government decided to initiate Peace for Galilee, as an operation designed to banish the PLO to a distance of forty kilometers, in order to remove the northern settlements from the terrorists' range of fire. At the time, Begin knew, and he expressed this opinion to me and to others, that implementation of the goal of the operation – banishing the terrorists from Lebanon – would require crossing the forty-kilometer line. He considered this advisable because to him, the main purpose was to banish the terrorists from Lebanon. For this reason, and for other military reasons, the details of which I am not familiar with, the IDF crossed the forty-kilometer line in the first days of the war, and reached the outskirts of Beirut, while eradicating terrorists and destroying their bases. Begin was deeply involved in every detail and well informed on the operation proceedings, and viewed the IDF's advancement positively. I remember well that on one of the first days of the war, after the IDF had passed the forty-kilometer line, I was bothered by the media reports and rumors, as if the advancement had been made without Begin's knowledge or against his opinion. I went into his office and began to talk to him about my concerns. Begin knew my opinions and intentions better than anyone, and he hushed me, saying, 'Yehiel, onward!'

"Begin was deeply hurt by the conclusions of the national investigative committee on the massacre at the Sabra and Shatila refugee camps. In his opinion, the committee had done an injustice to the State of Israel and to Defense Minister Ariel Sharon. Begin did not want to remove Sharon from his position, and when he was forced to do so, he told me it was 'the most difficult period of his life.'

"In August 1983, Begin announced his resignation from his position as prime minister, implementing his previous announcement that he would resign when he reached age seventy, and due to deep exhaustion, physical weakness, and heavy depression due to the death of his dear wife, Aliza, who died in November 1982. There is no connection between Begin's resignation from the government and the result of Operation Peace for Galilee in general, or to any issue involving Defense Minister Ariel Sharon in particular. Begin did not see the results of Peace for Galilee as a failure – on the contrary. Begin viewed it and its results as an important step in the advancement of Israel's security."

Yehiel added to his statement: "Menachem Begin was well aware of the harsh criticism voiced by the media against Peace for Galilee and against his and Sharon's involvement. Begin rejected this criticism outright. He believed in the justice of the operation's goal and its importance, and he was convinced until the day he died that Peace for Galilee achieved its goals and removed the threat that faced the State of Israel. Begin mourned the fallen deeply, but he asserted that the results were desirable, important, and prevented danger to the state. He was not 'disappointed,' 'full of bitterness,' or 'deceived' in anything related to the operation. Begin viewed Minister Sharon as the one who faithfully and determinedly implemented his will and the will of the government in destroying the PLO state [sic] in Lebanon and removing the threat to the State of Israel, and he was very grateful to him for that. I never heard Begin say a word; I never noticed any sign or indication that he thought that Defense Minister Sharon had lied to him. From my extensive, deep, and long-term acquaintance with Menachem Begin and with his opinions, views, and reactions, and noting the close relationship between myself and him, I state that if he had thought that Minister Sharon had lied to him, I would have known about this. Begin did not hesitate to direct my attention to matters on which he thought that anyone, including Ariel Sharon, was not exact in his words. For example, when Sharon expressed himself on the issue of Jordan being the equivalent of Palestine, and ascribed to Begin things he did not say,

Begin instructed me to refute these words publicly, and I did so. This public refutation led to a newspaper interview in which I was asked in this same context whether Ariel Sharon had lied to Begin, and I replied then, as I do now: 'Ariel Sharon did not lie to him.' Begin greatly esteemed Sharon as a military leader and excellent strategist and tactician, and this esteem did not change until the day Begin died. Begin went out of his way to express this esteem for Sharon. For example, Begin pointed out to me the decision in Sharon's libel trial against *Time* weekly magazine, which Sharon showed him, expressing great satisfaction at Sharon's achievement in that decision. Afterward, Begin even sent a telegram congratulating Sharon on the results of the trial."

As previously mentioned, at the beginning of 1982 the settlements in the Rafiah salient were evacuated. Some residents of Yamit had to be forcibly removed by the IDF. Yehiel had his own opinions on the matter, but he did not mention them to Begin.

"It was not my role to state my opinion," Yehiel recounted. "He didn't need to hear anything from me. Regarding Yamit as well, I'm sure he could read my negative opinion on my face."

But Yehiel was Begin's right-hand man, and he used that same hand to cover his mouth and prevent himself from saying things that did not correspond with Begin's worldview or decisions. In December 1981, a letter reached the prime minister's office from a girl named Goni Sorek who lived in a moshav in the Rafiah salient. She wrote: "I live in Moshav Ugdah. I think it is forbidden to evacuate the salient, because if the late Sadat wanted real peace, we shouldn't have to evacuate the settlements. I'm asking you to take action on this. Thank you." She received a reply from Yehiel: "Dear Goni. The prime minister received your letter and of course he understands your feelings. Although we all share the ache and distress of the need to give up our settlements in Sinai, you would certainly agree that the pain of peace is preferable to the pain of war. Therefore, dear Goni, despite the pain, and in order to achieve peace, we must keep all the promises we made in the agreements we signed."

***

Begin continued to serve in his position, although it became harder for
him every day, as each day brought a new burden. In November 1982, a
trip to Los Angeles was planned.

"We flew to the US in a military plane," Yehiel recollected. "We made
an intermediate stop at an American airfield in England, 186 miles north of
London, and there we received the bitter news of the collapse of an Israeli
government building in Tyre, Lebanon, following a gas leak. Seventy-five
soldiers died in the disaster. Begin had suffered many tragedies, despite his
weak health, and weathered them all. After we reached the United States,
three days after the Tyre disaster, on 28 Heshvan 5743 (November 14,
1982), thousands of miles from Israel, he received word that his beloved
wife, Aliza, had died."

Begin had not been looking forward to that trip to the US. But his wife,
who was already hospitalized and attached to an oxygen tank, reassured
him that everything would be fine, and that he should definitely make the
trip.

"We reached Los Angeles on Friday morning," Yehiel recalled. "We
went to the hotel. Begin was supposed to speak on Saturday night at 7
p.m. at a giant Israel Bonds dinner that was planned in a fancy hotel. In
the afternoon Begin lay down to rest, and at 6 p.m., we had planned that I
would go into his room to check if he was ready for the speech. But at 4:45
I was called to the phone, which was in one of the hotel rooms that served
as the Israel consular office during our visit. Benny Begin was on the
line, and he gave us the terrible news: Aliza was dead. I looked hurriedly
for Dr. Gottesman, the physician on the delegation, but I couldn't find
him. I found out later that he had gone to synagogue for the afternoon
prayer service. Dr. Gottesman carried a beeper with him, and one of the
security officers sent a message, but he didn't respond. We later found
out that at that minute, Dr. Gottesman had been called up to the Torah at
the service, so he didn't hear the beeper. It was clear to me that due to the
tragic circumstances, our visit would be cut short. I called a meeting of
the airplane staff, who were not in the hotel, and asked them to prepare the
plane to return to Israel. The security personnel managed to locate them
rapidly, and informed me that the plane would be ready to fly at 9 p.m. At
the same time, I contacted the bonds heads and informed them of what had

happened and that we would have to cancel the dinner.

"In the meantime, Dr. Gottesman returned to the hotel, and I told him the sad news. We went into Begin's room together. Hart Hasten of Indianapolis, one of Begin's close friends, was also with us. We found Begin sitting in an armchair, reading a book. He was ready for the speech, dressed in a suit and tie. Begin looked at us and immediately understood that something had happened. There was no reason for all of us to come into the room together, and furthermore, our expressions revealed that something was wrong. Then I told him the sad news, that his son Benny had called and told us that Aliza had passed away. When I said the difficult words, he said, 'Why did I leave her alone?' He stood up and went into the bathroom to take off the tie. When he returned, I told him, 'We're going back to Israel.' He murmured, 'Yes, of course.'"

Several minutes later Yehiel said to Begin, "I want to call Haim Corfu in Jerusalem to tell him about the gravesite. Where do you want Ala to be buried?"

Begin looked at him and said, "Yehiel, I already wrote it down in the will I entrusted you with!"

"Will?" Yehiel inquired in astonishment.

"Yes!" Begin replied. "I gave it to you when I was hospitalized in Ichilov."

Yehiel tried to remember what Begin was talking about. His memory had never failed him, but the topic of the will didn't light any bulbs. Suddenly he remembered something – perhaps that was what Begin meant. Before the elections that had led to the "turnaround," Begin had been hospitalized in Ichilov Hospital, and Yehiel went to visit him there. Begin awaited him, and in his hand was a long, sealed envelope. He gave it to Yehiel, saying, "Take care of this." Yehiel didn't ask extraneous questions. He took the envelope, and when he arrived home, he stuck in a small tin box that had once contained chocolates, and buried it in a cubbyhole in the bookcase. "That was my will," Begin informed Yehiel in Los Angeles.

"I never opened the envelope," Yehiel said in a whisper. "I don't know what it says."

"It was my will," Begin said in choked voice. "I wrote that when the time comes, I ask to be buried next to the graves of Moshe Barazani and

Meir Feinstein on the Mount of Olives."[11]

Yehiel left the room and called Haim Corfu, who was the Herut Party's contact person for the burial society. He asked Corfu to arrange the closest places to the graves of Barazani and Feinstein. Shortly afterward, the prime minister and his entourage were on their way to the waiting airplane.

The flight to Israel took sixteen hours, including a short stop in New York. The whole time, Begin closeted himself in the bedroom that had been installed in the plane, his world destroyed. The funeral was held the next day, shortly after they arrived in Israel.

Among those who flew on that plane to Israel were Hart Hasten, a businessman and director of Herut in the US, and one of Begin's close friends. Theirs was not a long friendship, but it was a strong one, as if they had been together in the underground.

Hart first heard of Begin after the Holocaust, while in a displaced persons' camp in Austria. He later moved to the United States. His brother made aliyah on board the *Altalena*. The first meeting between Hart and Begin took place in 1969. For years, Hasten was the one who introduced Begin at the Israel Bonds meetings. Yehiel first heard of Hart on March 1, 1976, at the *brit milah* (circumcision ceremony) of Josh, Hart's youngest son. Menachem Begin, who was then in the US on a speaking tour together with Eli Ben Elissar, was *sandak* (honored with holding the baby during the ceremony). Begin changed his route in order to attend the *brit*, as a sign of esteem for Hasten. After the circumcision ceremony, which was held in Indianapolis, Begin intended to continue to Los Angeles, his next destination.

"The moment the *brit* was over, the phone rang in our home," Hart recounted. "I picked up the phone, and a guy named Yehiel Kadishai from Jerusalem asked to speak with Menachem Begin. I passed the receiver to Begin. Later I learned that due to political developments and social unrest in Israel, economic decrees, corruption and bribery scandals within Rabin's government, and preliminary talks about pushing up the elections,

---

11 Barazani and Feinstein were fighters in the pre-state underground who had been sentenced to death by the British for their Zionist activities, but who had committed suicide before they could be hanged.

Yehiel proposed that Begin change his plans and return to Israel at once, as 'the smell of elections was in the air.' At the end of the conversation, Begin said to me, 'Yehiel told me that I have to go home at once.' At that occasion, he told me who this Yehiel was. It turned out he was absolutely right, and Begin's place at that moment was in Jerusalem. Begin canceled his trip to Los Angeles, rushed back to Israel, and in the elections that took place the following year, he was elected prime minister."

Here they were again in Los Angeles, and again they had to cancel the trip, but this time under tragic circumstances.

"I was with Begin in Los Angeles when we received the tragic report of Aliza's death," Hart reported. "On Saturday afternoon, I went up to the floor where he was staying, and the moment Yehiel saw me, he motioned me into one of the rooms, and there he told me that Aliza had died. He said he was trying to find Dr. Gottesman and that he wouldn't tell Begin without the doctor present. Then Yehiel asked about my wife. 'Where's Simona?' I told him that she was at her mother's house. He asked for her to come immediately, so that she could be with Leah, Begin's daughter, when she received the news. At 6 p.m., we found the doctor, and he gave Begin the news. We couldn't find Leah. Later she arrived and was shocked to find her father sitting in his room and crying, surrounded by people. 'What happened?' she asked, fearful. Everyone thought that the doctor would tell her, but no one spoke. Finally, she said, 'Mother. Something's happened to Mother.' Then I took it upon myself and said that yes, that's what happened. When the decision was made to return to Israel, Simona and I helped Begin and Leah to pack their suitcases. Begin told me that he wanted us to fly with them to Israel. We told Yehiel that we didn't have our passports, but he said we shouldn't worry, because this was a special plane for the delegation. So we flew with Begin to the funeral, and we accompanied Aliza on her final journey."

The connection between the Hasten family and Begin continued during his period of isolation following Aliza's death and his resignation from the government. Hart related, "Every time I visited Israel, I brought him books. He loved biographies, and I brought him dozens. He would finish a book a day. He sometimes wanted to talk to me about a book, but I would say I hadn't read it, I only bought it."

From the "turnaround" of 1977, Hart had gotten to know Yehiel closely and observed the close relationship between him and Begin. "Begin valued Yehiel's sensible judgment," Hart recalled. "By the way, Begin never called him 'my assistant,' but always 'my colleague' or 'my advisor.' He trusted Yehiel's honesty, decency, and boundless loyalty. Begin knew that Yehiel would never exploit anything for his personal good. I never knew anyone else so dedicated to another person as Yehiel was to Begin. This was a love story that was hard to describe. As regards his character, when needed, Yehiel knew how to walk on tiptoe, how to be strict without shouting."

CHAPTER 20

MAN WITH NO SHADOW

Begin did not stop torturing himself for listening to his wife's advice and flying to the US for his speaking engagements. He returned to Israel in mourning, broken and shattered. There was no straw that broke the camel's back, as every incident in itself was like an iron rod that broke Begin and brought him to declare, "I can't continue any more." If Aliza had still been alive, possibly the chain of events that developed would have signaled to him: enough. This despite the fact that she was always the one who encouraged him and pushed him. To him, she was the female figure addressed in Nahman Bialik's poem: "Take me under your wing / Be my mother and sister / Let your bosom be my shelter / A nest for my distant prayers." She was his support, his home. When she passed away, it was like the destruction of his home.

The year 1983 was marked by terror attacks in Israel and Begin's resignation from the top position in government.

- January: El Al renewed flights after four months of strikes. The stock market collapsed, and investors lost a total of one hundred billion shekels.
- February: The Cohen Committee published its conclusions, including harsh accusations against several individuals, with Defense Minister Ariel Sharon at the top of the list. Sharon resigned from his position and became minister without portfolio, and Moshe Arens replaced him.
- March: The physicians went on strike for four months, during which they breached a court ruling ordering them back to work. Chaim Herzog was chosen sixth president of the state.
- April: Moshe Levi replaced Raphael Eitan as IDF chief of

general staff. American Secretary of State George Schultz visited Israel in an attempt to push forward negotiations with Lebanon.

- May: An agreement with Lebanon was signed, but attempted terror attacks continued against IDF soldiers in the north.
- June: A series of attacks targeted IDF soldiers in Lebanon. The number of dead since the beginning of the Lebanon War reached five hundred. Israelis demonstrated against remaining in Lebanon.
- July: Israel decided to retreat south from Beirut to a new line along the Awali River. An attack was carried out against the Islamic College in Hebron, to avenge the murder of yeshiva student Aharon Gross.
- August: Nine months after the death of his wife, Aliza, Menachem Begin announced his intention to resign.

On August 28, 1983, Begin entered his office full of thought. Even before he managed to ask, in time-honored tradition, "Where's Yehiel?" Yehiel had already entered the room to check something.

"I'm glad you're here," Begin said, "I want to tell you that in today's cabinet meeting, I'm going to announce that I'm terminating my position as prime minister."

If the sky did not fall on Yehiel's head, it was only because "this was not great surprise to me," as he admitted. "Why? Because he had already said it more than once, and I always responded, 'What's the rush? You'll get through it.' During that period, there were times when he said to me, especially after a day when he wasn't at his best: 'Tomorrow I won't come. I'll rest at home.' I said, 'What can you do? Sometimes a person doesn't feel so well.' But the next day he would arrive full of energy. Then I said, at two or three opportunities, 'You're the proof that the spirit conquers the body.' But the matter ran much deeper. The main thing with him was the feeling that he could no longer do perfect work, as a result of his emotional and physical state. He was a perfect perfectionist by nature, or perfect in a perfectionist manner. He didn't like things that weren't done properly. I don't mean that he was a pedant about everything. But everything that he did had to be perfect. For example, he never used Russian when speaking, even though he understood and spoke that language. But because he couldn't speak it perfectly, he couldn't express everything he wanted to, and so he felt that an educated person like him should not speak Russian. This was the case with French as well. He understood French; he read *Le Monde* every day. But he would not speak French in public. Sometimes he would give an interview on French radio, and he would say some introductory words in French, ten or twenty sentences – because the French don't appreciate it when you speak to them in any other language. He would go to his sister, Rachel Halperin, who was a French teacher, and read her his written notes of what he planned to say. She would correct his pronunciation or the accents. He would practice it four or five times, until he could speak the text properly. Sometimes he would also consult with his nephew, journalist Emmanuel Halperin, who would help him to correct his French. Because Begin wanted to speak perfectly – without mistakes. His resignation was also a direct result of this feeling. He sensed that he was no longer perfect in his actions. He said to me several times, 'Look, I'm not the same man that I was.'"

As was his habit, Yehiel did not attend the dramatic cabinet meeting at which Begin announced his intention to resign. Yehiel accompanied him up the stairs to the floor of the cabinet meeting room. On the way, Begin met Azriel Nevo, and he told him of his impending announcement. The ministers were surprised to hear that he intended to resign, and tried to convince him to retract, or at least reconsider. But Begin was unwilling to acquiesce to any request. He was firm in his decision. During the meeting, he called Yehiel in and asked that he bring him the Knesset bylaws, so that he could see the exact wording of the paragraph referring to a prime minister who announces his resignation. Yehiel brought him the text, and he wrote in his handwriting: "To the President of the State of Israel: Mr. President, in accordance with paragraph 21a of 'Basic Law: The Government,' I hereby inform you of my resignation from the office of prime minister." Finance Minister Yoram Aridor stood up and said, "I don't understand what's going on here. Even if you submit your resignation right now, you'll still go into the prime minister's office, because some time will pass until the Knesset receives the notice, something like twenty-four hours, maybe more. It's a formal process. So why are you in such a hurry to submit your letter of resignation right now?" Begin gave the impression that it was urgent for him to end his position right then, that he felt he had to leave the place immediately. But Aridor's argument convinced him, and he didn't send the letter to the president right then and there. The Knesset meeting ending, Begin returned to his office, and then he went home – never to return to his position. The letter of resignation was sent to President Herzog nineteen days after Begin announced his intention to resign, by Cabinet Secretary Dan Meridor. The Herut Party central committee elected Yitzhak Shamir as Begin's successor in the prime minister's office, and President Herzog appointed him to assemble a new government. Meanwhile, Begin closed himself up in his home, and was only next seen in public in December 1983, when he moved into a new apartment at 1 Zemach Street in Jerusalem. His isolation continued for nine years, eight in Jerusalem and one in Tel Aviv.

Begin left behind a profound enigma. But for Yehiel, it was no mystery at all.

"The articles in the newspapers, the open letters, and the endless attacks in the media, the demonstrations – these did not affect him at all," Yehiel confided. "Neither did the demonstration [of the 'four hundred thousand'] in the square. For him, what embodied the verse in Psalms, 'they swarmed about me like bees' (118:12), was the increasing burden on his narrow shoulders, the accumulation of disasters, the constant chain of grim events and the victims that Lebanon continued to demand." The story was told that Aliza Begin once called Simcha Ehrlich and asked him to avoid calling Begin at night to inform him of victims, because he would get up and cry all night and couldn't go back to sleep, so deep was his sorrow. In addition to all this, the death of his wife Aliza and his shaky health caused him to collapse internally.

Yehiel added, "At one point, he said to me: 'In my state of health, thin as a rail, when I'm able to fit two, even three fingers between my shirt collar and my neck, when my voice is barely heard – how can I go like this to President Reagan?'"

Yehiel followed Begin, resigning from his position as chief of staff. He became Begin's personal secretary once again, and continued to work in the state archives for several months. He poured over Begin's materials along with journalists who came to interview him, related stories of Begin's service, answered questions, explained and clarified. Simultaneously, from the resignation until Begin's death, he visited the leader's home daily.

"Begin continued the same routine he had followed for many years," Yehiel recounted. "He was awake at dawn, listened to the early morning news on the radio, read the papers that were delivered to his house – *Al Ha-Mishmar* in Tel Aviv, *Haaretz* and the *Jerusalem Post* in Jerusalem. Later in the day, I brought him *Davar* and the afternoon papers, and on the weekends the newspapers' weekly magazines. I also brought him his mail, and as in the past, he dictated replies to the numerous letters he received. His replies were typed, and the next day I would bring them for his signature. Regardless of his physical state, his mind functioned brilliantly, his memory was clear, he listened to the news and was aware of current events. He continued doing all the things he always did, with one big difference – now he was free of the heavy burden of directing state affairs. There was a small number of close friends he wanted to see, and they would come visit: Ya'akov Meridor and his wife Zipporah; Dan Meridor, who came once a week; Esther Raziel-Naor, Natan Silver, and sometimes Moshe Nissim. Ambassador Sam Lewis and his wife Sally came two or three times during his period of seclusion. Shamir came on occasion, mainly before or after a trip abroad, when he had something to relate. Some tried to consult with him on political affairs, but he refused outright to give advice. When the state faced crucial issues, I tried to obtain his opinion. I would express my thoughts, and if he agreed, he would nod his head and say, 'Yes, yes.' When he thought differently, he would say, 'Yes, but…' He categorically refused to get involved in current events. Begin insisted on remaining inside his house in Jerusalem, except when he had to leave for medical examinations or treatments in the hospital, and for the memorial ceremony for his wife. Later, when he moved to 4 Glicksberg Street in Tel Aviv, he went out three or four times, no more, to a park near the apartment. This was after he was released from Ichilov Hospital for a repeat operation on his hip, after a similar operation at Hadassah Hospital in Jerusalem had been unsuccessful. One of the reasons he avoided going out in the street was because of his nature: he felt obligated to answer any person who addressed him. If someone asks me something in the street but I don't feel like talking to him, I say good day, and keep walking. If someone called him on the phone and he didn't feel like responding, he would say, 'Thanks for calling,' and hang up the phone. But he knew that if he went out in the street, he was certain to pass someone, an acquaintance or stranger, who would address him: 'How are you, Mr. Begin?' Then he would answer, 'Fine, thank you for asking, and how are you?' The next question would be, 'Why are you sitting at home?' or 'What do you think about what Moda'i said, or Rabin, or Peres, or anyone else?' Because of his gentlemanlike character, he couldn't just flap his hand as if waving off an annoying fly. He preferred to stay home in order to avoid all this."

One day, when longtime refusenik Ida Nudel arrived in Israel, a journalist from *Haaretz* phoned Begin's home. He picked up the receiver, and the journalist asked him what he thought about Nudel's arrival. "I'm very happy that she's finally come to Israel," Begin replied. "I wish her welcome." He hung up the phone. Five minutes later, the phone rang again. The journalist tried to ask him another question, on a political issue. "You're working very hard," Begin said, and hung up. This time the journalist got the hint, and didn't bother him again.

"For example, he didn't want Moda'i to come and give him a whole lecture about the party or political issues," Yehiel explained, "because let's say Begin didn't respond. Then Moda'i might go out, meet a journalist, and relate that he had visited Begin. Then he would repeat to the journalist the whole long lecture he had given Begin, and because Begin didn't refute him – when actually he hadn't responded at all – Moda'i would present it as Begin's opinion. A few days later, Gideon Pat or Abrasha Sharir or someone else would come along and say the opposite of what Moda'i had said. Begin wouldn't react, and the same scene would repeat itself. This is exactly what Begin wanted to avoid. Thus from the outset, he decided to take preventive measures. He knew what might happen, he knew some people would try to use him for all kinds of purposes that he agreed with or didn't agree with, and he simply gave up this privilege."

Before the fateful personal transformation that led to his resignation, Begin had mentioned to Yehiel several times that when he left the job, he would write a book about his life. He was mainly referring to the period prior to World War II, from 1930 to 1939, as well as his period in the role of prime minister. He had already written several books, including *The Revolt*, on the Jewish battle against the British from 1944 to 1948, and *White Nights*, the story of his imprisonment and suffering in Siberia during World War II. The missing part was his life in Poland and Czechoslovakia. The events after 1948 were recorded in the Knesset proceedings and the newspapers – they were already written, and only needed to be thoroughly researched and organized. (Of course, some of the media reports about him would have to be viewed critically.)

One of the last visitors to see Begin in seclusion in Tel Aviv was businessman Avraham Friedman, Honorary Consul of Finland in Israel. He had been a member of the Haganah high command, but despite this, he had personal ties with Begin, who maintained a high opinion of him. They had become friendly in 1948, after the Irgun came out of the underground to a certain extent, after the British announced their intention to leave. The financial situation of the Irgun was dire – they did not have enough cash to feed and clothe their six hundred soldiers. Begin contacted Friedman, who had already become a successful businessman, and explained the problem. Friedman was manager of a bank, and he arranged a loan that helped solve the problem. Begin never forgot this gesture.

One morning, Friedman called Yehiel and said, "Reb Yehiel, is there any reason why I can't see Menachem?"

"I'll check into it," Yehiel replied.

During his meeting that day with Begin, Yehiel asked him about the possibility, and Begin replied, "Why not? Please tell him to come."

Yehiel called Friedman and said, "Reb Avrum, please come tomorrow at 10 a.m."

This was ten days before Begin died. Yehiel was in his home in the morning, and at 9:55 he went down to the building entrance, just as Friedman's car parked in front. He escorted Friedman into the apartment. Begin and Friedman were happy to see each other, and immersed themselves in nostalgic conversation. At one point, Begin said to Friedman, "Do you recall our meeting in 1945? Do you remember what I told you about the Haganah people?"

"Yes," Friedman replied. "I definitely remember."

"I won't say it again," Begin continued. "You say it."

Friedman recalled, "You said: They'll attack us, they'll imprison us, and in the end they'll kill us."

Begin's shaky health led to several hospitalizations. In March 1992, he was hospitalized in Ichilov Hospital in Tel Aviv following excessive weakness. His condition declined, and he was transferred to the intensive care unit. Yehiel did not leave his side. On March 8, 1992, at 8 p.m., Yehiel was in the corridor, as Begin was no longer permitted visitors due to his condition. Yehiel left the hospital and went home, expecting to see his leader and friend again in the morning. His hope was not to be fulfilled.

At 5 a.m. on Monday, 4 Adar II 5752 (March 9, 1992), Benny Begin phoned Yehiel and told him the terrible news that his father had returned his soul to his Maker. After a silence, Benny added that he would like to meet with Yehiel in the Begin home at 6 a.m.

"I went to the chest of drawers in my living room," Yehiel recalled, "where I had placed Begin's will, which I had kept since 1977 in a tin box that had once held chocolates. It was still in an envelope of Hasharon Hotel. When I arrived at Begin's home, I opened the envelope in the presence of his three children – Benny, Hasia, and Leah. It had only three lines. This was the first time I had ever seen it. The previous time it had been relevant, when Aliza died, Begin had told me about it. It read: 'My dear Yehiel, please read aloud before my beloved relatives and friends my request, as follows: I ask to be buried on the Mount of Olives beside Meir Feinstein and Moshe Barazani. I hereby extend my thanks to you and all those who are involved in fulfilling this request. Yours with love, Menachem Begin.'"

The funeral was held on the same day, and its character was determined by statements about funerals that Begin had made to his son over the years. Begin also once said to Yehiel that in Brisk, the custom was not to "play around with the dead." In other words, they didn't place great emphasis on pomp and ceremony. When a person died, he was given a Jewish burial and that was the end of it. The funeral had no state character, no honor guards, no eulogies – ironically, this was Begin, who appreciated ceremony and formalities. At the moment of truth, his true character was revealed to those who had yet to become acquainted with it: modest, simple, not high above the nation, but one of the people.

The announcement of Begin's death was broadcast on Israel radio at 7 a.m. The announcement of the time of the funeral was made around noon. In between, thousands of people spontaneously made the trip to Jerusalem, without knowing exactly when the funeral would take place. Thousands gathered near the funeral parlor in Sanhedria to pay their last respects, and from there they continued on foot to the Mount of Olives.

"Begin was unique in his simplicity," Yehiel specified. "He never made a big deal of himself. Most of his life, he barely had his own office. But there was not one case – in his good days, of course – when someone asked to meet him and was refused. All his life he lived in that small, wretched apartment. Millionaires in Israel and abroad offered to purchase an apartment in their name, and he could live there to 120, the rest of his life. He never agreed. My apartment, which he visited on more than one occasion, was nothing special, but it was a palace alongside his. He was never impressed by external displays of wealth. He respected wealthy individuals who donated to good causes, to do good works. He was the embodiment of the simple Jew, and that was how he wanted people to relate to him. He never looked for titles. He agreed to accept an honorary degree from Yeshiva University, only because he didn't want to insult them. The ceremony and everything it involved was a real nightmare for him. I walked beside him when he received the degree, but the hat, the gown, he almost collapsed due to them. True, he was always careful about his appearance and he had special characteristics of external dignity, but mainly he had internal dignity. This was the main component of his behavior."

When Begin was laid to rest, Yehiel walked behind the coffin, grounded in reality: "I didn't think about Begin's passing in kabbalistic or apocalyptic terms, like 'the light of our eyes has been extinguished,' or other such expressions. I saw the process day by day: he faded slowly, and then he disappeared."

After Begin's death, Yehiel found in his home a touching letter, which reveals worlds about its writer. The letter shows Begin's warmhearted attitude toward every human being, from any sector of society, no matter what his or her views.

Yehiel related: "This story took place in the 1950s. A young woman named Lidia, secretary of the Labor Party faction in the Knesset, became friendly with Dov Alpert, secretary of the Herut Party in the Knesset. The two became close.

"To Labor Party members, the relationship was a desecration of their sacred values. Alpert had grown up in an extreme ultra-Orthodox, anti-Zionist family; then he had joined the Irgun and was imprisoned by the British at Latrun. How could someone from the Alignment fall in love with a member of Herut? And a former Neturei Karta member to boot? And worst of all, he had been in the Irgun. She was fired from her job.

"At the time, Begin was in Montevideo on a fundraising trip for Shelah. In one of his phone calls to his fellow party faction members, they told him about the incident. He wasted no time, but sat in the hotel in Uruguay and sent this letter to Ya'akov Meridor. He asked him to find a job for this young woman: 'Perhaps in our Knesset faction, even though we don't have the budget, we'll raise a few *lirot* so that we can employ her. We must help her!' In the end it did no good, and Lidia, who was deeply wounded by the incident, left Israel. Later I discovered that she became a successful professor of psychology in New York."

Yehiel also said, "In our party, we always helped people. Most of my work was focused on helping people, and I never gave a thought to whether they were 'our people' or not. If a citizen came and asked for help with an institution that had mistreated him, I picked up the phone and asked why did this happen, and that was it. Shouldn't that be taken for granted?"

***

In 1983, Yehiel's position as chief-of-staff ended with Begin's resignation from the post of prime minister. His job as personal secretary to Begin ended when his leader's soul resigned from this world. All in all, Yehiel had accompanied Begin for twenty-eight continuous years, six of which he served as chief of staff in the prime minister's office (1977–83), and twenty-two as his secretary (1964–77; 1983–92).

"For Yehiel, Begin was not a tool for advancement in life," Benny Begin emphasized. "And for Begin, Yehiel was not a tool to fulfill his demands. I would say that for my father, Yehiel was a friend who was there to help. Above all, the two families enjoyed a long history of friendship, true friendship. Their friendship smoothed the road for working together in the office. Yehiel was graced with the ability to make peace, to refuse politely, and especially – discretion. Lack of discretion made Menachem Begin angry, it really drove him up the wall. He refused to accept leaks. What's more, chiefs of staff are usually ambitious youngsters who use the job as a springboard, or people who know how to get things done, and by nature are not nice people, people for whom only results matter. But for Yehiel, the end did not justify the means, as my father wrote in *White Nights*, and on this issue, there was complete agreement between them. The difference in ages between them was relatively small, only ten years, and their acquaintance, meant that he was more of a friend than a clerk or assistant. Above all, Yehiel was an experienced person who had done something in his life. He had experienced the war in Europe, and he was very faithful to that concept of public service, from childhood. Yehiel was knowledgeable, he read and quoted, he traveled with my father for many long hours in cars and airplanes, and they had long conversations. In a speech at Metzudat Ze'ev, after the Likud won the elections, my father used the verse from Jeremiah: 'I remember the lovingkindness of your youth…how you went after Me in the desert, in a land not sown' (2:2) – Yehiel was part of that following in the desert."

Many public figures knew Yehiel well, and were able to describe his relationship and work with Begin.

Aryeh Han, former secretary of the Mafdal (NRP) Knesset faction, related: "Begin almost never moved in the Knesset without Yehiel, his right-hand man. One day I sat in the Knesset cafeteria with Yehiel. Begin was then in the opposition, and Yehiel was secretary of the faction. Begin entered the cafeteria, went to the buffet, then came to our table and said to Yehiel, 'I would like to remind my secretary that you need to remind me about such-and-such a matter.' It was a cute joke, but in actuality it had no basis, because he never needed to remind Yehiel about anything."

Dan Meridor added: "I met Yehiel in the late sixties after I was released from the army, after beginning university studies and activity in the Herut Party. I was a director of the Jerusalem branch, and quickly I became a central committee member. Once every month or two, I went to Metzudat

Ze'ev, where we sat in many meetings together. Despite his official title, I wouldn't say that Yehiel was Knesset faction secretary, rather that he was the man beside Menachem Begin. We became very friendly, because Yehiel was very well educated, particularly in Jewish topics, well versed in the weekly Torah portion and its commentaries. Although we were twenty-five years apart in age, we talked about these topics as friends, in Hebrew, of course, although here and there spiced with Yiddish. Above all, we talked about the Herut Party and Jabotinsky's writings, as I had also grown up with those topics and I was also informed on them, so we had a lot in common. In December 1981, when I was working as a lawyer, Yehiel was the one who called me and said I was going to be appointed as cabinet secretary. He also apologized in Begin's name that he hadn't called me personally, because just before that he had broken his leg, and he was in terrible pain. I asked Yehiel to give me half an hour. I consulted with my wife, and then I phoned him back and gave him my agreement, and shortly thereafter I began the position."

Another indelible memory for Meridor was the day Begin resigned. "When we went up to the cabinet meeting," Meridor recalled, "Yehiel told me that Begin was going to resign."

Azriel Nevo, Begin's military secretary, once consulted with Yehiel during the Lebanon War. This occurred after Ephraim (Freuka) Poran, the previous military secretary, had concluded his job. One of the senior military journalists wrote in an article in a popular newspaper, "Freuka, you're guilty" – the experienced Freuka had left the job, and a younger man, Nevo, took over. The journalist implied that had Freuka only remained, things would have been vastly different.

"I was deeply hurt," Nevo admitted. "I went to Yehiel and asked him what I should do. He replied, 'Forget it.' This answer didn't satisfy me, and I went to Begin. Even before I told him what I wanted, he grasped my hand said, 'You've probably read the article by the military writer today. Don't take it to heart, because tomorrow they'll be wrapping fish in it.' By the way, to the military correspondent's credit, a year later he published an article in the newspaper under the title "Oy, I goofed' – and he mentioned that exact article."

Further, Nevo mentioned, "It was a pleasure to talk to Yehiel. His head was exploding with knowledge – history, Bible, etcetera. On occasion, when I was pondering over some issue, and I came to consult with him, he could always pull out an answer or an idea. At the time, there was no Internet – Yehiel was our Wikipedia."

Sara and Isaac Ulkenicti, close friends of Yehiel and his wife, recounted that their granddaughter wrote her doctoral dissertation on diplomacy and space. She looked for governmental material and scoured private libraries. At her parents' suggestion, she checked Yehiel's rich library, and reported: "Not only does Yehiel have all the relevant books, he always knows what's written in each one of them."

Another story told by Azriel Nevo illustrates Yehiel's image as advocate for the ordinary citizen: "Begin had an election meeting in Beit She'an. Yehiel went with him, of course, and I also made the trip, because it was during a period of tension on the security front. A guard also rode in the car, and an escort car drove behind us. After the election meeting, we drove back to Jerusalem, when suddenly we received a message on the car radio that the prime minister was wanted on the phone. Of course, phones weren't what they are today. So we searched around for a way to call. At the exit from Beit She'an we passed a gas station. We went inside and told the shift manager that the prime minister was in the car, and we asked if he could use the phone. He was too shocked to reply, but we understood that he agreed. Begin went in, sat on one of the chairs – that chair is probably still on display at the gas station – Yehiel dialed, and Begin spoke. Before we left, Begin even apologized to the shift manager for disturbing him at such a late hour. As we drove off, we noticed two young women under a streetlamp, wearing short, seductive clothes. 'What are those girls doing here?' Yehiel wondered. I explained the facts of life, and he murmured, 'It can't be, they can't be Jews...'"

After the end of the chapter of his life connected to Begin, Yehiel began to become involved in philanthropic activity on behalf of Assaf Harofeh Medical Center at Zrifin. In fact, his contact with the hospital began years previously, during his service in the British military. As part of their physical fitness training, he and his fellow unit members went out to run an obstacle course. One of the obstacles was insurmountable for Yehiel – he stumbled, fell, and broke his leg. A military ambulance collected him and took him to the hospital at Zrifin, where his leg was put in a cast. He was hospitalized for two days there, then returned to his battalion, and until he recovered, he was given clerical jobs.

The second connection with the hospital was years later, when Aliza Begin paid a visit to a friend who was hospitalized there. Aliza returned in shock. "The situation there is simply unbearable," she related to her husband and her close friends Yehiel and Bambi. "There are no curtains inside the rooms to separate the beds, so everyone who walks by the rooms and peeks inside can see all the patients. There's no privacy. Ill people are completely exposed, and this makes it even more difficult for them to fight their illness."

No sooner had Aliza Begin spoken then she acted on her words. She contacted several friends who had more than a few coins in their deep pockets, and rapidly raised one hundred *lirot*, which in those days was considered a sizable sum. She sent this money to the hospital, and soon there were curtains in the rooms. Then someone told her that they also needed urns for use on Shabbat. Another phone call to her generous friends, and the urns were obtained. From then on, Aliza became a friend of the hospital, and when Assaf Harofeh directors needed donations for special life-saving projects, they knew how to contact her and enjoyed her assistance.

In 1982, when Aliza Begin died, the hospital decided to name a series of new wards after her, as a sign of appreciation for her activism and initiative. Until that time, the wards looked more or less like their counterparts in the Third World. The entire hospital looked more like a tent camp than a medical institution, because the majority of its budget came from donations. The hospital rooms were in cabins, some of which were not tiled. In the best case, they were partially covered with concrete.

One of the volunteers who worked to raise funds for the hospital was Tel Aviv businessman Shmuel Gottfarb, an acquaintance of Yehiel. He contacted Yehiel as a representative of the hospital, and asked him to join the friends of the hospital, whose main goal was fundraising.

This was just after Begin's resignation, and Yehiel suddenly found himself with free time on his hands. At a meeting with the hospital directors, who had invited him to discuss their proposal, he said, "I don't know what exactly you know about me, but I'm certainly no great fundraiser."

"But you know endless numbers of good Jews around the world," they replied. This knowledge could lead to donations, which in the end meant saving patients' lives. "We're counting on the fact that in time, you'll become a great fundraiser." The hospital board proposed that his first fundraising trip as a hospital representative should be to the United States.

Yehiel did know that in the Jewish world, there were hundreds and even thousands who were thirsty for details about the fascinating personage of Begin in all its complexity. There was no one better than himself, who had stood at Begin's side for decades, to tell them about him. Yehiel gave his positive answer, and in his trips overseas he was always introduced as the man who was closest to Begin, the one who addressed him by his first name. Only when others were around did he punctiliously use the full title, "Mr. Prime Minister."

"Whom do I need to convince to donate to the hospital?" Yehiel asked the hospital directors.

"You tell us," came the reply. "You have acquaintances all over the world."

Yehiel did not try to dredge up from his memory the names of potential benefactors. Instead, he contacted Haim Landau, who was well informed in the field. He proposed that Yehiel meet with Joseph Gross, a Jewish millionaire in the US who had made his fortune in the petroleum business.

Yehiel arranged a meeting with Gross in his office in one of the most exclusive skyscrapers in Manhattan. When the appointed hour arrived, Yehiel sat with Gross, and after a short conversation, the wealthy businessman came directly to the point: "Yes," he asked, "how can I help?"

"I'm representing Assaf Harofeh Hospital at Zrifin," Yehiel began. "The hospital's financial situation is desperate."

"I don't give money," Gross said.

"Look," Yehiel continued, "do as you wish. The hospital will find another donor who'll save us, but you'll remain with the knowledge that you stood alongside when you could have helped."

"I don't give money," Gross repeated.

Yehiel stood up to leave. "I wish you good health," he said, and walked toward the door.

As Yehiel stood beside the door, Gross explained: "You don't understand what I'm saying. I don't give money without a goal, but I am willing to give you a donation for the purchase of specific equipment. What do you need?"

This time he was speaking a different language, but Yehiel didn't know how to answer him. He asked permission to make a phone call from Gross's office to the office of Dr. Mordechai Waron, director of Assaf Harofeh. Gross's secretary connected him from a nearby room.

"What equipment do you need?" Yehiel asked after Dr. Waron came on the line. "I'm here with a donor."

The director related that the hospital was then negotiating with the Philips Company in Holland for constructing a catheterization room. The cost of the equipment, including constructing the room with all the necessary elements, was $1.18 million – an impossible sum in those days.

Armed with the numbers, Yehiel returned to Gross's office.

"I want to see their equipment list," Gross said to Yehiel after hearing the information.

Another phone call to Dr. Waron, and from that point on the connection continued directly between Gross'office and Philips. The deal was done, and Philips engineers came to Israel to establish the catheterization room, the last word in the field at that time. Gross funded the project from beginning to end.

"When I returned to Israel," Yehiel said, "the hospital people thought I was a genius at fundraising. I had barely finished unpacking my suitcase when they handed me a list of some more well-off Jews across the ocean."

Yehiel traveled to the US twice more, and helped establish New York and Los Angeles branches of the American Friends of Assaf Harofeh. Donations quickly rose to $45 million. A few years later, the American Friends held a benefit concert in honor of Yehiel and Bambi in a room at Carnegie Hall in New York. Eight young violinists played a special concert for them, and hundreds attended. After the concert, the committee heads invited Yehiel and Bambi to a gourmet Manhattan restaurant.

At that opportunity, Yehiel gave a speech, focusing on the story of Aliza Begin's life and the history of the hospital.

"Afterward, they made me president of the Friends' Committee," Yehiel added. "In the Friends' Committee bungalow at the hospital, there's even a room with a lovely copper sign with my name on it – although I've never even been inside that room."

Meanwhile, one of the side effects of the meeting with Gross was the firm friendship that developed between them.

"On one of my trips to the US with Bambi," Yehiel recounted, "we stayed in Manhattan over Shabbat. In the morning, we went to pray at the synagogue on Fifth Avenue, which the Zionist elite attended. Joseph Gross went to that synagogue, as well as Mirken, the well-known Wall Street banker who was friendly with Begin and admired him greatly. When I arrived at the synagogue, I noticed that Gross was absent. Mirken approached and invited me to Shabbat lunch at his home after the service. When it was over, I noticed that in the meantime, Gross had arrived. He saw that I was there, and extended an invitation on the spot: 'Yehiel, you're coming to me for Kiddush.' I told him that Mirken had already invited me, so he said to Mirken, 'I'm taking Yehiel.' 'All right,' Mirken acquiesced. 'I'll have to give him up for you.' Bambi and I went to Gross's home. He was a widower by then, and he had two maids, one Polish, the other Irish. He made Kiddush, we tasted the gefilte fish that the maids served, and then he said, 'Now let's go to Mirken.' We went down in the elevator and walked over to Mirken's home. At his place there were fifty guests enjoying a feast fit for kings. Mirken and his wife were thrilled to see Gross, because he had never been in their home. From then on, I became very friendly with Gross, whose contributions to Israel swelled. He also donated generously to institutions in the US. He brought over Israeli Supreme Court Justice Menachem Elon, along with his family, to teach Hebrew law at New York University. A year later, Gross asked me to find another Supreme Court justice for a year-long lecture series. I contacted the president of the Supreme Court, Justice Meir Shamgar. He liked the idea, but he couldn't release another judge from the court for a whole year, so the initiative was nipped in the bud."

Yehiel was closer to Menachem Begin than any other man, and when the song of his lifetime ended in service to the leader, Yehiel continued the relationship through activity for the Begin Heritage Center in Jerusalem, eventually joining its board of directors. The center was conceived in the early nineties by friends and admirers of Begin, but progress on the project was slow and unfocused. Serious efforts for building and operation began in the late nineties. Today the center is full of life, a beehive of activity for all ages and sectors of society.

Center director Herzl (Herzi) Makov had a difficult time remembering exactly when he first met Yehiel.

"When did I meet him?" he repeated the question hesitantly. "I don't know. I only know that he was always there. Since the day I formed my social, ideological, and political opinions, Yehiel was always in the background. But I got to know him closely as a result of our shared work at the Begin Heritage Center. We had many conversations, and with Yehiel, there were no empty conversations. Every conversation was ideological. He was a Betar member with all his heart and soul. He was always ready with a quote from Jabotinsky. He knew a vast amount of material by heart: poems, dates, articles, anecdotes, the wisdom of the Sages, Bible verses, Chassidic tales – a bottomless well. In this, he never showed the effects of age. Just like in his younger days, as he grew older, he was still able pull out a quote at the right time and place. I learned from him that when he worked with Begin, he didn't view himself as dealing with policy. He was more like the Rebbe's *gabbai* [assistant]. It wasn't his job to make decisions on *halachah* [Jewish law], but to take care of the Rebbe. He didn't get involved in issues, he saw himself as an aide. But despite his polite and gentle character, whenever anyone spoke badly of Begin, or desecrated Begin's memory, he risked getting raked over the coals by Yehiel. In the office, he considered himself the unofficial social worker of the entire State of Israel, and in this spirit, he took care of anyone who came to him and tried to solve their problems, and in many cases he was successful. This approach was actually a continuation of his work for Shelah. In that organization, the work was ideologically based, and he took care of our people. In the prime minister's office, it was no longer based on his private ideology, but work on behalf of all the Israeli public. During all the 'Yehiel hours' I booked over the years, I discovered a man the likes of whom I never met elsewhere: he never had a negative word about anyone, even those who probably deserved it. He had stories about people and events from fifty or sixty years back, but whenever he found himself in a difficult corner, he would hesitate and declare, 'It's better not to bad-mouth.'"

"I worked side by side with Yehiel [in the Begin Center]," Herzi reported. "When I made plans, Yehiel set the standard as far as I was concerned. I consulted with him, discussed with him, listened to his advice, adopted his ideas, and mainly checked whether certain activities were appropriate to honor Begin's memory. Whenever we published materials, booklets or films, Yehiel was the man to whom we gave the material before it was published, to hear his comments and apply them. Furthermore, every time Yehiel came to the center for a meeting, he never failed to bring along an important paper, a document of vital historical value, or rare photograph that he pulled out of his personal archive."

At the ceremony celebrating Israel's fifty-seventh Independence Day in 2005, held on Mount Herzl on the eve of the national holiday, Yehiel was given the honor of lighting a torch. The event was a perfect opportunity for Eitan Haber of *Yedioth Aharonoth* to pen a critique of the Likud. He addressed his denunciation to Ruby Rivlin, then Speaker of the Knesset, who spoke at the ceremony:

> Like all of Israel, I heard your lament at the torch-lighting ceremony. We haven't heard such a dirge for a long time.... You mourn the settlements of Gush Katif and northern Shomron, and fear disaster. Perhaps it will happen, but I'm telling you: it's not the evacuation. No Arab army can defeat us today. It's us. It's the party you represent. It's the corruption that you inadvertently support – this is what will destroy us. Want an example? Beside you during the torch-lighting ceremony stood Yehiel Kadishai. What were you thinking about as you recited the words, "For the glory of the State of Israel?" Here is a member of the nationalist party who dedicated his entire life to the party and the public. Even when he reached a position in which he could do anything for himself and his own pocket, he did nothing but act on behalf of the citizens. To this day, Yehiel lives in a small apartment on Ben Zion Avenue in Tel Aviv. He and his wife Bambi are supported by a

small pension. When he worked in the office of former Prime Minister Menachem Begin, he traveled to Jerusalem by bus or in a taxi that he shared with other employees. He always took money from his own pocket and his own private funds in order to give charity to a host of petitioners. That's the man. That is the Yehiel Kadishai that you, Ruby, and I know. What were you thinking about when you lit the torch? I'll tell you what you should have been thinking about: the long path that the party you represent has followed, away from concern for the individual, for the little guy (Jabotinsky's principles, remember?), to today's member of the Likud central committee who charges $1500 to arrange a meeting with a Likud minister...

After Begin's resignation, Aharon Bachar, one of the wittiest journalists at *Yedioth Aharonoth* and one of Yehiel's political rivals, dedicated a column to the right-hand man. His remarks were published in the Yom Kippur Eve 5745 (October 5, 1984) edition:

The journalists never granted you more than two or three lines, somewhere in the gossip section. Yehiel Kadishai, former chief of staff for the prime minister, collected a sheaf of papers from his desk, and before going on his way, his successors threw him a small going-away party. They clinked their glasses together with his.

A few days later, Yehiel was seen with the usual smile on his face, alongside the man he accompanied on a long path, without ever trying to stand out. Yehiel stood beside Begin when he left the hospital. The next day, he faded away from political life.

The halls of government are full of Young Turks who pound the corridors, roaring like lions in their constant restless attempt to attract the spotlights of publicity and fame, to climb, to reach the top. Yehiel was carved out of different human material. He sat at the very heart of authority, as Menachem Begin's closest advisor. But he never demanded glory for himself. Not only did Kadishai distance himself from publicity, he loathed the trappings of power. He traveled from Tel Aviv to Jerusalem for work on a bus or shared taxi, like an ordinary person. Every disenchanted person in this country found in him a listening ear; he assisted every orphan and widow – quietly, modestly, always from behind the scenes, always with a thin smile on his face, a friendly thump on the shoulder. If there is any substance in the exalted qualities that the Betar movement claims to uphold – then Yehiel represents the true Betar member, a "man of majesty" in the beautiful sense of the term. He was also a convivial person whom it was a pleasure to debate. Now he is going home, down his own path, back to his own private life, to that philosophical peace he has earned at his age. What could be more appropriate for a man like him, who knows how to appreciate a shared shot of whiskey, then to raise a glass from here and wish him all the best with all our hearts, health and a long life. *Le-hayim.*

Yehiel also wrote his own letters and articles that reveal much about his personality. For example, he wrote the following to Ora Namir, minister of labor and welfare, on November 13, 1995:

> My request to you is personal and human. The person asking for your assistance is S.G., a widower approaching eighty. This man is a Holocaust survivor. His health condition is described in the attached document, which details his chronic illnesses. I have known him personally for many years, and in the past few years we have worked together on the Committee of Friends of Assaf Harofeh Medical Center at Zrifin, of which he served as chairman until recently. For the past four years he has been unable to walk without assistance or in a wheelchair. The National Insurance Institute defines his disability at 95 percent. He does not need financial assistance (he is a regular contributor to charitable causes). His problem is that he needs a visa for the Polish woman who has been caring for him, as she does not have one. Can you please advise this man and

help him to solve this personal and legal issue? *Schar mitzva mitzva* – the reward for doing a good deed is the chance to do another good deed.

Often, Yehiel replied to items in the newspaper that from his point of view were incorrect. He wrote the following to *Haaretz* on December 19, 2003, in response to an article by Ze'ev Schiff, "The Hit That Wasn't Carried Out," published on December 2, 2003:

> Mr. Schiff writes emphatically that if Ehud Barak's plan to eliminate Saddam Hussein had been proposed to Prime Minister Menachem Begin, "We may assume that he would not have hesitated for long before authorizing it…, similarly to his view of the proposal to destroy the nuclear reactor in Iraq in 1981, which he authorized quickly, even though representatives of intelligence and the Mossad objected to the idea." How easy it is to type words on the keyboard that are merely words, with no basis in fact. I hereby declare that the process of deciding to destroy the Iraqi reactor lasted for over four years. Menachem Begin accepted the idea, which was in an embryonic state, as a legacy of the Rabin government, in June 1977, and the bombing was carried out in June 1981. It was a long process, involving intelligence, the Mossad, the IDF, diplomacy, and repeated investigations, which in the end led to the decision over the bombing. Although the final decision was made by the prime minister, the issue was weighed and involved deliberations. The heads of the Mossad and intelligence opposed the plan, but they admitted afterwards that they had erred in their objections. By contrast, their assistants supported bombing the reactor. In the past, Mr. Schiff has denied or belittled the importance of Operation Peace for Galilee and of banishing the PLO from the territory of the state of Lebanon, and he continues to do so at present. He pretends to understand better than others the security issues of the State of Israel. He has fixed opinions, and is unwilling to accept another point of view. Therefore I recommend that a

responsible reporter such as Mr. Schiff exercise caution before his fingers rapidly type facts that have no basis in fact.

Yehiel was a man of the people who lived with the people. He could not stand arrogance or snobbism. He once wrote to *Maariv* in response to two articles – one by poet Dalia Ravikovitch, the other by journalist Avi Raz. At the beginning of his letter, he quoted Ravikovitch:

> The girl was very young. Perhaps seventeen, lovely and scared. Her shift began early in the morning, as opposed to the workday or vacation day of the guests, which began at ten or eleven.... The chambermaid works and the guests enjoy themselves.... The guests are princes, the maid is Cinderella.... I wanted to ask her, how did an attractive girl like her find herself such a Sisyphean job as the daily cleaning of rooms, which only return to their unkempt state every morning? Of course I didn't ask. Why pour salt on her wounds? A chambermaid is only a passing shadow in the corridors. I don't know if the male guests tried to obtain night services for her in addition to the day services. The guests in the hotel were so involved in themselves that even their sexual needs were on a low level.... What do I wish for you, girl? That next year I won't find you in the hotel, if I go there once again.

Yehiel replied as follows:

> These things, the product of the thoughtful brain of Mrs. Dalia Ravikovitch, must move us to consider the poet's mood. What fault did she find in the income-generating job of the young woman? Is it not fitting for a young woman to work as a hotel chambermaid? From every possible viewpoint, every honorable job is a worthy asset for our country's citizens. Israel would be blessed to have more girls like her. Only an Israeli snob in 1989 is capable of producing such pearls of the pen.
>
> I wouldn't make this comment if I hadn't come across Mr. Avi Raz's article from last Friday in the weekend magazine,

under the title, "They Only Wanted to Get Home Safely." A person has to have a very negative attitude in order to see everything Mr. Raz saw on one bus trip on Dan line 5 in Tel Aviv. I'm also a regular passenger on Dan line 5 (and also line 4 and others on occasion). I can bear witness that in the dozens of years of my bus rides, never have I witnessed such incidents and phenomena as he describes in his shocking article.

Mr. Raz apparently belongs to the type of person who always sees the negative, and never the positive. Not only does he see, he also hears, and what's more, he has a well-developed sense of smell. In case he overlooked the smell of the passengers' sweat, he quotes an "elegant man" who "was discharged" from the bus. "After straightening his clothing slightly" and "lighting a cigarette with a shaky hand," he says, "I haven't been here for many years… I can't understand it: if everyone in this country has a car, and if everyone in this country travels abroad in the summer, how is it that there are no parking places, the streets are blocked, and the buses full?" And, "By the way, in such an advanced country as yours, haven't they heard of an invention called deodorant?"

I hold dear the young chambermaid who is earning an honorable income, and perhaps supporting her young sisters and brothers to boot. I prefer the odors of the bus passengers returning from an honest day's work to the snobby poet's scrawls and the fastidiousness of the member of Club Chanel No. 5.

In another article, Yehiel objected to any attempt to compare the Oslo agreements by Rabin and Peres to the Camp David agreements that Menachem Begin signed. Under the title "Camp David and Oslo – Two Completely Different Stories," he wrote:

The prime minister, the foreign minister, and senior or junior ministers usually assert that "The [Oslo] declaration of principles with the PLO is nothing but an improved version of the Camp David agreement – for Israel's benefit, of course."

I was in Camp David alongside Prime Minister Menachem Begin, and as an eyewitness to the proceedings, I can state that this assertion is the opposite of the truth. My statement can be proved by comparing the two documents. Perhaps some might argue that I am not fit to serve as a witness, since I am an "interested party." I thus prefer to refer to an independent source – a comparative study performed by Professor Michal Pomerantz, who teaches US foreign policy and international law at the Hebrew University of Jerusalem. What's in the declaration of principles that is not in the Camp David agreements?

At Camp David, the parties declared the legitimate rights of the Palestinians without any mention of political rights. At Oslo, mutual political rights were added. It is needless to explain the meaning of this.

At Camp David, the parties decided that the autonomy would be managed by an administrative council. At Oslo, legislative rights were added – in other words, a full and comprehensive quasi-political system.

At Camp David, the Arabs of Judea and Samaria were granted full autonomy without territory. At Oslo, they were granted, by extension, comprehensive rights over territory, including state lands and water reservoirs.

At Camp David, the Arabs of Judea and Samaria were considered part of the Jordanian delegation. At Oslo, an agreement was signed with a terror organization that declared itself a government in exile. Not only has it already received international recognition, it also received the status of a state. Who will inhabit it if not "the Palestinian diaspora"?

At Camp David, the parties decided that during the interim period, Israel would bear full responsibility for security in the autonomy. The strong local police would take on the role of assisting Israel in this. At Oslo, the issue of security was divided: internal security in the autonomous areas would be the responsibility of the Palestinian police, while external security would remain in our hands. Thus the "permitted and forbidden" in the realm of our right to self-defense were completely blurred over – for example, in the pursuit of terrorists or other criminals into the territories of the autonomy.

At Camp David, Jerusalem was not mentioned at all, except in separate, non-binding documents in which Israel, Egypt, and the United States repeated their positions. In those days, the agreement almost fell apart due to Israel's objection to a clause that did not reflect its viewpoint on the issue. At Oslo, the parties agreed for the first time to commit to discussing the issue in the final agreement. The Arab residents of Jerusalem were already given the right to participate in elections to the PA council, and by extension, to be elected.

The Camp David agreement determined that the administrative council would be established first, and after that the timetable would begin for implementing the agreement. At Oslo, the parties determined an accelerated, pressured timetable for the retreat of forces, the beginning of negotiations for a final agreement, and the end of the transition process – all these inhibit the possibility of holding negotiations calmly.

At Camp David, the framework agreement includes no clause covering resolution of disputes. At Oslo, the parties agreed on the possibility of third-party mediation, even for issues vital to our future such as the right of return, the future borders of Jerusalem, the rights of the autonomy authorities over the Jordan River bridges – the list goes on.

As opposed to Camp David, which enjoyed popular support, the Oslo agreement is based on the annulment of consensus principles. Before Oslo, these principles determined that we will not negotiate with the PLO; we will not return to the 1967 borders; we will not permit the establishment of another state between us and the Jordan River; we do not recognize the [Palestinians'] right of return; and at no stage will we discuss the issue of sovereignty over Jerusalem.

After all this, the conclusion is unavoidable: at Camp David,

Menachem Begin blocked the possibility of establishing a Palestinian state; at Oslo, Yitzchak Rabin and Shimon Peres established the Palestinian state.

In response to a newspaper article by Shulamit Har-Even, Yehiel wrote:

In 1946, when the British ruled in Eretz Israel, Ms. Shulamit Har-Even was a pupil in the eleventh or twelfth grade at Rehavia High School in Jerusalem. She is proud of the fact that Mati Sukenik [an IAF pilot shot down in the War of Independence], of blessed memory, never heard of the pupils in the classes there. Nor did those pupils not go to Birya to protect the "illegal" settlement or the weapons that the British confiscated. Yes, the issue was apparently "above their heads and mine," as she notes. Ms. Shulamit Har-Even characterizes the approach of "there's no need to hurry." And "in truth, we had no reason to hurry." This was also the attitude of many of our people's leaders at the beginning of the century, even of the Zionists among our people. Ms. Har-Even was there in those days, forty-seven years ago, a young woman of seventeen or eighteen, and that was her worldview: the slowly trickling spring...no rush.... These were the leaders of our people immediately following the Balfour Declaration...and after the mandate was given to Great Britain for the purpose of establishing a state for the Jewish people. Dr. Max Nordau shouted; Ze'ev Jabotinsky warned. But most of our leaders were in a mood of self-satisfaction.

Ms. Har-Even and those of similar character and worldview, and her intelligent friends, knew everything and understood everything, and now, they again know and understand.... They know how to give advice.... Have our sensible sages ever sat and thought, what would have happened to the Jewish people had our leaders followed a Nordau-ite or Jabotinsky-ite policy in the 1910s, the twenties, and the thirties? Is it possible that the Jewish state that Herzl envisioned would have arisen ten, twenty, or thirty years before 4 Iyyar 5708 (when the entire

Arab population of the Land of Israel, on both banks of the Jordan River, numbered no more than one hundred thousand)?

I remember Major General Har-Even. After the Six Day War, he published an impressive booklet, "The Myth of Czechoslovakia," detailing the lesson we should have learned from the history of this unfortunate country after 1948.

What is this impudent comparison of the PLO leadership, which "uses children" for its own purposes, to demonstrations of children who wish to remain in their homes in Eretz Israel? Is there no limit to inanity, impudence, and distortion of decent intelligence? Ms. Har-Even actually lived during the Holocaust, and she remembers it – does she not imagine that perhaps the Holocaust could have been prevented by establishing a secure refuge for the Jewish people years earlier? Had we listened to the voices of Ms. Har-Even and her ilk, the Jewish state would not have been established even in 1948.

Throughout his life, Yehiel earned many honorary awards, but one of the most precious to him was the award for life achievement in 2002 presented by the Jabotinsky Order of Israel. The judges' decision read: "Yehiel Kadishai faithfully represents in his activities and personality the generation of the Holocaust and the rebirth, and he is a definitive representative of those who fought for Israel's independence, to save Jews, and for the achievement of sovereignty in Israel. He is a true Betar member – who knows by heart the teachings and writings of the Betar leader; an Irgun member – who took part in several of its most daring operations; and Jewish Brigade fighter – who worked to save fellow Jews from the Nazi horror and bring them to our homeland. He dedicated his entire life to service of our people, state, and party, mainly as the right-hand man and faithful assistant to Menachem Begin, Jabotinsky's senior student. Efficient, organized, and knowledgeable, Kadishai helped Menachem Begin in an exemplary manner, both as head of the opposition and as prime minister, releasing him from tending to small but important matters."

At the award ceremony, Yehiel spoke: "I thank the judges' committee for finding me, albeit undeserving, worthy of joining the company of great individuals of wisdom and action, and I am pleased to be so honored. In truth, the award belongs to the lifetime project of the young men and women who from their childhood rallied to the flag of the Betar leader and internalized his national, educational and moral philosophy. I feel as if I am a representative of those few who still live among us. They are but a tiny number, lone remnants.… What brought us to join those groups of young people? It was the idea that brought us. The idea of Jewish rebirth; the idea of the Jewish state; to break the humiliating bonds of the Diaspora; the simple desire *li-hiyot am hofshi be-arzenu*, "to be a free nation in our homeland" [from Israel's national anthem]; a few words, each one of which says everything; to be, to be a nation, to be a free nation, to be a free nation in our homeland – the land of Zion and Jerusalem.… In the morning service for Shabbat and holidays, we recite the prayer Nishmat Kol Hai, 'Every living soul will bless Your name.' We express our thanks to the Supreme God and bless His name for the many thousands and tens of thousands of kindnesses He performed for our forefathers. This prayer is written in the plural. I would like to bless and thank the Holy One, blessed be He, for all the kindnesses He has done for me. I have been blessed, because at every one of the stations in my life, I was surrounded by good, dedicated people – beginning with my childhood in my parents' home – a family that lived with abundant frugality and abundant love; my schoolteachers, who imbibed us with love for the Jewish tradition; Hadassah Tel-Vardi (Rosenberg-Giladi), my first youth counselor at Betar Tel Aviv; my fellow Betar members at the Tel Aviv branch and at the counselors' training school, seventh class. At that school, we heard the philosophy of the Betar leader from Yisrael Epstein and Dr. Abba Ahimeir. Our commanders were people like Raphael Rosov and Yitzchak Farger (Yonah), David Linevsky (Niv), and Eliyahu Galezer; my commanders, such as Moshe Ariel and Tanchum Rabinowitz, and the other members as well – I'm not able to name all of the well-loved ones, but I must mention and remember the names of Simcha Rais (Raz) and Yoel Eilenberg, Ya'akov (Yankele) Shulgasser and Yehoshua Brandes Hacohen, Yisrael Feinerman, Yehuda Lampert, and Sioma Layzerovitch. These are only a small fraction of all those comrades-friends-beloved individuals – each one a true *mensch*."

Yehiel also mentioned Bambi, of course, "to whom I owe thanks for most of my credits," and concluded by recalling "the happiest period of our lives: twenty-eight years in the service of Menachem Begin. I would like to relate something I heard from Menachem Begin about the term 'miracle': 'When the Holy One gives a person the wisdom to do the right thing – that's the miracle.' When I was offered the job of secretary of the Knesset faction, I accepted the proposal willingly. That was the miracle. That was *the* privilege,and January 1, 1964, marked the beginning of the wonderful, heartwarming days in Menachem Begin's presence – I don't know why I merited to enjoy that privilege."

Some might say that in this case, it was actually Begin who enjoyed the miracle, in that he was privileged to enjoy a loyal assistant and soulmate such as Yehiel, whom he could trust with his eyes closed, the full one hundred percent. Benny Begin used these words to define Yehiel, the man who over the years was like a family member to him and his sisters: "Yehiel is a man without ego, transparent, self-belittling, with no self-image. He takes up no space in a room, and nothing is concealed. He is completely genuine. Yehiel is a man with no shadow."

INDEX

www.ingramcontent.com/pod-product-compliance
Lightning Source LLC
Chambersburg PA
CBHW050922140426
R18136000001B/R181360PG42813CBX00001B/1